LIVING *from the* HEART

HEART RHYTHM MEDITATION
for Energy, Clarity, Vision, and Inner Peace

Puran and Susanna Bair

Living Heart Media
Tucson, AZ

D1026409

Living from the Heart: Heart Rhythm Meditation for Energy, Clarity, Vision and Inner Peace

Living Heart Media

PO Box 86149

Tucson AZ 85754

www.livingheartmedia.com

First Living Heart Media edition
Previously published by Three Rivers Press, New York (An imprint of Random House).

Printed in the United States of America

Edition ISBNs:

    Softcover   978-0-9795269-6-1
    Audio 978-0-9795269-7-8
    E-Book 978-0-9795269-8-5

Library of Congress Control Number –

Over the years, *Living from the Heart* is the one book I have recommended more than any other. This book is a treasure of practical wisdom they have gleaned from years of teaching and exploration into the endless mystery of the heart. You will find science, poetry and inspiration, and much more, in these pages.

Dr. James L. Oschman, Author of *Energy Medicine: The Scientific Basis*

I've used HRM to lower my blood pressure to the point of reducing the medication I take for it, stave off migraine headaches, and to quiet heart arrhythmia when I'm stressed or overtired. Emotionally, I was able to come through a very difficult marital breakdown and negotiate a win-win divorce without the intervention of attorneys. I've healed many childhood wounds, and restored optimism to my life. I feel a deep sense of peace, harmony and gratitude now that I've been able to find my life's work, and a deeper connection to my faith than I've ever had at any time of my life.

Ronnie Howell, BA

I feel that Heart Rhythm Meditation has saved my life, prevented a heart attack and stroke, as I am diabetic with high blood pressure and 57 years old. After each Heart Rhythm session I feel calmer and rejuvenated. It has always worked and I am very grateful for its impact in my life. I know that it has helped me with stress at work, and it has saved my relationships with my students and girlfriend many times beyond measure. It has provided me with a new lease on life, a more complete and fulfilled perspective on what life and living is all about, and a greater ability to be more productive and functional in my average daily life.

Jim Cumming, MS, MA, teacher, former Army captain

Soon after being introduced to HRM and applying the meditation practices, my blood pressure began coming down, I became more accepting of myself and I literally found my heart! HRM opened my heart letting 50 years of emotion flow making my life more alive and real! I have a much clearer picture of who I am, what makes me tick, and live more from an open and accepting heart.

Porter Underwood, Petroleum consultant

Over the years I have practiced HRM, there have been profound shifts in my life. As a classical musician, I have greater ease of playing, creativity in expression, and higher concentration levels than ever before. My relationships with colleagues, friends and family have never been better or had the richness and depth of intimacy that they now have.

Robert Johnson, Assistant principal, Lyric Opera of Chicago

The forgiveness and gratitude practices of Heart Rhythm Meditation have been gifts beyond price, allowing me to open to my life now with so much gratefulness. It's like being able to breathe fully for the first time.

Jody Curley, MA, CBOT

I had elevated blood pressure for several years and was on medication for this. Even with medication my blood pressure would still occasionally run a little high. I starting practicing HRM in 2001; subsequently, my blood pressure started lowering into the 90's/50's. I gradually decreased my medication and was completely off of it within 6 months.

I've had lupus for almost 26 years and during that time have had numerous experiences of life threatening illness and hospitalization. I had taken prednisone on and off, but since starting HRM, I have not been on prednisone at all.

Betsy Hart-McMannis, Physical therapist

To Christina, Asatar, Kahlil, Ethan and Gerred.

ACKNOWLEDGMENTS

The purpose of this book is to introduce a type of meditation based on a coordination of heartbeat and breath. We learned of it from the teachings of Hazrat Inayat Khan, an Indian musician and mystic, the first to teach Sufism in the West, from 1910 to 1927. It is an ancient method, practiced by the early Christians as "The Prayer of the Heart." Heart Rhythm Meditation, as we called it, is developed here step-by-step, and then expanded upon through the four subtle energies called the "Elements."

We are deeply grateful for the encouragement and inspiration of Pir Vilayat Inayat Khan over our precious 33 years together, until his passing in 2004, and especially for his personal request of us to start a new school of meditation to focus upon the heart, using Heart Rhythm Meditation. We were blessed by his careful reading of this book and the thoughtful suggestions he made for improvement.

This is the second edition of *Living from the Heart*, incorporating principles we have learned from teaching this material over the past ten years since the first edition. The opportunity to update this book is entirely due to the support of Living Heart Media, for which we are very thankful.

What is the nature of the path we embark upon? This wonderful path of the heart begins with awareness of the heart, and the first step in that awareness is the sensation of the pulse, and then the heartbeat. As the practice unfolds, the breath becomes a source of energy that powers a transformation of the heart.

Life in the heart comes when consciousness is centered in feeling.[1]

---

1 Khan, I (1989, 309-310)

The more the heart quality is wakened in a person, the more he perceives the feelings of others. To him the thoughts and feelings of others are clear.[2]

The power of thought, speech, and action depends upon the power of heart. A thought, word, or action prompted by the power of heart becomes a living force. The power of heart means not only the power of heart from within, but also the power of the heart of flesh. A person with a weak heart physically must also experience the same. For the heart is the root of one's being and exists in every plane of one's being. In each plane the heart is the center, and the health, the power, beauty, wisdom and success of life all depend upon the condition of the heart.[3]

2 www.hazrat-inayat-khan.org: Message: Vol 2, Cosmic Language: 11. Mind and Heart.

3 Khan, I. Sangatha I, Tasawwuf, Metaphysics, *Esoteric Papers*

CONTENTS

List of Tables and Figures

A NOTE FROM THE PUBLISHER

Living from the Heart was originally published in 1998 by Three Rivers Press, an imprint of Random House. At the time, the Mind/Body/Spirit genre was hot; publishers rushed titles to the marketplace to take advantage of the trend. But unlike most of these books, *Living from the Heart* has stood the test of time, emerging as a spiritual classic. People have told us that they've read the first edition a dozen times or more; *Living from the Heart* has changed lives.

Living from the Heart launched the Institute for Applied Meditation (formerly known as the PSI Collegium), which has grown to become a dynamic global organization and has introduced a number of innovations to the teaching of the ancient art of meditation. IAM was the first organization to teach meditation online, creating an interactive, online community long before social networking sites existed. Even today, no other organization offers anything comparable to the richness and depth of IAM's online webcourses. Living Heart Media is proud to support IAM's mission to deliver the finest training in meditation available anywhere, and to be part of the emerging culture of the heart.

We're pleased to offer the first Living Heart Media edition of *Living from the Heart*. Readers familiar with the Three Rivers Press edition will note several changes to the text, which has been revised and expanded. Since 1998, Puran and Susanna Bair have taught Heart Rhythm Meditation to thousands more people, and have learned so much about how to effectively teach the method.

Although Puran and Susanna Bair wrote *Living from the Heart* together, Random House insisted that only Puran's name appear as author because their research showed that books with two authors did not sell as well. This edition corrects that mistake and recognizes as co-author Susanna Bair, co-founder of IAM and Puran's collaborator, teaching partner, and spouse.

In this edition, new stories by Susanna have been added to illustrate the points made in the text. Several new drawings and diagrams have been added, and sections of the text on the Walking Practice and Running Practice of Heart Rhythm Meditation have been added. The section on the stages of Heart Rhythm Meditation has been revised and expanded, and the distinction between upward and downward meditation has been further clarified. New material has been added to clarify the relationship between the four elements and the four dimensions of the heart (the topic of Puran and Susanna's book *Energize Your Heart in Four Dimensions*). New appendices have been added, providing more detail about the roots of Heart Rhythm Meditation, the Hazrat Inayat Khan database, and the goals of Heart Rhythm Meditation. New references have been added for clarification, the table of contents has been expanded, and an index has been added so the reader can easily access themes of interest from the text.

We hope you enjoy this new edition of *Living from the Heart*. May this book remind you of the truth you already know but may have forgotten; may the book inspire you to be the person you truly are; may you find in these pages a way to connect to the purpose of your life; may the method of Heart Rhythm Meditation strengthen your breath and add a sense of rhythmic peace to your days.

Jack Carpenter, President

Dr. Asatar Bair, Vice President and Editor

Living Heart Media

INTRODUCTION

The Heartbeat

The purpose of this book is to teach you Heart Rhythm Meditation: how to become conscious of the beats of your heart and thereby get in touch with your most basic rhythm and your deeper feelings. You will gain the ability to tune your attitude, approach, and actions to express the harmony and the other qualities of your heart, especially love, creativity, and courage. You can learn this practice by yourself or with a group, then apply it to your health, relationships, and goals. Success in what you choose will then come more easily, allowing you to take on larger challenges with less stress.

If we were to ask you, "Can you feel your heartbeat?" you might reply, "Of course I can," and press your fingers to your wrist. But that's your pulse, the echo of your heartbeat. If we asked again, "Can you be aware of your heartbeat in your chest?" you might ask for a stethoscope. But can you feel your heartbeat directly, in your chest, without any instruments, just by your awareness? We have found that you can learn to feel your heartbeat, the fundamental clock of your body, anytime you want, for as long as you want. We call this method of self-awareness Heart Rhythm Meditation.

As you learn Heart Rhythm Meditation, it will change your life.

- First, it will expand your concept of who you are and broaden the scope of your awareness. You will have done something that you didn't think was possible, which will lead you to challenge other limitations. You can practice this at work, even during a meeting, and everyone will be able to see the effects (without knowing the cause).

* Second, it will create a profound state of stillness with alertness, filling you with peace and contentment. This is excellent therapy for the stress of life which is so hard on one's heart. Awareness of your heartbeat will physically strengthen your heart and stabilize its rhythm; the relaxation will open your circulatory system; and the full-breath pattern will create much greater oxygenation of your blood stream. For all these reasons, Heart Rhythm Meditation will give you much of the cardiovascular benefit of exercise without having to leave your house, change clothes or break a sweat.

* Third, it will create brilliance in your mind, producing frequent "aha!" flashes and peaks of insight. These are by-products of linking the conscious and unconscious mind. Once the door to your inner consciousness is opened, inspiration will begin to flow both ways. You will then be able to see in your conscious mind images of the creative and intuitive faculty of the unconscious—and they are exciting!

* Fourth, feeling the incessant beat of your heart will give you an unstoppable self-confidence, and thinking about your heart will make you heart-centered. You'll be more open and helpful to others, more insightful and courageous. This will transform your health, relationships, and accomplishments. Keeping your attention on your heart will increase your magnetic field, producing personal magnetism or charisma. You will learn to project your heartbeat into the space around you, which makes your atmosphere into a presence that harmonizes, heals, and

facilitates growth. Success at whatever you choose will come easily, with less stress, when powered by your heartbeat.

You can learn Heart Rhythm Meditation without buying any equipment, and without any monthly fees. You can develop these four experiences with your own heart, using its rhythm and your breath.

Peace comes when self is in harmony with the rhythm of the heart. This is accomplished in silent meditation by entering into the life-stream in the heart.

If there is any form of concentration to be used in meditation, it consists in first getting into the rhythm of the heart, by watching the heartbeats, feeling them and harmonizing with them.

Then one centers all feeling in the physical heart and out of feeling selects love, and out of love, Divine Love. [1]

The practice of listening to your heartbeat will make you conscious of one of the key functions of your unconscious mind, and that will bring about a working connection between your conscious and unconscious resources. Your unconscious mind directs your heart to beat and adapts the heart's rhythm to your physical and emotional condition. When you become aware of your heartbeat, you will directly witness a behavior of your unconscious. Some of what was unconscious becomes conscious, and a doorway opens between your conscious and unconscious mind. Through this portal you can glimpse the power of your vast unconscious and begin to harness it to your purpose.

You rely upon your unconscious mind constantly. While you are making conscious choices, such as choosing a destination while driving, your unconscious is controlling the many small motions needed to control your car. Your unconscious continues to look for your car keys after you've given up. It remembers your life experience and stores away every event, every face, every disappointment and attainment as a resource for future use. It also

---

1 Khan, I (1989, 307-308)

tries to make connections between your various and probably conflicting desires toward the goal of integrating the many elements of your life into a cohesive whole.

Every person has a mission in life, and your mission includes and requires learning about yourself, in depth. Why do you feel the way you do; what is the relationship between your attitude and life's events; where is the limit of your influence and vision; how can you contribute to the larger mission of humanity? If you share this aspiration of self-knowledge, you will delight in using your heartbeat to probe your depth and height. Conveniently, your heart has a beat that you can feel clearly and dramatically, to make it clear when you have really directed your thoughts to your heart instead of somewhere else.

The questions about your purpose can't be answered with your logical mind, but you can feel the answers rising out of the depth of your unconscious mind, especially that part of the unconscious called the "heart." The great spiritual search – the journey to your Self – begins with the discovery of the heart, which is so hard for people to find. The practice of Heart Rhythm Meditation offers a simple guiding principle: you can find your heart by meditating on your physical heart. It's so obvious – it's in the right place and the name's even the same.

W E HAVE A STORY *to illustrate the way of the heart.*

Joan was walking the halls of the court house, breathing through her heart in the rhythm of her steps (a technique described on p. 163). The case against her was gathering steam, and her lawyer and the lawyer for the other side were meeting now in a conference room. Joan knew that what she had done was right—her intention had been to help her company's client, and her boss had assured her that their company would benefit as well. Even her boss's boss had okayed it, but when she left to join her client's firm, the president charged her with violating her employment contract and stealing proprietary information. It was untrue, a fabrication. But none of the approvals she had received were in writing and no one was willing to repeat them now. The client nobody wanted was now portrayed as a crucial alliance and the project the company was trying to get out of was suddenly the company's future direction. Then she heard that her company had lost four senior people in other divisions and that she was being used as a message to others who might want to leave that the company would make defections difficult. Her lawyer was pessimistic about her chances; the company could ruin her if it wanted to.

Joan stopped outside the conference room and checked her heart again. Through Heart Rhythm Meditation she had built up a powerful sense of her heart. From her conscious breath and heartbeat, her heart felt like a magnetic power. In that consciousness she felt neither guilt nor anger, as neither perpetrator nor victim, Although her lawyer had strongly advised her to leave the negotiations to him, she opened the door. As she stood in the doorway, all eyes quickly turned to her. Her glance slowly moved from eye to eye among the roomful of men. She didn't know some of them so she said, "I'm Joan," and then, confidently, "I just think we can work this out."

The impact she had on the room was enormous. No one spoke or looked away for some seconds. Joan said nothing more and actually couldn't have because her heart was speaking for her so loudly in the silence. Then a lawyer for the prosecution blurted out, "I didn't know it was you. This changes everything." Her lawyer studied the man and got a nod from him. He then turned and said to his client, "Thank you for coming, Joan. I think it will be all right now." She stepped back into the hall and closed the door. Her heart was pounding in her chest, not with the high-speed pounding of fear, but with the strong beat of a queen who has just freed the prisoners.

Her lawyer joined her in a few short minutes. "They've dropped the case. Before you opened the door we were negotiating the amount of the fines and penalties. I don't know what you did, but now they've dropped everything. Did you know that lawyer who spoke to you?" "No," said Joan. It was her heart that did the magic, Joan knew, not anything she had said. Her heart had freed her, and the lawyers as well.

The physical heart that pumps your blood and the poetic heart at the center of your emotional experience are connected through the unconscious mind. It's clear to us that this homonym of heart is not accidental. The poetic heart is a deeper facility than the mind. We define it as the depth of that faculty of which the mind is the surface. The emotions run as currents through the lake of the heart. Those currents stir the depth of the lake and produce ripples on the surface of the lake, the mind. The mind's images are inspired by, even determined by, the heart, but the mind shows only the surface of what is happening in the depth. The force that makes the currents of the lake has a pulse, a beat, a vibration. That pulse can be made conscious.

The difference between mind and heart is like the surface and the bottom. It is the surface of the heart which is mind, and it is the depth of the mind which is heart. The mind expresses the faculty of thinking, the heart of feeling.[2]

While your physical existence receives most of your attention, you also exist as a non-physical field of energy and light which is both radiated by the physical body and also focused into a continual re-creation of the body. You can begin the experience of the interchange between the matter and energy aspects of yourself by becoming aware of your magnetic field. The body has a measurable magnetic field, and that magnetic field pulsates with the heartbeat. So the heartbeat shows you where to look: narrow your search for the magnetic body to that which pulsates as the heart does. The discovery of yourself as a magnetic field is one of the great breakthrough experiences of life. It brings your conception of yourself closer to reality.

---

2 www.hazrat-inayat-khan.org: Message: Vol 4, Mental Purification: 15. The Secret of Breath.

Are you concerned about the health of your physical heart? It has been found that the unconscious mechanism that regulates the heartbeat can itself be regulated by adding the attention of your conscious mind. If you make your heartbeat conscious, your heart is strengthened. Every heartbeat you can feel is a step towards a healthier heart. An irregular heartbeat becomes less irregular because the self-monitoring creates a feedback loop.

Never boring, the rhythm of your heartbeat is rich in feeling and meaning. Even when the average heart rate is stable, neither increasing nor decreasing, the individual beats have a slight variation in rhythm, echoing the breath rate and the subtle frequencies of the nervous system.

The heartbeat is strongest in your chest, but you can feel it anywhere you direct your attention: hands, face, feet, etc. Wherever you look there is an echo of the heartbeat, and the quality of the echo tells you about the state of that part of the body and of the circulatory and nervous system. The circulatory system carries your heartbeat to all parts of your body and your nervous system carries the subtle echo signal back to your brain. So the heartbeat you feel is a built-in, self-diagnostic signal revealing the health of your whole body.

S AMUEL'S FOOT *was under the engine block when it fell over, crushing his toe. Through the intense pain he also felt a particularly painful throbbing of the pulse in his toe. After a few hours, the throbbing pain went away, and he was left with only a constant and strong ache in his toe. The next day it was still bleeding slightly and quite sore. When Samuel did his Heart Rhythm Meditation, he tried to feel his heartbeat in various parts of his body, as usual, but although he paid particular attention to his toe he couldn't feel the pulse there. This condition persisted for three days: blood continued oozing from his toe, which had no pulse that he could feel. On the fourth day, he could again feel the pulse of his heart in his toe while doing Heart Rhythm Meditation. On that day the bleeding stopped and the pain subsided. By the next day he was back to work.*

I AM PARTICULARLY SUSCEPTIBLE *to head colds. I can tell one is coming on when the pulse that I feel in my head takes on a peculiar rhythm. The beats become uneven in their strength, and some beats are absent completely. Normally, in Heart Rhythm Meditation I can feel each heartbeat reach my head strongly and clearly. When the pulse in my head becomes uneven and irregular, I use Heart Rhythm Meditation to try to restore the normal feeling. After concentrating on the heartbeat in my head and directing my breath there for some minutes, the pulse in my head begins to feel normal again. In this way I can heal the condition that would otherwise result in a bad cold. I am reminded of this when I neglect to do it and then suffer the result.* PURAN

Your heartbeat also tells you a great deal about your emotions. As you listen to your heartbeat and then think of people and situations in your life, you'll notice that the beat changes. These changes tell you which relationship needs attention, which situation needs more priority. This technique can also help you decide when to speak and when to listen, when to act and when to watch, when to reach out and when to draw in. It's most comforting and reassuring to listen to your heartbeat. It's a simple and natural method for diminishing anxiety and fear.

FRED WANTED TO *talk to his boss about the new project, in which he wished to play a larger role, but he faced a dilemma. Would his boss see his desire as self-promotion and dismiss it, or had his boss simply undervalued him and would welcome his volunteerism and eagerness? Fred used Heart Rhythm Meditation to find his heart and immediately strong feelings of worthlessness and self-doubt emerged. Whatever he would try to say to his boss, whatever words he would use, this combination of worthlessness and self-doubt would get communicated and would influence his boss's decision.*

Staying with the practice, beat after beat, Fred's feelings began to change. Like everyone else, he has layers of emotion -- one layer covers another. Under his feelings of worthlessness and self-doubt was a feeling of rejection and disappointment; under that, a feeling of lack of fulfillment; under that is his feeling of the capacity and abilities that lie unfulfilled. When he reached that core, his confidence returned. Throughout this whole inner process of discovery, like digging into the ground, his heartbeat was his guide, his spade, and his goal. When he found the deep pool of transpersonal capability under the cover of his personal regrets and disappointments, he knew he could communicate it.

Fred saw his boss and walked over to him. He smiled confidently and genuinely and his words came easily. "I have some skills that could be applied to the new project," he said. "I'm sure you'll need all the help you can get, and I can contribute more." His boss said, "I think so too, but I didn't know if you did." His role was enlarged, and thereafter Fred had to use the Heart Rhythm Meditation to maintain the higher level of performance and responsibility he had been given.

If listening to your heartbeat is so helpful in life, why isn't it commonly done? Because people don't know how to do it, or even that it can be done, and haven't correlated the signal with their own state. Someday, I hope, school children will learn how to monitor their heartbeat for the physical and emotional feedback it gives. If you have children yourself, perhaps you can teach them how to tune in to their heartbeat to help them through difficult situations in school or sports. Your own mastery of Heart Rhythm Meditation will develop a permanent asset, like a family trust, that you can pass on to your children and enjoy together. It will enhance not only your own life, but it can become part of that special experience and wisdom you give them which helps to define your family.

But why bother to learn a technique to listen to your heart instead of simply using a stethoscope or an electronic heart monitor? First, using a device gives you only half of the information that you would get from Heart Rhythm Meditation. When you listen to your heartbeat internally, you're observing your nervous system as well as your circulatory system. The way your heartbeat feels is an important part of the information you gain. In what areas of your body do you feel your heartbeat, and how strong does it feel? These are signs about your consciousness, reflected in your nervous system. (Details on how to interpret them are given in Chapter 9.)

Second, in order to listen to your heartbeat, you must be in a state which is itself very beneficial. It is a calm and clear state, centered and comforting. You think differently, you feel differently, and the world appears to be a different place. Anxiety and fear subside, and the stream of thoughts and emotions that come from those feelings just evaporates. Experiencing the harmony within allows you to experience the harmony of the world around you and with you. Sensing that harmony gives you the ability to move with it, which creates success in life's affairs. In this way, the heartbeat is a beacon that guides you to a state of being that is most desirable in itself. We're going to use the heartbeat as part of a technique for developing the meditative state, and conversely the state of meditation will allow the heartbeat to be felt.

Listening to your heartbeat can become the basis for your most personal and private time, as it reveals your most basic rhythm and amplifies your deepest feelings. As an activity for group meditation, moreover, it takes on an added dimension. As you begin to sense the heartbeats of others and tune your heartbeat in harmony with theirs, an overall, unified rhythm emerges. Research by Dr. Beryl Payne, a physicist in Massachusetts, has shown that the heartbeats of people who are meditating together tend to converge automatically.

In a retreat setting, after days of continual meditation, you can reach the height of Heart Rhythm Meditation: a state where you sense the Earth's heartbeat beating in your own chest. (You probably sense a harmonic of the slow periodic shifts of the Earth's magnetic field.) Your heartbeat, radiating as a pulsing life, will seem to recreate the waves of the ocean, the shimmering rays of sunlight, gusts of wind, and the fertility of the earth. In this state, there is no boundary between the self and the world, the inner and the outer. This is the state of unity, and the heartbeat leads the way. Attaining this experience of unity is the real aim of this book; listening to the heartbeat is the path. Along the way, you will learn a great deal about rhythm, vibration, energy, emotion, and yourself.

Heart Rhythm Meditation

Heart Rhythm Meditation is a heart-centered meditation in which you coordinate your heartbeat, brainwaves and breathing. To begin, let's try a preliminary exercise to verify that you can indeed feel your own heartbeat. This is a small part of Heart Rhythm Meditation, as dunking your head under water is a small part of learning to swim.

At first, you can feel your heartbeat best when you're holding your breath. The longer you hold your breath the stronger your heart's beat will feel. Just take a big inhalation and hold it. You can probably hold your breath for 20 to 30 seconds, and in that time you'll feel your heartbeat.

You might feel the pulse in your face, or your neck, or somewhere else than in your chest. That's helpful -- now you know the beat you're looking for. But keep looking for the source of the beat in your physical heart.

Although it is just a first step, for me this was an incredible experience: to first feel my heartbeat. All I wanted after that was to be able to make the experience continuous rather than an isolated event. KEN, *a Heart Rhythm Meditator*

This brief experience may give you confidence that you can indeed become aware of the contractions of your heart muscle deep inside your chest. You may find it surprising and exhilarating, or you may find it anxiety-provoking to have to hold your breath. When you learn the full Heart Rhythm Meditation practice you'll find it becomes sustainable and comforting. By following the instructions in this book, you will be able to sit calmly and have a clear and continuous experience of your heartbeat for as long as you desire it. The beat will open up to become a rich and profound experience of all that is within you, and you will marvel at what the sound of your heart tells you.

Let's try it again.

You can adopt a breathing rhythm that has a pause in it, in which you hold your breath for up to half of your breathing cycle. To do so, you need to take a full inhalation. It's easy to hold your breath when your lungs are full. (Never hold an exhalation. When your lungs are empty you are literally exhausted.) To get a full inhalation, you need to breathe out more fully.

Don't try to take an exceptionally big breath—that may work once, but it won't work continuously. Instead, try to extend your exhalation three seconds longer than normal. Then let the inhalation return immediately afterward. It will be much larger in volume and will sustain you between breaths. When you feel the urge to exhale, do so gently and silently, and always finish the exhalation. Never hold the exhalation, hold only the inhalation.

Now, while you're holding the inhalation, "look" into your chest, in your mind's eye, for your beating heart. You will likely feel it toward the end of the time you're holding your breath. When you start your exhalation, the motion of breathing will obscure the beat, but you'll get it back when your breath is still again after the next inhalation. After trying this a few times, you'll find that the sensation of the beat comes earlier and persists longer during the holding time. Try to keep the rhythm of the beat in your mind while you breathe out and in again, and see if your mental beat coincides with your next sensation of it.

If you need a clue, hold your left wrist with your right hand and gently press your right thumb against the artery (under your watch strap) next to your tendon. You will feel your pulse clearly here and when you can feel the same beat elsewhere you should stop pressing your wrist. The objective is always to feel your heartbeat within your chest.

With a little practice, you'll find you can feel your heartbeat throughout your breath cycle. With a little more practice, you'll be able to do so easily. That's when the benefits begin—when listening to your heartbeat is no longer an effort.

This experience of feeling the heartbeat is a major accomplishment in inner awareness. You will have gained a lifelong asset, a tool you can apply to your personal development and accomplishments in life. You'll be able to rely upon an experience that few people believe is possible but that is not a fantasy, nor supernatural. Learning Heart Rhythm Meditation can benefit everyone. It's for businesspeople, educators, artists, designers, scientists, homemakers, and managers. It is a technique that you can make your own and apply to the fulfillment of your life as you desire. It doesn't take you out of the world; it helps you be effective as yourself, in concert with the world.

Learning and using Heart Rhythm Meditation is a constant progression. To make it useful and to be able to build further meditation experiences upon it, we need to back up to the beginning, explore the steps carefully, and understand what we're doing and why. Then the heartbeat will make sense in a larger context, and when problems or difficulties arise, you'll be prepared.

In the following chapters, we'll start with the basics: examine the theory of Heart Rhythm Meditation and then do the preparations. Then we'll focus on our breathing, making the breath conscious, rhythmic, full, and retained. Then we'll be ready to focus again on the heartbeat: finding it, using it to time the breath, and adopting the Square Breath Rhythm. This will take us to the full-blown practice of using the heartbeat to develop the Elements of the Heart: Earth, Water, Fire, and Air, which will have powerful practical effects in your life.

You may gain the state that results from Heart Rhythm Meditation by other methods as well; it may even occur spontaneously. For many, a life-changing event occurs when they experience a single moment of the heart. But if you adopt a regular practice of Heart Rhythm Meditation, you will make this most valuable experience reliable. When you can reproduce this state at will, then living in the heart really begins. Your regular practice, repeated every morning, month after month, works within your unconscious to prolong the meditation state long into your day. Then the state of meditation becomes your home: you own it and can live in it whenever you wish. In contrast, a spontaneous moment of being in your heart is like being blindfolded and taken from a slum to a palace, then forcibly returned to the slum, with only the memory of that palace and no further access. That experience can make life even more miserable until one finds for oneself the path from here to there.

As with any meditation, the techniques of this practice do not guarantee delivery of the meditative state, for the practice is more than the techniques. Besides the techniques, an emotion is required. Some people have this emotion already, while others who practice the techniques skillfully cannot progress because they haven't developed that feeling. If the feeling is missing, then it can best be built up in the heart by contact with others who meditate.

Meditation can't be taught, but it can be caught.

The reader may be able to catch Heart Rhythm Meditation from the instructions on these pages. Indeed, that is our hope and objective. But it cannot be guaranteed. What can be expected is that you will learn so much about the practice and state of meditation that Heart Rhythm Meditation will come easily when the situation of a group or a teacher presents itself.

Perhaps you won't be able to find a genuine teacher or a sincere group in your area. If not, then you may feel empowered to start a group in which you and others can catch Heart Rhythm Meditation together. This book is intended to be a resource for such a group. Its step-by-step approach allows anyone to begin, and it advances to a level that will challenge meditators who have years of experience. The well-defined goals allow you to assess your own progress and build confidence.

Discovery of Heart Rhythm Meditation

PURAN: *I conceived Heart Rhythm Meditation during a two-week solitary meditation retreat in New Mexico in 1982, under the guidance of my meditation teacher. I had an experience there I'd never had before, of the affinity between my heart and the sun. In that state of consciousness I experienced that my heart was the sun, and the sun in the sky was my moon, a mirror of the light shining from me. Then when I looked over at the mountain range to my right, I saw my arm, and my arteries became its streams. My body stretched out supine as far as I could see, and it all pulsated, throbbed, with my heartbeat.*

What I discovered was that by meditating on my heart, I could find in my heart the power of the heart of the sun and the rhythm of the heart of the Earth. What started out as an inner-directed practice reached "that" deep within me that is not personal but is shared among all things. "That" is what I am, I realized, and all of "that" beats in heart rhythm.

After the experience of the heartbeat of the planet, I kept up the awareness of my own heartbeat as a focus in meditation. This led me to discover the benefits of this practice for my physical heart and to be able to stay centered in my emotional heart. Then I discovered that my teacher's teacher had written extensively about this particular form of meditation: in the 1920s he had recommended awareness of the heartbeat as a technique for developing a heart-centered life. Much earlier, the first Christians practiced a form of Heart Rhythm Meditation called "The Prayer of the Heart."

I knew the experience of the heartbeat could be taught to others to benefit their physical and emotional well-being and their spiritual development. The essence of what I experienced in the desert could be passed on without the years of training it had taken me.

It's all about the heart, and focusing on the heartbeat is the fast track to the heart.

SUSANNA: *I meditated on my own for ten years, then when I found a meditation teacher, my meditations became much more intense. I learned the art of breath control and visualization.*

When I moved in with Puran, I suddenly had four boys: three step-sons and my own son. One of Puran's sons had never lived with the others; they had their loyalties to their own mothers, and my son and I were thrust into their lives. Puran was working long hours to support us and I had to fulfill the needs of kids I didn't know.

My previous pattern for handling stress was to simply leave, but I wanted to be with Puran and I wanted to help his sons. I was not getting any help from the meditation I had learned. This situation required tremendous growth in my capacity to handle stress. My emotional heart was being hurt continuously, and I felt the pain in my physical heart. I focused into my body to listen to its signals and discovered that I could understand what my body was telling me if I felt my heartbeat.

As we refined Heart Rhythm Meditation and we got better at it, I found I could become creative and confident in my ability to handle a situation that I could not have otherwise survived. I took the experience into my heart, and it benefited not only myself, but all who came into my psychotherapy practice. I taught Heart Rhythm Meditation to all my patients and passed on the emotional strength I had gained.

While Puran has specialized in the theory and background of meditation, my own contribution to the practice has been to

> *make practical links to people's health, relationships and accomplishments. My interest is applying meditation to the most pressing challenges of practical life, and this is reflected in the name of our school, the Institute for Applied Meditation, which has the acronym "IAM."*

IAM is a name that fits Heart Rhythm Meditation as with each double beat we imagine the heart is saying, "I am."

IAM offers Heart Rhythm Meditation as its first course, and this book contains the source material for that course. Our curriculum includes three levels of instruction, with specific internal experiences that can be self-tested and with specific goals that can be observed in one's life. To learn more about the Institute, refer to our website: www.IAMheart.org.

I think you'll be pleasantly surprised at the power of this method and your ability to learn it. If you apply Heart Rhythm Meditation to your accomplishments, to your relationships, or to your health, I'm sure you'll find that all of these things are benefited. It is really possible to live from the heart, and Heart Rhythm Meditation can help lead you there.

Note to Readers

> IN THIS BOOK, *stories are enclosed in boxes, like this one. This allows them to be easily found or skipped. Some of these stories are about one of us or other meditators we've known, some are drawn from science, and some are teaching stories from many different traditions.*

> Instructions for the meditation practice are indicated by boxes like this one. To follow the practice, just jump from one such instruction to the next. The rest of the material is background to the practice.

We also have recordings which contain additional instruction, available at IAMheart.org. You can make your own recording by reading from the instructions. Then you can use the recording to guide yourself when you're sitting with your eyes closed. You may also find that you can lay the book flat on a table in front of you and open your eyes briefly from time to time to get the next step in the practice.

 To judge your own progress, test your ability to meet the goals that are indicated by this symbol, the logo for the Institute for Applied Meditation; we chose it because the heart has four dimensions of develop-ment, as described in our book, *Energize Your Heart in Four Dimensions*, and we have four basic energies to draw upon in our spiritual unfoldment, as described in Chapters 10-13.

Part 1

HOW
HEART RHYTHM
MEDITATION
WORKS

1. WHAT IS HEART RHYTHM MEDITATION?

The Natural, Ideal Condition

The wonderful thing is that the soul already knows to some extent that there is something behind the veil, the veil of perplexity, that there is something to be sought for in the highest spheres of life, that there is some beauty to be seen, that there is Someone to be known who is knowable.[1]

As we discussed in the Introduction, Heart Rhythm Meditation is a meditation using the heartbeat and the breath. Attention to the heartbeat sensation ensures that your consciousness is in your body and ensures that your breath is coherent with your internal clock. The basic technique is an ancient method of inner awareness, as documented in Appendix 1.

The joy in thinking about meditation is that the soul already knows what it's about and why it's valuable. Your soul has a sense of familiarity with meditation that does not come from your conscious memory. Once the experience of meditation is recreated,

---

1 www.hazrat-inayat-khan.org: Message: Vol 9, The Unity of Religious Ideals: The God Ideal.

you see that, "This is the state I was once in. This is my own natural condition."

The state of meditation is familiar, like the best of times or the most awake and inspired moments we have ever experienced. These memories of peak experiences drive our interest in going forward. Your best ideas and most creative moments have occurred when you were in a meditative state, which can happen spontaneously due to inspiration, exercise, relaxation, or even taking a shower. Fortunately, anyone can learn to meditate consciously, to attain the state of meditation at will.

Doing Heart Rhythm Meditation is like swimming in an infinite ocean of energy or, some would say, of love, spirit, or peace. As in swimming, there is a little technique to be learned, and there is a risk of the unfamiliar. When we learn to swim, entering the water seems like taking a risk, even though our bodies are mostly water and even though our natural buoyancy makes swimming easy. We don't have to support our weight—the water does it. The water surrounding us has a current, making movement in one direction easier than in others. We learn to trust the water and then to direct our motions to navigate through it, diving deeply, swimming far, and generally enjoying our fluid nature. Swimming, like meditation, allows movement through a space that would otherwise be a barrier and an experience of an otherwise inaccessible portion of the world. When there is a barrier on land, one can go by sea.

Babies know how to swim by instinct, but as we grow, fear blocks that knowledge. Heart Rhythm Meditation is similar. It is a natural skill that we have to relearn. As with swimming, we don't learn how to do it from a book but from practice.

The act of meditation is described in the words of the famous children's song:

Row, row, row your boat, gently down the stream.

There's a profound teaching in this song: Don't row against the current, and don't simply float with the current, but direct your will along the current. In meditation we are consciously aiding an experience that we do not create consciously.

To be effective, thought must balance action. Our lives are mostly activity-oriented; we need much more reflection, contemplation, insight, and planning. But in a life that mostly rewards activity, there is not enough time for creative thought unless one uses an intensive process like meditation. Heart Rhythm Meditation balances many hours of activity with an experience of half an hour. The result is more creative, higher-quality work with less stress and an improved attitude toward others and one's self.

The world we live in is a creation of our mind; that is, things are the way we see them. Any point of view can find its support in the world because the world we see is a product of our point of view. People have an uncanny ability to sense how we see them and to respond to us in kind. Actually, this world is an infinitely rich reality that we each customize by our vision of it and our attitude toward it. Spiritual development is a process of learning how each person individuates reality, breaking it down to make it their own, then reintegrating the individual fragments into a unity once again.

WHERE I LIVE *in the suburbs of Boston, the same neighborhood contains parallel universes for its different occupants. The children occupy it primarily for an hour or two in the morning and for a time after school and into the early evening. Most commuters occupy this same neighborhood in the morning and again in the evening. Another whole life to the neighborhood that few people have seen comes on after the house lights go out. Then the nocturnal occupants emerge: the raccoons, skunks, opossums, bats, owls, and others. In the hours before dawn, the birds begin to sing, with different birds joining the chorus at their respective times. Some mornings, before anyone is stirring, deer come across the lawn. I am among the predawn occupants, and I marvel at the natural symphony of the birds glorifying nature by their song. Were it not for my meditation practice, I would miss this splendor. As much as I value sleep, to be awake is the most wonderful thing. There is no end to awakening.*
PURAN

The state that Heart Rhythm Meditation brings upon us is our natural condition, the state in which we were meant to live. That state banishes fear and anxiety and brings out the natural human qualities of being creative, inspired, energized, generous, magnetic, clear, insightful, and filled with peace. In this state we remember our innate mission in life, we can do what we wish to do, we discover others in whom we see ourselves, and we understand whatever we concentrate on.

That such a state exists, accessible to all, is unbelievable to many. How can it be so easy? Why is it not generally known? It is because the average person is so unaware of his or her potential that this natural, innate treasure remains hidden. There once was a man who lives in a castle, but in the basement dungeon. He lives there in misery, with continual complaints about the place, but he hasn't explored the rest of the castle. He hasn't found the stairs, doesn't know of the grand rooms and the beautiful vistas of the upper floors. Exploration would require inconvenience and risk; he thinks it's better to stay among the familiar surroundings. He is not even convinced that there could be a place that is much better than the only rooms he knows, the rooms of the dungeon, in spite of the myths he's heard and the dreams he's had—none of them "real"—about a heavenly kingdom. Poor man, he already lives in that kingdom, and he himself is the king, whether he believes it or not.

Meditation is the ideal state because in that state one has no boundaries and no beginning or end in time. All the potentials of the soul are unfolded so that one sees the divine within. The emotion is very strong yet impersonal. In fact, the greatest emotions are not personal ones but the shared feelings that stir the universe: awe, rapture, ecstasy, harmony, and peace. As meditation is the ideal state, the practice of meditation is the ideal activity. But meditation cannot be attained by the power of will alone. If it could be, it would indeed be a common condition, as the world has no shortage of will. To reach the divine state, you have to use a divine method. That is, you must use your infinite unconscious, the natural buoyant quality of consciousness, and the power of the heart, and you must trust that the heart possesses an innate sense of direction, of guidance, that already knows the path.

The horse knows the way, to carry the sleigh . . .

Here is the central dilemma of learning meditation. We know that the state of meditation cannot be reached by an act of will alone, but we want to make the practice of meditation reliable, to be able to reach the state whenever we need to. How can something that is not willful be done on demand? By inviting it to begin and influencing the direction it takes. In many areas we don't have control but we do have influence, as when managing an organization or raising children, and in activities where conditioning has occurred, like playing the piano. The unconscious responds to the intention of the conscious, just as the unlimited universe responds to discrete events.

When you have a clear intention and you follow a practice step by step, your conscious intention attracts the unconscious resources needed to change the state of your consciousness. Over time, the unconscious is impressed by conscious repetition. The changed state of consciousness called meditation will also respond to your call. Even though meditative states cannot be brought on willfully, there are techniques that set up and trigger the experience, and in time those techniques become so reliable that a meditation state is always accessible. You will be able to shift your mind into meditative states whenever you want to, instead of waiting for a spontaneous occurrence of insight or creativity. In this way Heart Rhythm Meditation is like a ladder to help you climb from an emotionally blocked state into an inspired condition where you are more powerful and free to act.

I BEGAN MEDITATING *at young age, and I spent years using visualizations and mantras that I learned from books or other students. After some time, I came to a dead end. The meditative practices I was doing didn't have enough inspiration and power to carry me through the challenges I had to face. I knew I needed something more, so I took a summer retreat with Pir Vilayat. During that retreat I had the most expansive experiences within my heart that I had ever known. I felt the glory, depth, and vulnerability of my heart as tears of emotion streamed down my face. I left the retreat full of excitement and inspiration. At home, I tried to repeat the practices, and I found I couldn't do it; I wasn't able to catapult myself into the experiences I had on retreat. I felt like a failure. It was so hard to remember what the steps were that Pir used to make these inner experiences possible. It seemed so clear at the time, and later, it felt so complicated. I sat and sat, and became more and more lost in thought.*

I learned from this that willpower is a great foundation; my will kept up my practice. But willpower alone wasn't enough: The next step was to learn how to breathe. I thought I already knew how to breathe, but there was a lot more to learn: to experience breath as energy, to breathe through my heart, and to help my heart to open by listening to the rhythm of my heartbeat. In time, I began to hear in my heartbeat the symphony of the universe, and the glory of the One became tangible within myself.

SUSANNA

What Meditation Is Not

There are many popular misconceptions about what meditation is and what it is not.

- Meditation is not a trance; you can learn to hold the meditative state while talking and being highly aware of your surroundings.

- Meditation has nothing to do with drugs. It is the antithesis of any addiction or external dependence.

- Meditation is not about losing control of yourself. In fact, it is the ultimate in control. You can control your body, mind, and emotions in ways that you never imagined possible.

- Meditation is not "turning off your mind." Your mind continues to function during meditation, although with more brilliance. Your memory is sharp, and you can use it when you want to.

- Meditation is not a belief; it has no dogma. It is a series of tools by which you can expand your experience of yourself and the world. What you believe can then be based on your experience, not on your concepts.

- Meditation is not connected to any religion, and meditators do not belong to a cult. Once you learn to meditate, you can do it on your own, without any group affiliation.

- Meditation does not create a trance state. A trance can be dangerous, similar to being drugged, where awareness of your surroundings is reduced or distorted. But a trance is not meditation, and you can easily avoid a trance state by following the instructions in this book.

- Meditation is not a technique to control other people or events. It is a technique to control yourself, and it naturally results in being more influential.

- Meditation does not need to make you otherworldly or spaced out. It will make you aware of things that you used to miss, and it will greatly improve your concentration. Getting spaced out is undesirable, easily correctable, and a symptom of being unable to handle the extended spectrum of reality that you pick up in meditation.

A Refuge and a Rehearsal

Heart Rhythm Meditation can be done anywhere. A quiet space is preferable at first. Physically, we sit on a chair, a small stool, or a pillow. We get very still and breathe in ways that are slightly different from normal breathing, while thinking of some specific area of the body. We then create and hold a specific thought or mental image. Each combination of a particular (1) posture, (2) intention, (3) breath rhythm, (4) attention on an area of the body, (5) an image on which to concentrate and (6) an invocation of a being or ideal that defines a specific type of meditation.[2] There are hundreds of types of meditations, each with a different effect. It is amazing that such a simple activity is capable of producing such profound and varied results.

Certain combinations of breathing, attention, and attitude that include a focus on the heart and the heartbeat constitute Heart Rhythm Meditation.

Heart Rhythm Meditation creates a state of peace that is also an inspiration, a refuge that recharges. If we were to think that Heart Rhythm Meditation requires a quiet and peaceful atmosphere, we would have it backward. Through Heart Rhythm Meditation you create a quiet, peaceful atmosphere that reaches quite far into your life and increases its reach as your experience increases. You will feel that you are in the center of a vast ocean of peace. No meditator experiences the practice as lonely. In the meditative state, loneliness is not possible. There are many emotions in the various stages of meditation, but loneliness is not one of them because the experience of connectedness is so strong. Any loneliness, despair, or anxiety that you may feel will fade in the powerful light of the meditation. That doesn't mean you're repressing them, for in meditation your feelings become more conscious, not less. A whole new set of transpersonal emotions arise, as well as the personal ones you brought with you, and these transpersonal emotions show you dramatically that you cannot ever be alone.

Meditation is a refuge from the slings and arrows of life. It speeds healing from emotional wounds, allowing us to reenter life's challenges without burnout or bitterness. But Heart Rhythm Meditation is more than a refuge or relief *from* life; it is a rehearsal *for* life. Our objective is not to isolate ourselves away from life in a meditation refuge, but to develop a greater capacity for being in life, dealing with the problems that life hands us.

---

2 For more on the "Six Basic Powers", see our book *Energize Your Heart in Four Dimensions,* pp 98-105

Meditation is doing in a protected environment what we should be able to do anywhere. [3]

WHEN I STARTED *to meditate, I spent hours getting my meditation bench just right. If I had trouble getting into the meditation, I assumed it was because the bench was too high or too low. I also needed an environment that was just right. I experimented with eye patches to keep out light, ear plugs to keep out sound, and all kinds of pillows and pads to make my legs comfortable. The first inkling I had that all this preparation wasn't necessary was when I saw my teacher sit on his left heel on top of a rock. I remember, too, feeling the effect he had on a space — he turned a big, flappy tent into a sacred cathedral. In that tent it was easy for me to meditate. My mind didn't bother me, and neither did my legs or my senses. I was so inspired by being within the walls of the atmosphere that meditation had created that I could ignore the distracting sound of the plastic sheeting that formed those walls. I remember going there at night when it was empty and still feeling all around me the comforting presence of the group.* PURAN

IT WAS SUMMERTIME, *and the time of the retreat had arrived. I left New York city and drove north, to the Adirondack mountains upstate. As I got closer, the temperature dropped, the wind started to blow, and it began to rain.*

The next morning at 6, I was taking off my rain boots as I entered the meditation tent nestled in the woods. I was wearing all the clothes I had, wrapped in my sleeping bag, listening to angelic music, waiting for my teacher to arrive. I could feel him coming long before he could be seen or heard. A rush of warmth went through me, and I dropped the sleeping bag from around my shoulders. By the time he had assumed his seat I was in an inner state of ecstasy. As the music faded out and he began his instruction, the cold wind and rain became a soothing score for

---

3 Attributed to Hazrat Inayat Khan.

the rhythm of his voice and breath. His meditation was a masterpiece of inspiration and transformation. SUSANNA

Upward and Downward Meditation

There are two main ways to meditate: upward and downward. The upward form of meditation is exemplified by Buddhism and Vedanta. The popular Transcendental Meditation (TM) is a greatly simplified form of Vedanta, and some clinical stress-reduction methods, like Dr. Herbert Benson's Relaxation Response,[4] are a simplification of TM. Upward meditation turns one's attention away from the physical, from the self and the environment, toward the abstract, infinite, and impersonal. These methods open up the consciousness, producing relaxation, decreased central nervous system activity, an irregular heartbeat, and unfocused thought.

By contrast, Heart Rhythm Meditation is downward meditation, in which the goal is to focus the infinite into a center, strengthening the heart and reforming the sense of identity. Meditating downward focuses the mind on the heart, producing increased central nervous system activity and a wave-like pattern of heart rate variability (HRV). Both of these directions in meditation have their usefulness, but the downward method is especially designed to be practical in life.

In the historical development of meditative practices, it is clear that the concept of meditating upward came first. Upward meditation is associated with Vedanta, the esoteric side of Hinduism, and Buddhism, which had a close connection with Vedanta, as Gautama Buddha was a Hindu Brahmin who studied the meditative techniques of Vedanta, from which come the oldest texts on meditation.

Upward meditation corresponds to the transcendental view that the physical world is an illusion (maya) that, in myriad forms, covers an underlying unity. When, through meditation, you escape the artificial boundaries imposed by individual identity, you dis-

---

4 Benson (1976)

cover your connection to a greater dimension—an inner but cosmic dimension of yourself. This type of meditation is called Samadhi. Many stages of Samadhi were distinguished by Yogi Patanjali, and Samadhi was carried even further by Gautama Buddha in the meditations called the Arupa Jhanas. Following this revelation from Buddha, there was nothing more to be discovered about transcendence, the world of pure spirit, diaphanous light, and sheer intelligence. Buddha had made the ultimate ascent and found a pathway for human liberation.

Thousands of years were required to develop the idea of meditating downward. (For more on the history and development of Heart Rhythm Meditation, see Appendix 1.) Yet downward meditation is clearly a step forward, for the advanced techniques of upward meditation can be dangerous and are rarely taught. Some teachers of Yoga and Buddhism have modified the ancient practices to emphasize more of the downward direction in their meditation.

The development of downward meditation required a breakthrough that occurred later, in the western tradition of Judaism, Christianity, and Islam. Instead of seeing the physical world as an illusion that masks the true reality, we now understand the physical world to be the point of it all, the ultimate objective of all reality, the culmination of the divine intention. Each one of us is an embodiment of a single, all-pervading consciousness, and each one of us also contains within ourselves the whole of that which we manifest in part. We may be deluded by the appearance of things, seeing only the surface and not the depth behind it, but our delusion does not stem from the physical world being an unreal illusion. The physical world contains all the other levels. Liberation is not the goal but the halfway point; the goal after liberation is to experience love fully, and from love to co-create a world that is as beautiful in reality as heaven is in possibility. This is the purpose of downward meditation.

Which is more real, the house or its blueprint, the plant or the seed? The yogis pointed out that there is much more potential in the seed than any one plant can manifest. Similarly, the soul is much richer than the personality. The seekers who came later noted, however, that there is more beauty in the flower than in the seed, and the act of manifesting even a part of one's soul potential into one's personality is cause for a cosmic celebration. Upward meditation may disclose the soul, but the proof of that disclosure is developed in the heart through downward meditation.

The upward or downward orientation is expressed not only in meditation but also in one's approach to life's problems. Buddhism teaches that the solution to the continual suffering of existence is to reverse the "wheel of becoming," the chain of cause-and-effect, in order to attain a state prior to the first cause, where all is stillness and peace. The Buddhist practices of upward meditation were designed to attain this condition of serenity and transcendence. Naturally, such practices are very effective in alleviating stress. If one can step back from things far enough or view life from the vantage point of an ascetic on a mountaintop, the trials of life do seem unimportant. The Buddhist formula for becoming free is to transcend the battleground of life's trials by withdrawing from and disidentifying with all that is transient and subject to change. But almost all of what we know and love, and virtually all that we are aware of as our own self, is transient and subject to change. Surely that which is eternal in others and in ourselves is glorious and beautiful, but the body, the mind, the psyche, the feelings of the heart—all of which are constantly changing—are also beautiful. Not only is giving up the changeable a high price to pay for freedom, it is not a path that leads to the integration of heaven and earth, spirit and psyche, the "high" and the "low", or the dynamic and the static parts of ourselves.

If life in the world is considered important, and if the body and the mind are considered valuable, then the desires of the heart must be honored and the pain of the heart must be addressed without retiring to the monastery. In the path of the heart, one's true desire is taken as a voice of inner guidance. Since there is desire, there will be suffering, as Buddha said. Christ said, "Do not resist suffering." We say pain is the condition of a feeling heart; it's preferred to being a stone.

The pain of life is the price paid for the quickening of the heart.[5]

One objective of Heart Rhythm Meditation, then, is to heal the heart, to integrate all of one's experience of life, so that one can assimilate an even wider experience of life. What we learn is that the healthy heart is stronger than any stressor and bigger than any pain. Through even the worst stress and pain, the heart can still feel joy simultaneously, because joy is its essence and needs no external cause. We can learn to respond to stressful situations by using the emotion and energy of the heart, so that stress is no longer stressful and the body doesn't react to it.

Downward meditation expresses our modern understanding by bringing the potential of the universe "down" into ourselves and into our lives, transforming our world from the inside out. Downward meditation is centered in the heart, both the physical heart that pumps blood, and the heart chakra, or center, which is located at the thymus gland and the cardiac plexus in the center of the chest. Downward meditation is a rich, emotional, and intense experience that has a profound effect upon the unconscious. A very efficient process for effecting change, it inspires and awakens one's ideals. It is creative and develops flexibility in thinking and approaching life. Like food for the mind, it awakens a deep insight into the way life works while strengthening and increasing one's resourcefulness.

[Downward] meditation draws all strength to the center of one's being, to the heart, and from there it radiates to all parts of body and mind. [6]

ONE OF THE CHALLENGES *I had to face by meditating on my heart was that I had fallen in love with Puran. Our love was forbidden: as Pir Vilayat's senior student and representative, he was the teacher of a center in Boston, where he was married to another Sufi leader; they had a young child together. I was married,*

---

5 www.hazrat-inayat-khan.org: Message: Sayings: Gayan: Boulas

6 Khan, I (1989, 305-6)

too. In the beginning of this experience I was in ecstasy. But I soon began to deny my emotions. When I sat down for meditation, I felt an excruciating pain in my chest, like my heart was tearing and twisting. Meditation was not inspiring, nor was it uplifting; it felt more like an inferno. I had no one to talk to, for I had sealed myself off, believing that nobody would be supportive of my forbidden feelings. I cut off all contact with Puran; I had dozens of letters from him in a box, unopened.

It felt like the only answer was to stop meditating. At first I was only short-tempered, but I soon felt depressed and isolated. Sometimes I did sit down to meditate and the pain was always there. It became reassuring to feel this instant excruciating pain, my friend who was always present. The pain became my lifeline, for it told me that my love was still there although we had no contact. The pain opened a whole new level of experience with my heart and with meditation. SUSANNA

Although upward meditation provides relief from stress, downward meditation increases one's ability to handle stress. What was stressful before will no longer be stressful or as stressful. We cannot remove all stressors from our life, and life would be boring if we could. What we can do is increase our physical and emotional strength, the strength of the heart, so that we can better handle the stress we have. Then, without making any changes in our life situation, we are at ease where we used to be tense. Heart Rhythm Meditation shows us how to manage stress not by gritting our teeth to get through, nor by avoiding that which is difficult, but with the nobility of the heart. You experience in a few minutes of silence the power and guidance of your heart that makes it possible for you to live from your heart the rest of the day.

The Five States of Heart Rhythm Meditation

The practice of Heart Rhythm Meditation will cause a profound change in your consciousness, progressively shifting your awareness from being a separate individual to being an expression of the universe with the whole of creation within your own heart. This occurs in five well-defined states of being. These states always occur in order, though it is possible to pass through states in a very short time. The full experience of these five states of being is the whole work of human development, the fulfillment of the human potential.

If you are reading this book for the first time, it is not necessary to understand the five states before you begin the practice. You could skip this section. However, many people like to anticipate what can happen if they undertake a consciousness-enhancing experience. It is our feeling that this description will enhance your experience by allowing you to recognize the states you pass through. Even though the full progression will take many years to develop as a reliable experience, you will have momentary experiences of all these states from the first week of practice.

Figure 1 provides an illustration of the five states.

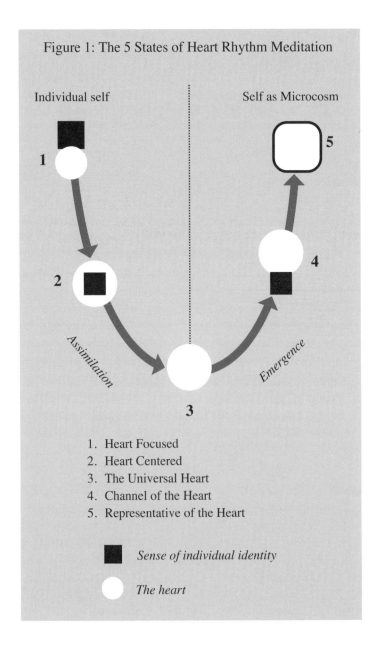

Figure 1: The 5 States of Heart Rhythm Meditation

Individual self · · · · · · · · · · Self as Microcosm

1
2
3
4
5

Assimilation

Emergence

1. Heart Focused
2. Heart Centered
3. The Universal Heart
4. Channel of the Heart
5. Representative of the Heart

■ *Sense of individual identity*

● *The heart*

Heart Focused (Concentration)

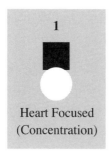

**Heart Focused
(Concentration)**

The first state is called "Heart Focused", and it occurs when you hold your concentration on your heart. Concentration means placing your full attention on one object. By focusing on only the object of concentration, all other thoughts and sensations fade away.

Concentration is the first stage of any kind of meditation. In Heart Rhythm Meditation, we focus our concentration on the heart.

Concentration is the beginning of meditation; meditation is the end of concentration. Once concentration is fully acquired, it is easy for a person to meditate. [7]

Concentration is an exercise to train the mind to hold a certain object steadily, without wavering, and by the power of concentration there is nothing in the world that cannot be attained. But concentration is a very difficult exercise to accomplish for the nature of the mind is such that when the mind takes by itself something, worry or trouble or a grudge against someone, or insult, it holds it without any effort, but when one desires to hold an object in mind for the sake of concentration, the mind acts like a restive horse. Once concentration is mastered, one has mastered life on earth. [8]

THE MASTER HATIM *was asked by a stranger, "How do I get to the house of Master Hatim? I have come to study with him." Hatim gave him elaborate instructions, and the man set off, thanking him for his careful description. The next day, the man*

---

7 www.hazrat-inayat-khan.org: Message: Vol 4, Mental Purification: 12. Mystic Relaxation (2): Concentration

8 www.hazrat-inayat-khan.org: Message: Sangatha II: Tassawwuf, Metaphysics.

returned to the same spot and, seeing Hatim, exclaimed, "Your directions have brought me back to this same house, where I was yesterday! What a miserable guide you are! I should report you to the authorities. What is your name?" "I am Hatim," the master answered. The man, astonished at meeting the teacher he sought, begged forgiveness for his rude language and asked, "Why, master, did you not tell me yesterday?" "Because," Hatim said, "I had to see if you could follow simple instructions before welcoming you to our school."

In concentration, you focus your mind upon an object which may be physical or conceptual, for example a flower in front of you, a person you know, a star you imagine, or a concept like peace. The ultimate in concentration occurs when the whole world disappears from your mind except for the object of concentration. In this state, you don't notice the passage of time or physical sensations. The focused mind can channel all the energy of the heart onto your object of concentration, illuminating it.

In Heart Rhythm Meditation, by focusing intensely on your heart, you focus the energy of the whole universe into your heart, strengthening it tremendously. The heartbeats become more regular, and the power of your heart is increased. Your entire circulation system is improved, the benefits of which reach every cell.

Most of what is popularly meant by the word "meditation" we would call concentration. It's no wonder that with this misconception, "meditation" has not become widely popular. Willful concentration is a mind game, and a boring one at that. Here are three cautions about concentration:

First, do not engage in fantasy, as for example, imaging yourself in a different place or time. Fantasy can become an addictive escape mechanism. Instead, appreciate the beauty of where you are and who you are right now. Isn't that enough to inspire you? Using suggestion in meditation has to be done very carefully or it will result in a delusion. The only suggestion we can use in meditation is to call attention to what is actually happening. For example, we like to imagine the magnetic field of the heart in order to help us discover its reality. We do not want to fool ourselves into imagining something that isn't real. The purpose of meditation, after all, is to experience reality and incorporate it into ourselves.

Meditation has a great advantage over suggestion for it not only keeps the heart in rhythm, it places the center of lifeforce there. [9]

Second, concentration is hard to do unless one has help from the breath, as we do in Heart Rhythm Meditation. The sensation of breathing is easily felt, and that sensation can center you so that your thoughts don't fly around. Concentration is hard because the mind, like the body, likes to move and is uncomfortable with stillness. You can have no success at concentrating your mind if you are not first able to hold your body absolutely still. Then, if your breathing is regular and balanced, your mind will be too. If you've tried to concentrate on something without making your breath conscious, you know how hard concentration can be. Concentrate on your breath first; only after you can do that should you attempt concentration on anything else.

Third, using your will to control your mind is pointless, like trying to control children by making rules. Your mind will fight your will, but it will surrender to your heart. This is a great secret of concentration: use your emotion. It's easy to think of what you love.

No one has to remind the lover to remember the beloved, for the lover sees the beloved's face everywhere.

---

9 Khan, I (1989, 305-6)

Following this advice, concentration is no longer a chore but a joy. Whatever one loves, one can easily hold in one's mind. Anyone can do it. A further step is to concentrate on anything by finding the love that one has for it. Your heart can easily direct your mind because although mind rebels against will, mind surrenders willingly to love.

It is the stream of desire flowing in the heart that gives us our sense of direction. When we are unaware of this stream of emotion, we waste our time in pursuit of things whose attainment doesn't bring us happiness, and neglect those things that would fulfill us. The Heart Focused state can be disruptive to a life organized to avoid emotion and fill time with unimportant activities. Your heart will remind you of what you have always wanted, and then the question is, "What are you doing about it?"

AFTER I FINISHED SCHOOL, *I pursued my dream of being an actor. I was working on a play based on Euripides' Medea with a group of four other women. The concept was to do this play with an all-female cast, to make an artistic statement and focus attention on the roles that women assumed in modern society.*

Though we did some great work together as a group, the play never gelled, and we missed our deadline to finish the play and go on tour. Our money had run out, and we had to return to work. The disappointment was immense for all of us. I had put my heart into this play and I really wanted it to happen. But how? I had no money, no cast, and no venue. Then I got a letter from a woman in Basel, Switzerland who had invited us to make a stop there on our tour. Her note said I should come anyway, even without the play, as they had a group of women that I may be able to work with.

I was terrified. I knew no one in Basel. I wasn't sure I was a good actor, let alone writer, director, or producer. My friends were against it, as was my boyfriend, and my family. I trembled as I got into my battered VW bug. My heart was hammering in my chest, so I began to breathe through my heart. It felt like my heart was all I had to hold on to.

Six months later, we had an opening at the premiere theater in Basel. Our shows sold out and we took the play on tour to Berlin and Zürich, cities that were on the cutting edge of experimental theater in those days.

Though the play was a success, looking back on it the greater success for me was that I had started to feel the life force in my heart—and in relying on it, my heart became my guide, my torch, and my rock. SUSANNA

The Heart Focused state brings great benefits: by concentrating on your heart, through attention to your heartbeat, pulse, and breath, you learn how to concentrate, and concentration is the key to accomplishing any goal. The Heart Focused state also provides important health benefits, making the immune system and physical heart strong. By maintaining your concentration on your heart, you will also gain relief from stress. Your stress is forgotten during concentration, and when you leave the Heart Focused state, your mind will be relaxed, for the mind relaxes after the exertion of concentration. The Heart Focused state also leads to a state of confidence and peace, for you gain self-knowledge, which takes away anxiety and makes you more self-assured.

The greatest application of concentration is to think of another person. By often thinking of the same person, a connection is formed in your heart and when the other person reciprocates, the connection is formed in both directions. Through this connection you come to know another person, and ultimately to know yourself.

To discover one's self it is helpful to see one's qualities mirrored in those of another. [10]

Heart Centered (Contemplation)

2

Heart Centered (Contemplation)

The second state is called "Heart Centered." As the Heart Focused state deepens, the concentration on the heart becomes stronger, until it passes over into what we term "contemplation." Contemplation occurs when your concentration on a particular object becomes so strong that not only are all other objects forgotten, but you forget yourself. If you're not aware of yourself, then who are you? You become what you're focused upon.

As Pir Vilayat describes it: "You, the subject, exchange places with the object of your concentration. Then you become within that which you saw without, and the object studies the subject."[11]

Contemplation is similar to concentration, but it is distinguished by a changed point of view. In concentration, the object remains outside yourself, separate and distinct. In contemplation, you become the object; you are within it and it is your self.

- In concentration, you look at a flower intensely. In contemplation, you identify with the flower and look back upon the one who you were when you were looking at the flower. You also feel all that the flower feels within itself, as if it were within your own self. If the flower is thirsty, the contemplative feels thirsty. Your body feels to you exactly as the flower's body feels to the flower.

- In concentration, you study a pool of water and how it is filled drop by drop by the rain. In contemplation, you feel fluid and absorb the rain into your own being.

---

10 Vilayat Inayat Khan, quote contributed for this book
11 Khan, V. (1983)

- In concentration, you are entranced with another person and are able to notice and appreciate all the aspects of that person at once—the details of his or her form, the nuances of movements, the subtle sounds within the voice, the minute changes in facial expression. In contemplation, you feel all those things within yourself, as your own. Then the leaps and connections that the person makes in his or her mind become your own mental realities. You feel the emotions that cause the shifts in the expressions you saw in that face, you feel as she or he feels; you think as the other thinks. Your body becomes the other's body.

- In concentration, you become aware of the breath going in and out of your body. In contemplation, you become the breath and feel how it fills and empties the body.

- In concentration, you can feel your heartbeat in your chest. In contemplation, you pass into the Heart Centered state. Then instead of feeling that your heart is within you, you feel you are within your heart, which has become as large as a huge room.

A TEACHER CHOSE *a deer as the object of concentration for his student, Robert, because Robert had told him that he loved deer. The teacher instructed him to go into a meditation hut and think of a deer; after some time the teacher called him, and he answered in the sound of a deer. The teacher said again, "Come out of the hut." And Robert said, "My horns are too long, I cannot get through the door."*

This is contemplation. The teacher knew that Robert could use his love to easily attain concentration. Robert made the leap from concentration to contemplation when he identified with the deer.

The physical sensation associated with the Heart Centered state is a feeling of expansion; your heart feels very large, and your body may also feel much larger. There is often a feeling of pressure within the chest, as though your chest were physically too small to contain your heart.

The Heart Centered state brings even more profound benefits. By entering this state, by becoming heart itself, you gain a much deeper unity with your heart. You are no longer listening to your heart, you *are* your heart, and you are intimately aware of the heart's exquisite sensitivity, as well as its great power. By forgetting yourself in the heart, you take a leap of faith, which allows you access to a much greater power.

In Heart Rhythm Meditation, the heart is so strengthened by your mind's concentration on it that it finds its voice and responds to your mind. Then you can truly experience what it is to listen to your heart. The heart's guidance is different from logic, and its concern is not self-centered. The method of listening to your heart is different too. You listen to your heart by imagining you are inside it, that you are your heart. This is contemplation of your heart. Feel what it's like to be intimately connected to every cell of the body, cells that are individuals as well as the building blocks of an organism. You, the heart, not only supply all these cells with the blood that carries every nutrient they need, you are also sensitive to their feedback, and you adjust your rhythm to their needs. You pick up, through the nervous system, every tremor that any cell feels, and through your pulse you retransmit an appropriate response to the whole body. As the drums of a Native American village broadcast a message to all the villagers, the complexities in your heart rhythm communicate the state of your body to all your body's cells.

The Universal Heart (Meditation)

3

The Universal Heart (Meditation)

The third stage of Heart Rhythm Meditation is called "The Universal Heart" and it is here that meditation really begins. In the Heart Focused state there was no change in your identity as you observe others, even though your observation is enriched substantially by adding your heart-energy. Back in the Heart Centered state, your self-concept was shifted, but your consciousness remained dualistic— your own heart remains separate from the hearts of others. In the Universal Heart state, there is no separation of subject and object.

In meditation there is no duality because subject and object have merged. Where concentration was difficult, meditation is simple. It requires no effort, once the ability to meditate is gained. Identity, which was maintained in concentration and reversed in contemplation, becomes so fluid in meditation that one has an "oceanic experience." One is conscious of being and of other beings, yet they are not separate and distinct.

- In contemplation, you feel as the flower feels. In meditation, you feel as the flower feels in its soul. Instead of the rose, you become rosehood, or even flowerhood, and then you experience the qualities of that archetype—the beauty, the clarity, the openness—which are embodied in the flower. Those qualities are not unique to the flower in front of you, or to all flowers; they exist in people as well. Through the soul of the flower, you discover universal qualities, qualities which appear in the flower, in all flowers, in everything, and in your own soul.

- In contemplation, you feel as other people feel: their point of view, their self-concept, their motivation, their attitude. In meditation, you experience what other people experience when they meditate—the archetype of which they are an example. You discover a source, a common reality, that you share essentially. The other person is not different from yourself, rather, both of you are examples of the same qualities that permeate all of existence.

- In contemplation, you have a specific object in your mind and intention in your heart. In meditation, your desire is to allow an experience to emerge. In concentration and contemplation, you use your will to direct the experience. In meditation, you are a willing participant but not the director.

Meditation is a training of the mind not in activity but in passivity: the training of the mind to receive some inspiration, power or blessing from within. [12]

Realizing that the personal will must limit the experience to something personal, you surrender the notion of individuality to become aware of the consciousness that is flowing through all things. That consciousness has an experience, and that experience becomes your own. It is not an individual experience; it is the experience of the whole occurring within one individual.

The third stage is meditation. This stage has nothing to do with the [personal] mind. This is the experience of the [impersonal] consciousness. Meditation is diving deep within oneself and soaring upwards into the higher spheres, expanding wider than the universe. It is in these experiences that one attains the bliss of meditation. [13]

The one who experiences meditation is not the same as the one who initiated the meditation. The experience of the universe cannot be felt by an individual, but an individual can, through the stages of concentration and contemplation, open his or her identity to include the universe. This is a state of unity called Alpha Consciousness.

How are these three stages—concentration, contemplation, and meditation—achieved?

Concentration is achieved by focusing the mind so that there is no room for anything else but the object of concentration.

Contemplation is achieved by changing places with the object of concentration: you become that object and you see the world, including yourself, from its point of view.

---

12 Khan, I (1990, 465)

13 www.hazrat-inayat-khan.org: Message: Vol 4, Mental Purification: 12. Mystic Relaxation (2): Meditation

Meditation is achieved by introducing the concept of per-
fection, infinity, or eternity. The notion of perfection which
hoists one beyond the constraint of one's limited self-
image may be likened to eternity in time and infinity in
space. [14]

These three key concepts that initiate meditation—infinity,
eternity, and perfection—are all aspects of the same thing. Infinity
is the perfection of distance, eternity is infinite time, and perfection
is eternal.

In Heart Rhythm Meditation, the individual reaches the state
of meditation where the heart expands beyond its personal identity
to become the heart of humanity. At first you are conscious of your
heart inside you (concentration). Then you are conscious of yourself inside your heart, which is greatly expanded (contemplation).
Ultimately, you find that the whole world comprises one cohesive
heart-reality (meditation). Then you feel the experience not just of
your personal heart but of the whole heart, the heart that is infinite,
perfect and eternal.

Pure meditation aids one to reach into the inner recesses
of the heart. Concentration is principally concerned with
mind, whereas meditation, while not entirely disconcerned
with mind, centers the soul where it belongs: in the
heart. [15]

By going deeply and intimately into the personal experience
of your own heartbeat, you can find the fundamental rhythm of the
whole being of life. Such an effort makes no sense in cold blood,
but it is quite accessible if one goes through the earlier stages of
concentration and contemplation.

---

14 Vilayat Inayat Khan, quote contributed for this book
15 Khan, I (1989, 307-8)

The Channel of the Heart (Contemplation)

4

The Channel
of the Heart

What experience could there be beyond the Universal Heart? What happens next is that the Universal Heart appears as a reflection in your own heart. Duality reappears—as multiple appearances of the One Reality. Each person's chest reflects the Universal Heart just as each wave in the ocean can reflect the same sun and make light appear at innumerable spots on the water.

An analogy to music can help us understand these stages. First, the musician focuses intently on the technique. Then a great musician transcends technique and any concerns of performance as she feels the music flowing through her. In shorthand, we say (1) the musician plays the music and then (2) the music plays the musician. By identifying with the music itself, the musician can become so completely effaced that she disappears; there is no more musician at all; (3) the music alone exists. This is the state of meditation. The music at this stage is not "a piece of" music; it is music itself. It is this source of music that J. S. Bach "heard" and wrote down. (4) In the next step, the source of all music becomes a stream of music that flows through the musician.

We call the fourth state the "Channel of the Heart." In the Heart Centered state, you had contemplated your own heart to find yourself within it. In the Channel of the Heart, the Universal Heart is contemplating your heart and finding Itself in it. This is the Universal Heart contemplating Its creation of Itself as a human heart. The human heart is the focus of the whole universe, where the spirit is quickened and a soul is born continually.

You become as a riverbed, through which the river of Divine Love flows. You still experience the Universal Heart, but your individuality re-emerges. This new sense of individuality, your true self, appears within a vast and rich atmosphere of heart that surrounds you. This state could be called "Living in the Heart."

Your sense of self-concept has progressed in this state from the whole, Universal Heart to that cone which channels infinity into a point. You were the ocean; now you are a funnel that gathers the ocean into a stream. You were the still waters; now you are the flowing channel that carries the water into life.

Your heart is not your own: it is the instrument of the Universal Heart. Through your heart, the Source of Love is able to appear in the world in the form of human love. You have gone from the passive state of "Let Thy Will be done," to the active state of "Let me be the instrument for the transfiguration of the world." When Isaiah heard the divine question, "Who shall I send; who will go for Me," he responded, "Send me!"[16] This was the response that none of the angels could give, for in their experience of unity (State 3), they had not yet discovered their individual ability to initiate action, even when inspired and powered by the One Source.

When you are able to repeat the commitment you made in a time before human existence, you will find within your heart the inscription of the purpose for which you were sent. The experience of the opening of the heart is a prerequisite to our human responsibility to discover the purpose of our lives and to pursue that mission with all our heart.

Representative of the Heart (Concentration)

5

Microcosm

The fifth and final state is the culmination of human development; we call it the "Representative of the Heart." In this state, one operates as a conscious microcosm of the Universal Heart. This is a further stage of unity, called Omega Consciousness.

To understand the difference between the Channel and the Representative of the Heart, consider a political analogy. A king might have two kinds of ministers: an emissary and a representative. The emissary is entrusted to carry the king's message to a foreign land, as in communicating his terms in a negotiation with another king. The other king would then reply, and the emissary would carry the reply back to his own king. This emis-

---

16 Isaiah, 6:8

sary is a conduit for the message of his king, and is charged with carrying and delivering the message with the decorum of the one from whom the message comes. This kind of minister is like a conduit, a channel, for the king. This is like the Channel of the Heart.

The second kind of minister, the representative, is empowered to negotiate on behalf of the king. When the representative makes an agreement, the king is committed to what his representative has agreed. The representative is a full delegate and can stand-in for the king at any time.

Jesus addressed all His disciples and said, "And so I tell all of you: what you prohibit on earth will be prohibited in heaven, and what you permit on earth will be permitted in heaven." [17]

One's identity is a microcosm of the Heart of God, the Universal Heart. One's mind and heart work cooperatively, with the mind acting as a lens to focus the radiance of the Universal Heart toward those people, situations, and aspects of the self that need the Heart's understanding, courage, creativity, and peace. The Heart radiates peace, sending out wave after wave of vibration that harmonizes all those it reaches and creates an integrated, purposeful harmony.

One becomes the embodiment of love, harmony and beauty. The microcosm not only channels the whole, but reciprocally the macrocosm instantly experiences all that the microcosm experiences. The whole is the part, and the part is the whole, even though the whole contains the part.

This fifth state, the Representative of the Heart, completely confounds the mind. Those who have experienced this state throughout history have recognized that words cannot begin to convey the experience. When they have deigned to speak of it at all, they have usually done so in poetry, paradox, koan, or parable. In the words of Jesus Christ:

---

17 Matthew 18:18-19

I and my Father are one.[18]

I tell you the truth, anyone who has faith in me will do what I have been doing. He will do even greater things than these.[19]

In the words of Hazrat Inayat Khan:

My heart is the key to the hearts of men.

Make God a reality, and God will make you the Truth.

The soul in its journey onward strikes a plane where it exclaims, "I am the truth."[20]

The Parable of the Rainbow

The rainbow, *concentrating* on the sun, recognizes something of itself in the sun: the light that is the rainbow's own essence, the sun shows much more intensely.

Contemplating the sun, by identifying with it, the rainbow delights in the experience of a much brighter form of light, with all colors integrated into white.

Now *meditating* as the sun, the rainbow enjoys realms of light beyond the forms of rainbow and sun. It discovers the nature of light itself, before it radiates throughout the universe or is differentiated into colors.

The sun, which is now experiencing itself as pure light, re-members again its rainbow form. Just as the rainbow longed to be free, the light now longs to be expressed.

In *contemplating* the rainbow, the light of the sun feels that its own being is revealed in a splendor that had been an unseen potential in sunlight. The rainbow reveals the inner colors of the pure white light of the sun, which the sun can now experience by its contemplation.

---

18 John 10:30

19 John 14:12

20 www.hazrat-inayat-khan.org: Message: Sayings: Gayan

Finally the sun, in an act of joyous love for the rainbow, *concentrates* its glance through the cloudy skies to illuminate the rainbow to full brilliance. It pours itself into the rainbow without limit or reserve. The sun becomes the rainbow, and the rainbow is recreated as an expression of the sun.

Your personality, compared with your soul, is like the rainbow compared with the sun. Your objective is to illuminate your personality with the light of your soul. The first three steps bring you into your soul; downward meditation brings your soul into life.

In the first three steps, you first feel the beat of your own heart in your chest; then the beat of your heart fills your body. Your whole body seems to be inside your heart. Then the beat of your heart is revealed to be the rhythm of the Heart, the infinite and all-pervading heart whose beat creates every rhythm in life.

In the last two steps, you develop a simultaneous awareness of the beat of the cosmic Heart and the beat of your own heart in syncopation, within yourself. Then the overall Heart rhythm gives rhythm to your own heart, strengthening and perfecting its rhythm. At this point you feel the experience of every heart, every emotion, within your own heart. Your heart is in your chest, yet it is not your own. It feels and operates as the heart of everyone. Finally, your heart reveals itself completely as the Heart of the universe. It is the beat of your heart that beats all hearts and that moves the ocean waters into waves and the air into gusts of wind. The whole world sighs when you sigh and smiles when you smile. This is an extraordinary state that must seem to be metaphorical or poetic until one realizes the truth of it.

Thy music causeth my soul to dance; in the murmur of the wind I hear Thy flute; the waves of the sea keep the rhythm of my dancing steps. Through the whole of nature I hear Thy music played, my Beloved; my soul while dancing speaketh of its joy in song.[21]

---

21 *Ibid.*

When my heart is perturbed, it upsets the whole universe.
When my heart is asleep, then both worlds fall into a deep
slumber. The whole creation wakes up with the wakening
of my heart. When the shell of my heart breaks, pearls are
scattered around. [22]

Meditative Consciousness

In the past, people felt that what was not perceivable was not real, or if real, not relevant. Now science has shown that the universe is incredibly complicated and that our usual perceptions of it are more limited than the experience of a rose without color and fragrance. For example, contrast the usual experience with what is possible in meditation:

Usual Condition	Meditation Condition
We use only small portions of the brain, and only one of the two hemispheres of the brain at a time.	Both hemispheres work simultaneously, and some brain waves involve the entire brain.
We have only very limited access to the memory in our unconscious mind, including the memory stored in our muscle tissue.	Memory can be released from the muscles and we can "stir" the unconscious memory.
We are unable to control the basic rhythms that regulate the body our metabolism, energy level, and the like.	We are better able to adapt to the task at hand.
We identify ourselves with only the particle aspect of our material bodies in space, giving a limited self-image.	We discover the wave aspect of our bodies, localized co-existent with all other waves, giving an expanded self-image.

---

22 *Ibid.*

The stages of meditation can be described in terms of brain-wave patterns:

- Beginning meditation appears on an EEG as mostly alpha waves in both hemispheres of the brain simultaneously, indicating relaxation. The blood pressure falls.

- More advanced meditation shows beta and theta waves simultaneously with the alpha waves, indicating lucid awareness, heightened mental powers, and creativity.

- In very advanced meditation, delta waves occur as well, which normally only exist in deep sleep. Yet the meditator is awake and can later relate what happened in the room. The heart rate slows considerably.

WHEN PIR VILAYAT *was tested at the Himalayan Institute, it was found that he could recall a conversation that occurred while he was producing delta and theta waves. I was later tested at Dr. Herbert Benson's clinic in Boston. The amplitude of the delta waves I produced during Heart Rhythm Meditation was as high as the amplitude of the alpha waves I produced. I was fully aware of my surroundings throughout the session.* PURAN

Because these brain-wave patterns are so characteristic, it is possible to identify meditative states of consciousness with some certainty and to distinguish the states of meditation from trance or sleep or normal consciousness, for example.

If we were to rank the degree of deliberate intentionality that is present in our consciousness, it would range from deep sleep without dreams, where there is no awareness, to concentrating on math or other mental problems, where the mind is completely focused on a specific task. Generally, the various states of consciousness, shown in the graph on the next page, can be divided into two categories, called "asleep" and "awake." Meditation is then a third state, with characteristics of both and neither of the other two states. Figure 2 shows our subjective appraisal of these states.

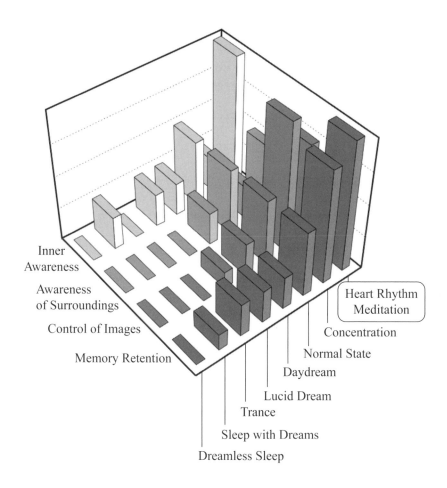

Figure 2: Comparison Between Heart Rhythm Meditation and Other States of Consciousness

Like awake consciousness, meditation consciousness has memory and awareness of surroundings. But the control of thoughts during meditation is not the same as the control or lack of control that we have in either asleep or awake consciousness.

We do remember some of our dreams, and we do forget some of our daytime experiences, but no one would deny that our memory is much lessened when we are sleeping than when we are awake. In sleep, our thoughts are not formed deliberately or willfully but take a direction of their own. Our sleep can be interrupted by environmental factors such as loud noises and temperature, but we cannot make ourselves "pay attention" to these things while we sleep. Dreams have very little deliberate intention, but lucid dreaming, where we are aware of a dream as it is happening and can modify it to some extent, has some intention. In a daydream, we have memory and awareness of our surroundings, but we only partially direct our thoughts. In normal consciousness, we mostly direct our thinking along rational lines, but most topics are initiated by sensory perception. That is, we think about what we see and hear, primarily, and we remember our perceptions, thoughts, and actions.

In the concentration state, as we focus on an object, sensory input is greatly diminished in importance. The bus stop goes by when we are reading on the bus; the light gets dim as we are reading at sunset; we forget to eat when we are engrossed in some topic. But this loss of awareness of our surroundings is different from the loss of awareness in the dream state, because the awareness is given up by us rather than taken away.

Where does meditation fall on this spectrum? Meditation is like each of these states, but it is different from all of them. In meditation, the delta brain waves that define "deep sleep" may be present, even while we are aware of our surroundings. In most meditation practices, inspiration continually comes up without our consciously directing it, much as in dreaming, and some of it is quite surprising. Memory is always present in meditation. During most meditations, the brain waves show the presence of the beta waves of directed thought, similar to the concentration state. Concentration is the first step in meditation.

Heart Rhythm Meditation, as described in this book, creates a state like concentration but with much greater awareness of the inner condition, less control of the mental images, and more relaxation, like the sleep state. This meditation state is not like a trance: you will not "blank out." You will always be aware of your thinking, but you will be thinking differently.

One of the advantages of meditation is that it gives us insights that are not directed, expected, or logical.

While the body is resting in meditation, it is not in the same condition as in sleep. The reason is that the body is also in meditation, the body also breathes; it breathes through the pores of the skin, and it is necessary to keep the whole body in meditation.[23]

In psychological terms, meditation is an activity of both the conscious and unconscious mind. It builds a relationship of cooperation between the two, in which both are valued and trusted for their respective skills. In the beginning of meditation and at certain periods recurring, we need to purify the unconscious so that it can be more useful. That part of our consciousness of which we are not generally aware—the unconscious—may be divided into two parts: the higher consciousness and the subconscious. The higher consciousness is responsible for intuition and emotions of rapture, awe, and ecstasy: joy without reason. The subconscious holds in an emotional form a lifetime of individual experiences and the es-

---

23 Khan, I (1989, 225)

sence of the experience of our species, which it sorts out and files until they are all integrated into one overall understanding. In meditation, the light of the higher consciousness falls on the subconscious and makes its integrating task much more efficient.

What most distinguishes meditation, as a defining characteristic, is the meditator's sense of identity.

THE "I" THAT I THINK I AM *changes from the personal to the impersonal. When I am meditating, I am aware of myself and my surroundings. I have my own individual set of memories, and I am aware of the need to initiate and to engage in meditation. I also have a feeling that "I" am not the one who is meditating. Rather, I am allowing, or facilitating, or even encouraging, a larger consciousness to operate through my consciousness. So I am both directing the experience and observing it passively.*

Metaphorically, in my meditations I am creating a river bed, and I am then amazed at the river that flows through that bed. I can change the course of the river by changing the banks, but the life-giving, beautiful, and powerful flow of water is not created by me. The stream has neither its origin nor its destination in me. Both are infinitely beyond my finiteness. I prepare the river banks, I invite the water, and I patiently strengthen my call by building up the rhythm of my breath.

Rhythmic breathing, like pushing a swing higher and higher, carries my wish outward and brings back an answer. In stages, without requirement or demand but with expectation and desire, I surrender my breath and allow Breath to breathe me. Rather than breathing, I am breathed. My heartbeat echoes back to me from the Heartbeat of everything around me.

Eventually, inevitably, I am swept up in the flow of the river. I stop identifying with the river banks and lose my dominant sense of self in the undeniable reality that I am the water, the stream, the spring source, and the ocean goal. It no longer makes any sense to distinguish the water from the channel: all is river, and I am that.

Then, again, I am the river bed, with the water flowing through me. The river bed directs the water where it will; the river follows the banks. The inspiration I feel surging through me, pulsing in every cell, is directed by my interests and applied by my hands, eyes, mind, and every part of me, to the challenges of my life, at this time. PURAN

2. THE BENEFITS AND ELEMENTS

No one need ask, "What shall I gain by meditation? In what ways shall I benefit?" If one only knew, it is by means of meditation that all is gained, not only things are gained, not only attributes and qualities are gained, but even God is so gained. [1]

Early Stage Benefits

The first benefit you will receive from Heart Rhythm Meditation is a wonderful relaxation. This relaxation is different from sleep or any other "restful" activity. It comes with a heightened sense of awareness, so you will not be sluggish or drowsy afterward. Of this state, people say things like "That is the most relaxed I can ever remember being." You may feel as if you can't move your body—it's too heavy—even though you know you can. You won't want to move.

The second benefit results from the alertness: you will have the "aha!" experience of having brilliant ideas spring into your mind. Because the mind takes over normally unconscious tasks (like breathing), or monitors them consciously (like the heart rate), parts of the unconscious are freed up. Consequently, the mind operates differently in meditation: the unconscious is more accessible and more responsive to the will. This "aha!" state is very valuable

---

1 www.hazrat-inayat-khan.org: Message: Githas: Meditation

as it helps us solve the puzzles of our lives and meet our challenges with new creativity.

The third benefit is the experience of power in your heart. It comes as a direct result of listening to your heartbeat. You feel that your heart has expanded and can no longer fit in your chest. You have a sensation of pressure, but not pain, in the chest. You feel that your scope, your reach, and your influence have expanded outward into the world at large. These feelings correspond to the discovery of your magnetic field. The magnetic field of the human body is a measurable reality, and when you become aware of it, you feel its energy. The value of this experience is its powerful effect on your self-confidence and self-image.

These three benefits come in the early stages of learning Heart Rhythm Meditation.

Later-Stage Benefits

Following these three early-stage benefits, further experience and skill in Heart Rhythm Meditation yields additional practical benefits. These benefits can be placed in four categories, linked to the effects of the four Elements on the heart (described in Part 3). The four Elements, Air, Fire, Water, and Earth, were originally described by early thinkers who were attempting to classify objects, forces, and qualities in the world around them. Although the Elements are out of favor scientifically, there is a relationship between the scientific concept of phases of matter and the Elements. There are four phases of matter, solid, liquid, gas, and plasma, which correspond to the Elements Earth, Water, Air, and Fire respectively. The Elements are also valuable as categories of human experience because they relate to the kinds of inner experiences that we have.

We have Fire experiences that rise up and lift our emotions, leading to exaltation, Water experiences that flow downward and lead to grace and acceptance, Earth experiences that spread out horizontally and give us stability and control, and Air experiences of the mind, independent of direction, that give us awareness of the hearts of others.

Element	Direction	Benefit
Air	Independent of direction	Awareness of heart
Fire	Rising up	Exaltation, ecstasy
Water	Flowing downward	Creativity, grace
Earth	Spreading out horizontally	Stability, control, integrity

The Elements have special experiential meanings in Heart Rhythm Meditation, because each Element can be developed by using a particular version of the meditation that focuses on it, as described in Part 3 of this book. Adding the Elements to Heart Rhythm Meditation is a practical way to tune yourself to and bring out the different qualities and abilities of your heart, strengths you can apply to the challenge at hand.

The Elements in You

To be more specific about the Elements, the discussion in this chapter is interspersed with a dozen short scenarios taken from the lives of Heart Rhythm Meditators. The scenarios are categorized according to the Elements. Some of these stories may be interesting to you, and some may feel very familiar. Other stories may make you uncomfortable. These reactions are all valuable, full of information. If you have a group of people with whom you practice meditation, even one other person, you can benefit from discussing your reactions with them.

After reading these stories, ask yourself, perhaps prompted by another:

2. The Benefits and the Elements

1. Which stories attracted you the most? Were any of them repulsive? Wherever you had a strong reaction to a story, either positive or negative, the important thing is the strength of the emotion, not its direction.

2. Considering that the stories are grouped by Element, determine which Element produces the strongest emotional reaction in you. You will likely respond to several stories. Are all these stories in the same Element? If not, which one is strongest? This is the Element that you are drawn to develop in yourself. It is probably the one you need most in your life, as the needs of life and the desires of our hearts are usually aligned by Element.

3. Which Elements are the strongest in yourself now? Those that you have already developed are probably those that are not interesting to you. However, some Elements don't create any emotional response in you because they are outside of your range of experience, neither developed nor developing in you now. Considering that there are two reasons for having no response to an Element—it may be strongly developed already, or it may be largely outside your experience— determine which Elements are strongly developed already.

4. In which Element(s) are you most different from what you desire to be? This is the Element to which you should direct your attention by forming a goal to be achieved through meditation.

We recommend that you make a note immediately upon reading each story so that you can capture your reaction while it's warm.

Stress Management and Inner Strength (FIRE)

The body responds to emotional or mental stress in exactly the same way as it responds to physical stress. For this reason we tend to overreact when emotionally stressed, as if we were at risk of physical harm. When you experience stress, anger, or fear, your adrenaline level increases sharply, which releases a tremendous energy in your body. This energy can be life-saving, appearing at those moments when you must make emergency efforts for survival. But this type of energy is most conducive to gross actions, quick movements, and short-term gains: fight or flight. The release of adrenaline is useful to the large muscles, but it clouds the mind and makes one confrontational and defensive. If your adrenaline goes up when the market goes down or when your child acts up, your reaction will not be your best, because the adrenaline will cause you to oversimplify into good-bad categories and to emphasize the short term, which blocks creativity.

Once it is elevated, the adrenaline level stays high enough to facilitate further fight-or-flight reactions until the "danger" has passed. Unfortunately, it can take hours for the adrenaline level to descend again, in the meantime causing the familiar feeling of "bringing the office home." Prolonged stress also causes a multitude of health problems.

AS A CHILD, I USED TO WONDER *why it was that my father had to have all the lights off in the morning. In the bathroom, in his bedroom, in the kitchen during breakfast, the lights had to be off. Light was more than annoying to him, it seemed to be actually painful. As an adult, I realized that father's problem was symptomatic of severe stress. When the body is stressed, the iris of the eye, which normally closes down in bright light, actually* opens up. *His iris, instead of protecting him from light, was actually assaulting him.* PURAN

Stress can make the body take other reverse actions, contrary to its normal self-regulating mechanisms. Stress can cause a person to eat or drink too much, putting additional stress on the heart, arteries, veins, liver, pancreas, and so on. Stress can also cause the body to react to food as if it were an aggravating poison, resulting in eczema, hives, other rashes, upset stomach, or diarrhea. Under stressful conditions, we need better problem-solving skills than normal, but stress can cause a restriction of blood flow to the brain, resulting in headaches, or sleepiness, the typical "overwhelmed" response. These reverse actions make it more difficult to solve the problems that caused the stress initially.

WHEN I FINISHED HIGH SCHOOL *I knew I wanted to study Psychology at the University of Vienna. It was either university or work in our family's hotel. The thought of spending my life working in the hotel was stifling. I had to get out. But I had no support. The university was paid for by the state, but how would I live? My family wouldn't support me financially. I had no job and no contacts in Vienna. My boyfriend at the time invited me to stay with him at his parents' apartment close to Vienna. I was grateful for the opportunity, but had only known him by then for a year and had only met his parents a couple of times.*
That time was really stressful for me. I was up late studying and up early to take the train to class, but the most stressful aspect was the unfamiliar family structure and finding my place in it. At that time, living with your boyfriend in his parents' home was an unusual arrangement in a Catholic country with traditional mores about marriage and family. I developed a cough that wouldn't go away. The doctor diagnosed it as a weakness of the lungs, and the prescription was an antidepressant. I remember taking one of

these pills feeling the effect of drowsiness in my body, a relaxation, but a strange one. I didn't like it. I got in touch with my heart, to find out what I really felt. I got clarity in that moment that I needed space, and I found the strength to make it clear to my boyfriend that we had to leave his parents home or I would leave by myself. Within a few months we had jobs and our own apartment in Vienna. My cough disappeared and has never returned. SUSANNA

A first approach to stress management is to try to *shed the stress*, as if it were water running off your back, the way you naturally do on a long vacation. It has been found that the adrenaline level falls off more quickly for meditators than for nonmeditators. Even beginning meditators have an improved ability to recover from stress as a result of the conscious relaxation that occurs in meditation. Consequently, meditation makes you less likely to take the stress of work home with you—you will unwind more quickly. Meditation will also likely replace the use of alcohol, nicotine, or other depressants.

A second approach that people employ in order to manage stress is to *increase their long-term power* so that what once was stressful is no longer. Recall what used to be stressful to you as a child. Whatever it was, it's probably not stressful to you now because you have more personal power at your disposal. With Heart Rhythm Meditation, you can further increase your energy level and take more in stride.

This is a completely different approach: instead of removing yourself from the stressor, or removing the stress from yourself, you will be able to handle more tension with less physical and emotional reaction. Your objective is to teach your body a new mode of response that doesn't rely on adrenaline—by using your heart, the powerhouse of emotional strength. This strength will increase your capacity to handle both short- and long-term stress so that you can deal with it rather than battling it or succumbing to it.

GORDON WAS OVERCOMMITTED *in his work at the software company, but he tried not to show it. He was the one who proposed the project of extending the single-user software to multiuser and so he was the one assigned to make it happen. Subsequently, it became vital to the company and to his self-esteem, reputation, position in the firm, and financial security. On the surface he seemed to be handling the stress pretty well, but he couldn't hide it from his body or his family. He didn't want to reduce his commitment level, but the project would take another nine months. So he had to find a way to survive the pressure and even thrive in it.*

Everyone told him to work smarter, not harder, but they didn't tell him that the way to do that was with his heart, not his head. Gordon came to Heart Rhythm Meditation for stress reduction and found a method to tap his heart's power. Making his heartbeat conscious led him to consider his heart's desire and objective. His heart's objective, he felt, was not to just survive this stressful period, nor even to succeed with the project. The heart's objective was to succeed with style, with beauty, and with a reserve of power left over for dignity. Although this attitude seemed to raise the stakes and make the task more difficult, it changed Gordon's approach so dramatically that it became easier. By involving his heart, Gordon was able to tap into a reservoir of power that was not available to him otherwise. He unleashed his creative qualities, and the work became fun.

Sometimes Gordon found himself slipping back into his old way of working. He would become anxious about failure, or be seized by fear. Or he would become mechanical and start counting his hours. The work of one hour doesn't equal the work of another hour, so time measurement is irrelevant. What is important is maintaining concentration, because all problems yield to a fo-

cused mind. He tried to will his mind into focus, but no one's will is strong enough to maintain concentration week after week; only the heart can do that. He found he could use his will to do Heart Rhythm Meditation every day, and that practice would calm his fears and remind him of his heart and his love for what he was doing. When he remembered his heart, he loved the tasks involved in his work, he loved the interaction with the people at work, and he loved being able to contribute to the support of his family. In this condition he had no stress where stress had previously prevented him from attaining this condition. He broke the vicious circle by doing Heart Rhythm Meditation.

One experiment we use in teaching Heart Rhythm Meditation demonstrates stress management through enlarged capacity. It was demonstrated to us by a doctor who specializes in stress therapy. In order to study stress, he needed a way to be able to induce a standard level of stress in each subject; he did it by using intense cold.

THE DOCTOR CAREFULLY *packed my right arm in crushed ice, from my fingertips to above my elbow. Without meditation, that will usually induce intense pain within a minute. Using Heart Rhythm Meditation, however, you can have more of an effect on your environment than your environment has upon you. When he was finished piling up the ice, I started the practice and I had a feeling of power throughout my body. My arm never got cold. I remember looking at the ice surrounding my arm and thinking, "That poor ice is doomed; it's all going to melt." Because my arm wasn't cold, I didn't feel any pain. My adrenaline level, which indicates the degree of stress or shock, didn't rise. But my arm wasn't numb, and I didn't just "survive" the stress by "guts." It was easy; I was smiling.* PURAN

If you try to "guts" it out, your arm will turn as white as a sheet, indicating a reduction of circulation, but with Heart Rhythm Meditation your arm will be fiery red, showing increased circulation instead. This means that with Heart Rhythm Meditation, the body is dealing with a traumatic situation by using an unusual but innate power, without resorting to its emergency fight-or-flight adrenaline response. The "flight" response shuts down the circulation in the arm to prevent the cold from spreading to the rest of the body. The arm is sacrificed for the survival of the body, and the arm turns white. The "fight" response raises the adrenaline level dramatically, the heart races to increase circulation to the muscles, emotions are intensified into anger, panic, or fear, and the whole body prepares for rapid action. Heart Rhythm Meditation enhances the circulation in the area that is under attack, but the heartbeat increases only slightly, and there is no anger, panic, or fear. There is simply the confidence that the power of the heart to change the environment is greater than the power of the environment to change the heart.

A big ship is less affected by the waves than a little boat.

Peak Experience of Energy (FIRE)

Heart Rhythm Meditation brings out a type of energy that is both more powerful and more refined than an adrenaline rush. This energy, which can be accurately directed and usefully harnessed, is accompanied by a heightened sense of awareness and mental clarity. It can be used to make an extraordinary effort of personal breakthrough or magnanimity toward others. It can make you feel more powerful, more positive, and more in control, more "centered." This feeling of being positive and in control is crucial to the next stages of meditation.

With meditation, you may be able to make an extended physical effort, such as working all night, while staying alert mentally. You may need less sleep generally. The amount of sleep that we need physically is generally less than what we need mentally, as the mind uses that time to sort and file the many impressions that it received through the day.

GLORIA, A BANK MANAGER, *wanted a meditation that would allow her to sleep one hour less per night and work one hour more. Heart Rhythm Meditation brings about a state of conscious sleep that is more efficient than regular sleep, allowing the sorting and filing processes to take less time. Using this method, Gloria was easily able to reduce her usual eight hours of sleep to six and a half, without feeling tired. She spent 15 minutes in meditation before going to bed and 15 minutes upon rising. She actually reduced her sleep by one and a half hours a night, but she increased her meditation time by half an hour, so the net gain was one hour. The extra meditation time makes it possible to sustain a daily rhythm with less sleep.*

At an advanced stage, those who have learned Heart Rhythm Meditation report a peak experience of energy and power far beyond any state of excitation they've ever experienced. This is one of the reasons why advanced meditators are so committed to the practice: there is simply nothing else like this peak experience of energy.

B EFORE HE LEARNED *Heart Rhythm Meditation, Phil experimented with drugs. He loved the feeling of exhilaration and god-like power that he got from cocaine and other stimulants. He was also attracted to dangerous sports, like race-car driving, which he said made him feel more alive than anything else. Phil's lifestyle changed when he became a meditator. The energy that now came from within himself was very tangible. It replaced his need for external stimulation with a desire to understand himself better. He became less frantic and more considerate.*

The "high" of meditation is more satisfying than the effect of drugs and danger, and once a person has felt it, external stimulants lose their appeal. Meditation's effects are:

• long lasting
• easy to control
• ecstatic
    • without side effects

2. The Benefits and the Elements

The excitement of danger is a result of adrenaline, which causes a short-term orientation and blocks "big picture" thinking. The excitement of Heart Rhythm Meditation is like the feeling of great joy. Drugs don't produce energy in the taker; they only borrow it from the next day. Taking drugs is like taking out a short-term loan with high interest. Heart Rhythm Meditation doesn't borrow energy from one's self; instead it increases the total energy one experiences by increasing the interaction between one's self and nature.

Courage and Power (FIRE)

To do extraordinary things, you need extraordinary energy. The energy discovered in meditation can give you the courage and confidence to:

- Face a crisis or an opponent with confidence, but not anger; forcefully, but without descending to personal attacks

- "Seize the high ground" by remembering the important issues when others are quibbling in the swamps of urgent problems

- Do what's right, although it's hard

- Radiate power to others during disappointing times, inspiring and empowering them to rise to the occasion and find creative solutions

Meditators have demonstrated incredible examples of generating and using energy—looking into the sun, for example—that strain our imagination and understanding. The objective of Heart Rhythm Meditation is not to look into the sun, but rather to apply that same inner power to face everyday situations with an intense glance and a temperament of fearlessness and undefeatable joy. Think of a situation that saps your confidence, whatever you find hardest to do.

THREE MEN IN *a Heart Rhythm Meditation course were asked to share their experiences of courage from the heart.*

An entrepreneur talked about having to go back to his investors to ask for more money because his project had slipped. They wouldn't reach break-even cash flow for another six months, and he needed bridge capital. It took a lot of courage—it was not the easy course—but he found an inner confidence that carried the day.

A doctor spoke of an operation he had just performed that had not improved the patient's condition. He thought a second operation would be successful, but there was always a risk of additional shock. He had to convince the hospital administration and the patient's family that the risk was justified. He had been anxious about the responsibility he took upon himself by making this recommendation, but his heart felt good about it, and the surgery worked. The patient recovered.

A portfolio manager described a situation he had faced when the investment policy he put in place did not increase the return of his fund after three months. He had repositioned the assets and changed the risk factors according to solid principles that he knew would work over the long term, but the returns were still unaffected. He felt that he had to hold his course while his changes took effect, and he needed the chief investment officer above him to keep his faith. There are many ways to look at performance in the short run, but only total return matters in the long run. Being in his heart allowed him to present his case to the CIO plainly and simply, with the power that comes from real confidence, not phony bravado. His heart inspired the CIO to respond from the same place, and he got the time he needed. The market correction in the next month hurt the competition but not his fund, proving the validity of his strategy.

Courage is like being the sun in the darkness. It's not imagining that you have the power of the sun in your eyes; it's acting like the sun itself. A meditator becomes sunlike. Meditation is about being, not just thinking.

2. The Benefits and the Elements

Using Your Feelings (WATER)

When once the heart begins to live, another world is open for experience. For generally what one experiences in one's everyday life is only what the senses can perceive and nothing beyond it. But when once a person begins to feel and experience the subtle feelings of the heart he lives in another world, walking on the same earth and living under the same sun. [2]

We sometimes distrust our feelings because feelings cannot be analyzed objectively or controlled willfully. In business, "personal feelings," it is said, cannot be allowed to interfere with decision making. The most successful people, however, admit to using "gut feelings" and other non-rational processes as an important part of decision making. A person who tries to act only mentally, without emotion, is fooling himself.

Emotion is "behind" thinking. If your feelings change, your thought-stream will quickly follow. When you're depressed, you'll think pessimistically about everything, but when you're happy, you'll think optimistically about the same situations. The objective is to match your feelings to the job at hand. Thinking your way through a situation can be effective, but feeling your way through it is much more involving, drawing upon what you know beyond your understanding.

- To turn around a bad situation, first go into the full emotion of disaster, letting yourself feel it fully without flinching from it. Then work yourself out of that feeling and into a hopeful feeling. Whatever worked for your personally, to transform your emotion, will likely work to transform the situation, when you make an appropriate translation.

- On the other hand, to make the most of an opportunity, first feel the full glory and joy of it. Then, instead of expressing that emotion directly, suppress it and let it emerge through you in activity that is appropriate to it.

---

2 Khan, I (1989, 287)

The difficulty with using emotions is that it takes practice to notice them as they emerge and to discriminate between them. We tend to identify with our feelings, like "I *am* depressed" instead of "I am *feeling* depressed," which makes it difficult to work with the feelings. Bringing your emotions into your identity makes them too close to see. With certain kinds of meditation, however, you can notice even subtle emotions clearly and distinctly, without identifying with them. You can then easily build a rich vocabulary for different kinds of feelings.

Perhaps one situation in your life makes you feel betrayed, but another makes you feel recognized. You need to concentrate only on the emotion appropriate to the situation at hand, or else your motivations and actions will be confused. Suppose someone who is sponsoring an idea that you favor is also someone who you feel has hurt you personally. You want to be able to respond positively to the idea with genuine feeling, putting aside your hurt feelings until you can talk with the person alone. Heart Rhythm Meditation makes all your emotions more conscious, so you can use them in ways that will help you most.

One feeling is often a cover for another feeling. For example, anger can cover hurt. We feel angry, but under that anger we feel hurt. We feel good when we can express the anger, but it is more honest to express the hurt. Saying "that hurt" instead of "you made me angry" is more likely to cause an opening in the other person than produce a defensive reaction on their part.

By developing a larger capacity for emotion, you open up a very broad band of communication with others. One result is that you are able to be more intimate with your spouse. Another result is the discovery of deeper and more genuine friendships.

M ARSHA WAS SERIOUSLY *depressed, which manifested as antipathy toward everything, extreme fatigue without drowsiness, and pessimism or indifference toward all that she once admired or coveted. She had no complaints, really—she wished she did have, because that might create a desire to get out of bed and do something about it. It was an unspecified discontent that arose in her. Her depression was actually not an emotion, it was a lack of emotion. Her husband urged meditation on her; she was unexcited and resented the intrusion. However, she soon found that meditation was neither disagreeable nor strenuous. Further, in Heart Rhythm Meditation, she found in her breath some glimmer of emotion, like a memory of something she'd lost long ago. After more practice she sensed that a very powerful emotion was trapped under a heavy floor of fear. She saw that a battle between this hidden emotion and her fear of it was what was annihilating her feeling for life. As she continued to meditate, the deep-sourced emotion grew stronger, but her fear of it also increased, keeping the emotion just beneath her awareness. She began to get hints of what it was she couldn't let herself feel: a profound discontent with her life and a longing for something else, even though her life's circumstances would be the goal of many. By letting meditation take her into the most uncomfortable part of her feeling space, she could hear the voice underneath the inner scream. She then knew how it frightened her to face a change in herself.*

Without meditation, we rarely get so much information about our inner state. In too many cases, the distress call that depression signals receives no answer, and the condition persists, sometimes for decades, eventually poisoning the physical body and causing disease. In Heart Rhythm Meditation, however, we feel both the fear and the longing that fear holds in check so much more intensely that a natural resolution must occur. Like two warriors who become so familiar with each other that they gain mutual respect and even admiration, the fear sees the longing's compellingness, and the longing hears the fear's warning of the fragility of life. Together they finally emerge as allies, freeing the emotional blockade they caused.

Reading Others (WATER)

Some people use a sophisticated intellectual and verbal screen to hide their feelings, perhaps even from themselves. People often don't know their real feelings. Even when they do, they seldom share them with others. You can help people if you can feel their emotions of which they are unaware. They may only hint at their feelings by verbal communication, but there is a way you can read their feelings directly and nonverbally:

- First, become aware of your own feelings, by placing your hand on your heart and directing your breath and attention to the center of your chest.

- Then, in the Heart Centered stage of Heart Rhythm Meditation, you let yourself become receptive to the other person, without resistance or judgment. You'll find the emotion of the other person emerging within yourself, as if it were your own emotion.

- Check out your experience by sharing with the other person how they make you feel in yourself. Notice if they were feeling the same way.

The prerequisites for this ability to read others emotionally are the ability to feel subtle emotions within yourself and a familiarity with a wide emotional range. Whenever someone sings into a piano, only those strings that correspond to the sung notes vibrate in response. Your response can become as fine as a musical instrument, so that the emotional vibrations of others vibrate within you.

W HEN A FIRE *breaks out at the hospital where you work, Dave is accused of starting it because he was seen in the area shortly beforehand. You always liked Dave personally. He absolutely denies any involvement and asks you for your help in defending himself against this charge, which would ruin his career. When you meet with him, you are receptive, but then you are surprised by a feeling that comes over you: you feel guilty yourself, as if you were the one who started the fire. Dave seems sincere, and you feel sorry for what may happen to him, but you have to counsel him to take responsibility for his actions because you know that he feels guilty inside himself.[3]*

Y OU ALWAYS ASSUMED *that Laura was a trustworthy associate and was loyal to you personally, but something she has just done has left you wondering. You could easily interpret her action as a deliberate attack with self-serving motives, perhaps as a favor to your rival. You need to know whether you can continue to trust her and rely on her support, or whether you have to assume that she is looking for a way to trip you up. You meet with her and meditate with open eyes as she talks. In the meditative state, you feel nothing but admiration and loyalty for her, which you therefore can interpret as her feeling for you, reflected within yourself. You realize that she is loyal; she was simply unaware of the effects of her actions on you.*

Creativity and Charisma (WATER)

Magnetism is a good example of a part of reality that you can feel but not see, although it can be sensed by instruments, some birds and other animals, and sensitive people. Human beings, plants, and animals have a kind of magnetic field, and they exchange energy with each other through these fields. You know what it means to be a magnetic person. There are now preliminary scientific methods for measuring this kind of magnetism. When we hold magnetism within ourselves, it produces creativity, and when it is expressed outward, it is charisma.

What people want from you, essentially, is your magnetism, because magnetism is capable of charging others with energy, just as a dynamo charges batteries. People who are tired, physically, mentally, or emotionally, need the energy that they can get from

---

3 Pir Vilayat and I met with "Dave," and Pir immediately felt that he himself was guilty. -Puran

your magnetism. You extend this magnetism through your presence, so people like to be around you; through your eyes, so people like your attention; through your words, so people like to listen to you; and through your smile, so people like to make you happy. To get the most out of others who work with you, you need to give them magnetism. You recharge your own magnetism from your deep emotions, which are accessed best in meditation.

VINCENT WAS GIVING *a presentation to the team from the customer's office. He spoke clearly and eloquently and was feeling sure of himself. Then the customers began to ask questions. Some of the questions were ones he could answer, but some were totally unexpected, forcing him to think carefully. There seemed to be no end of their questions; they were always ready with another one. His mind was getting drained; his speech became jumbled as he abandoned sentence structure. His eyes wandered. He was feeling attacked, under fire. Nothing seemed to satisfy them, and every question seemed like another attack.*

Then Vincent remembered that what people want is magnetism, not simply answers. The customers wanted to probe him, to find out how deep his resources were. They didn't really want the facts that would answer their questions—they wanted inspiration and creativity that they could apply to their problem themselves. He stopped struggling with answers that didn't satisfy them anyway. He just said things like "We'll have to work that out together" and smiled at them. It wasn't a tentative smile, and it wasn't an act. He reached into his emotion, and it came out as a smile that radiated reassurance and commitment. The customers stopped asking questions, and shortly after that they folded up their notebooks and left, satisfied. The rest of Vincent's team were ecstatic at how he turned around the customers' assault. The customers needed energy, in the form of inspiration, to find a creative solution to their problem. Vincent recovered his magnetism through his emotion. They got it as energy and used it to solve their problems themselves.

It is easy to get drained by the demands of those around you. If you let them, people will take as much magnetism as you have. You know when you've given too much when a meeting with another person leaves you feeling somewhat depressed. You can recharge your emotional energy, the source of your creativity and charisma, even while others try to drain you. Meditation is the quickest way to do it. You can feel the result immediately in your body, especially in your chest, and others can verify it.

Happiness (WATER)

Then there is the question of happiness. A person thinks that when his friends are kind to him, when people respond to him, or when he gets money, then he will be happy. But that is not the way to become happy: sometimes it proves the opposite. For lack of happiness makes him blame others, believing they are standing in the way of his becoming happy; in reality that is not so. True happiness is not gained, it is discovered.

Man's way itself is happiness, that is why he longs for happiness. What keeps happiness out of one's life is the closing of the doors of the heart, and when the heart is not living, then there is no happiness there. Sometimes the heart is not fully alive but only partly; at the same time it expects life from the other's heart. But the real life of the heart is to live independently in its own happiness; and that is gained by spiritual attainment, by digging deep into one's own heart.[4]

Truly, happiness comes from inside oneself, not from outer events.

---

4 www.hazrat-inayat-khan.org: Message: Vol 6, The Alchemy of Happiness: The Aim of Life

2. The Benefits and the Elements

SINCE SHE STARTED *Heart Rhythm Meditation, Christina has found that she is genuinely happy. She carries this happiness with her to her work. When work goes well, she is as pleased as anyone else. When work doesn't go well, she remains hopeful. She isn't working to make herself happy—she is independently happy.*
At first her boss thought she didn't care about or feel the problems in the company. But over time he has realized that she feels everything very deeply—she just has such a wealth of emotional energy that disappointments don't faze her. This is the unstoppable worker—it's done with emotion, not will power. One day he asked her, "What is the source of your optimism?" She said, "Optimism comes from the heart, not the head."

Most people think they need this or that to be happy, but it's not so.

One may live in a community where there is always amusement, pastimes, merriment, and beauty; one may live that life for twenty years; but the moment one realizes the movement in the depths of one's heart, one feels that those whole twenty years were nothing. One moment of life with a living heart is worth more than a hundred years of life with a heart that is dead.[5]

Happiness is a natural condition of the living heart.

There is the happiness of realizing that you don't need a reason to be happy.[6]

The religious sometimes de-emphasize personal happiness in favor of ritual and morality. The way of the heart is all about happiness. But the religious needn't worry—this isn't hedonism. Hap-

---

5 www.hazrat-inayat-khan.org: Message: Vol 10, Art: Yesterday, Today, and Tomorrow: 11. Poetry
6 Vilayat Inayat Khan, a common expression

piness, as distinct from pleasure, doesn't come from any particular sensation or event; it doesn't even come from getting your way or being rewarded. Happiness is truly a spiritual experience of harmony between your life and your heart.

Beside the obvious benefit that happiness has for yourself, your happiness is also a benefit to others. If you're happy you can be sympathetic, just as you must be (or feel) rich to be generous. Otherwise, your own problems are so consuming that you can't think of anyone else.

That person is living whose heart is living, and that heart is living which has wakened to sympathy. The heart void of sympathy is worse than rock, for the rock is useful, but the heart void of sympathy produces antipathy. [7]

The purpose of life is to be happy. As a Buddhist, I have found that one's own mental attitude is the most influential factor in working toward that goal. In order to change conditions outside ourselves, whether they concern the environment or relations with others, we must first change within ourselves. Inner peace is the key. [Dalai Lama] [8]

What does it mean to say that your happiness comes from your heart? It's your heart that remembers your purpose in life and guides you toward that purpose through your interests and passions. And it is progress toward the fulfillment of your purpose that produces happiness.

EVEN WHEN THE *heart is removed from the body, the heart muscle continues to contract rhythmically. The muscle cells of the heart are made this way; they love to beat. The heart muscle maintains its beat while the mind sleeps, even while you hold your breath. There are two sets of muscles for breathing, but the heart muscle has no alternate. The life of the heart is not boring;*

---

7 www.hazrat-inayat-khan.org: Message: Vol 13, Gathas: Metaphysics: 3.2 Sympathy

8 Epstein (1995)

it has to adjust to the needs of the other parts of the body. Sometimes it must beat very fast, accelerating instantly; it beats slowly while keeping a night vigil. The heart's echo is felt in every cell.

The heart is a metaphor for your happiness: Do what you love. Do it with a passion. Do it for yourself without needing attention from others. But listen to others and adjust what you do to suit their true needs. Be aware of the circle of your influence, and promote rhythm throughout that scope.

Concentration (AIR)

Concentration is the secret to accomplishment, yet few people have good concentration. Your ability to concentrate will improve dramatically when you use the techniques of Heart Rhythm Meditation. The practice you'll get at concentrating on your heart will immediately carry-over to all other concentrations.

AT A HEART *Rhythm Meditation course, a group of executives were introduced to a simple concentration exercise where it would be obvious if anyone lost their concentration. They were asked to sit still for 30 minutes. About half of the participants were able to do it; the others had some unconscious twitch or conscious discomfort that moved them. At the end, it was clear that each person knew which group they were in, so we didn't even mention their success or failure. We just asked them to do it again, using their heartbeat. A second attempt is usually less successful than the first because concentration is tiring, but with Heart Rhythm Meditation, they were* all *able to do it. The ones who had managed to keep still before found that the second time, it was pleasant instead of difficult and the others were delighted that they could succeed so easily where they had failed before. (The instructions for this exercise are in Chapter 5.)*

Distractions come from inner and outer sensations, but we have found that advanced Heart Rhythm Meditators can meditate even in the midst of noise and confusion.

AT THE MENNINGER INSTITUTE, *three meditators at different levels of experience were wired to separate EEG machines to test their ability to meditate. After all three showed the characteristic brain waves of meditation, the door to the lab room was opened and slammed shut. According to his brain waves, the beginner lost the meditative state and never regained it. The advanced meditator showed erratic brain waves for a few seconds, then slowly regained the state of concentration. The master had no change in his brain waves throughout the whole disturbance, indicating that his concentration never wavered.*

Relaxation is more difficult than it looks; it takes a lot of concentration to relax fully. Our muscles retain a considerable tension even when we are still, and that tension can remain unbroken for years. (The degree of muscle tension can be measured as a voltage in the tissue.) With practice, you can learn "profound relaxation," and it is a very pleasant way to increase your concentration power.

With concentration power, you will be able to switch your mental state from linear to creative, and vice versa. Left hemisphere dominance in the brain is better for logical and linear thinking, while right-hemisphere dominance is better for conceptual and creative thinking. A simple meditation allows you to monitor which hemisphere is dominant and change from one to the other. Someday this will be taught to schoolchildren. In the meantime, those who know how to tune their minds to the task at hand will have a clear advantage. The trick is that the left-right energy in your heart controls the right-left hemisphere dominance in your brain.

SUSAN SAT IN *another endless meeting—about integrating her two retail departments—that jumped from one detail to another without solving anything. She realized that the level of detail corresponded to the scope of what people could grasp at one time. She shifted her mind into the right hemisphere, using a simple breath she learned through Heart Rhythm Meditation, and started to see the synergy of the two departments in an over-all shopping experience. Then she spoke from that viewpoint and took everyone with her into a broad-based examination of the whole retail concept. As they agreed on the higher-level issues, the details fell out easily. The two departments were merged into one larger department with newly designed revenue units. The total sales far exceeded the combined sales of the two old de-partments.*

The mind follows the tuning of the heart. If you try to control your mind directly, it easily escapes. But your thinking follows the desire of your heart like a raft follows the current.

Insight (AIR)

We all live in the same world, and yet we perceive this world so differently. The meditator develops a power of insight that sees beyond the appearances of things. Through a keen sensitivity to vibration, it is possible to sense an essential quality in things.

JIM WAS A *buyer of organically grown produce. The ideal of healthy food was important to him, but he was aware that the higher prices paid for organic vegetables attracted some less idealistic farmers, so he was careful about checking out the growers for strict organic practice. As he was inspecting one farm, he began to suspect that the farmer was hiding something. One field had just been fertilized and Jim asked to see it. He picked up a handful of earth from the field. The farmer assured him that the fertilizer was a hundred percent organic, but Jim felt a strange sensation in his hand. Standing there in the sun, he meditated for a moment with his eyes focused on the soil in his hand. Then he noticed that a faint but clear bad taste was devel-oping in his mouth. Jim told the farmer that he knew it wasn't organic fertilizer. The farmer was caught and admitted that he had used "just a little of the chemical variety" to get a better yield. Jim said, "I can't buy your produce."*

Insight also applies to yourself, picking up the inner signals that can guide you into harmony with your immediate situation, resulting in effective action.

Insight into other people not only recognizes their present strengths but sees what they could be. The key to insight is to see with your heart, not your analytic and judgmental faculties. Consider people's motivation and desire more than their words and deeds.

W HEN C HARLES ADVERTISED *for an executive assistant, he knew that what he wanted was a person who would have the capacity to replace him ten years from now. How could he find the right person among the people waiting to see him? He gathered them all together, gave each of them a piece of paper, and asked them to write down their name and their qualifications. When they had all done that, he asked them to crumple up their papers and throw them into the wastebasket. Then he asked each one, "Why did you throw your paper away?" Everyone said roughly the same thing: "You told me to do it." Only Alice said, "Because I wanted to." It was Alice that Charles chose as his assistant.*

Intuition (AIR)

At the New York Stock Exchange, careers were made and lost over Black Monday—the largest single-day drop in the stock market ever recorded, in October 1987—depending on who had been able to see it coming and who hadn't. Some people clearly had seen it coming. They moved money out of the market, wrote newsletters, told their friends. Those who "knew" didn't attribute their insight to anything like psychic abilities or extrasensory perception; they spoke of economic indicators and "hunches." There is no question that we have intuition at times, or even regularly, but it might get lost in the "noise" of our other mental processes.

I don't believe in foretelling the future, but some of the factors shaping the future are already visible today. Meditation causes the mind to operate in such a way as to incorporate factors that seem logically unrelated into a single reality. With meditation, you should be able to discriminate between the reliable voice of intuition and the unreliable voices of fantasy and wishful thinking. Consequently, intuition will come more often and speak more loudly. As a result, your ability to sense future trends should improve greatly.

Julius Caesar said, "To govern is to foresee." Your job may require you to look ahead to the obstacles that are already forming in your future and to steer around them, avoiding danger for yourself and those you are responsible for. You already know much more than you believe you know, and meditation will help you extract that knowledge.

Another use of intuition is to see what is happening in the present at a distant place. You can learn to reach a colleague at a distance and share something of his or her experience, directly.

JOHN HAD AN *important sales call coming up. He had met Bob before, but he didn't know whether Bob would be receptive or hostile to him. Consequently, John didn't know whether to pitch the plan in a conservative way, expecting trouble and covering all the problems, or as an exciting opportunity, playing to the upside. John meditated on Bob and realized that Bob was very favorably disposed to him, that Bob would rather share in his excitement than raise stumbling blocks. So John prepared for a friendly audience—and got one.*

NANCY HAD RESPONSIBILITY *for a group in The Hague that she had never met with. She knew the manager there only slightly, from the few trips he had made to meet with her. She got weekly reports from him and monthly figures from the account-ant there, but she didn't feel that she really knew what was going on. Was the manager just telling her what she wanted to hear? Was he really doing all he could to find new business? The day before she met with him, Nancy did the Heart Rhythm Meditation she usually did, all the while thinking of her subordinate. She felt a deep conflict in her own emotions. The next day she asked him why he was feeling conflicted. He opened up and told her that he had discovered some facts about the company's operation that he felt were unethical, and he had been in a terrible conflict about how to handle it. She got him to share the information with her, and then she called a meeting with the head of the European division so that he could present his findings in the open. Subse-quently, he felt safety and understanding in his relationship with Nancy and never hesitated to share his concerns with her.*

Self-Mastery (EARTH)

The first step to integrity is to develop self-mastery. A person without self-mastery can't be trusted—your intention might be good, but a slip-up can ruin it. To be trusted, you must be able to trust yourself, knowing that your motivations and your conscience are clear. Then even if you act unconsciously, your actions will be consistent with your purpose. To be considered responsible by others, you must be responsible for yourself.

JACK WAS BOTH *admired and feared. He had the ability to make his subordinates feel that they were part of a family, or he could make them feel completely insecure, threatened, and an-gry. It all depended on his mood, and nobody knew what that depended on. At one moment, he wouldn't want to hear about anything. At another moment he would be yelling, "Why wasn't I told?" He fired people on the spot. Jack was never at fault, in his view, but his people frequently were. He was impulsive, making decisions quickly and sometimes reversing them just as quickly.*

His decision seemed to depend on who had talked to him last. On other issues, Jack was compulsive, holding to fixed concepts in which only he believed. He polarized people. His circle of admirers was large, but his circle of enemies was even larger. Although he had tremendous experience and a track record of success, he couldn't be trusted because he was out of control.

Jack started to build his self-mastery by learning the Heart Rhythm Meditation. It was easy for him to do the practice when his mood was "up," but he couldn't even think about it when he was "down." Slowly, the effects of the practice carried over from the up times to the down times. His temper still flared, but he could find his way out of the anger by remembering his practice. Eventually, he learned to control his breath, which controlled his moods. He could feel from his heartbeats that his heart was much less stressed, and so were the hearts of those who worked with him.

Heart Rhythm Meditation is a method to increase your self-mastery. Self-mastery is defined here as the ability to do what you want to do instead of what you don't want to do. For example, with self-mastery you would:

- Be able to master your desires, compulsions, and addictions (We are all addicted to something.)

- Have a deliberate positive effect on your physical health, especially your heart, nervous system, and some glands

- Be disciplined and purposeful about your use of time to accomplish goals

- Say what you mean and mean what you say

- Be patient with others

Even a slight increase in self-mastery will have a substantial effect on your accomplishments and your feelings about yourself. Self-mastery requires controlling the mind. To control your mind, you must first be able to control your body. To control your body, the key thing is to control the nervous system. Among meditators, the degree of self-mastery is astonishing; some can control their heart rate, blood pressure, metabolic rate, body temperature, and even the rate at which wounds heal.

To be what you want to be, you need the help of your closest allies: your body and your mind. If you have trained them through concentration and rhythm, they will respond to your wish.

Trusting and Trustworthy (EARTH)

We build trust by the consistency and stability of our behavior and our relationships with others, but unforeseen events test that trust.

KATHY'S MOTHER DIED *when she was young, and her father, an alcoholic, was unavailable to her emotionally. Kathy didn't have anyone to trust, so she learned how to get through on her own—a survival mechanism that hindered her adult relationships. She was suspicious and critical of trust, consistency, and intimacy because they had not been familiar to her in her childhood. Because of her conditioning, she unconsciously expected to be abandoned and consequently could not accept being loved. When she married, she constructed unconscious tests of her husband's commitment. She belittled him in front of others, found fault with everything he did, and withdrew emotionally and sexually. He survived these tests, but she was still not satisfied because she could only imagine that he would leave her.*

When she first tried meditation to go into the depth of her heart, she found it too painful to bear. Fortunately, her meditation teacher helped her realize that her adaptation to her circumstances was preventing her from having the experience of the heart that she longed for.

Her Heart Rhythm Meditation developed in her, over some years, the beginning of an ability to trust. It came out of her experience that every time she looked for her heartbeat, it was there. The emotional impact of this obvious fact is unbelievable to one who has never done it or who has no issue with trust. It is not a fact like one would record after a medical examination; it is an intimate experience of feeling the heart in unceasing motion within one's self. Kathy learned that she could, and must, trust at least this—that her heart sustains her very life, every moment of every year, and that her unconscious sustains her heartbeat.

Through the direct experience of her heart, she opened herself to love; through the constancy of her heartbeat she opened to trust; through both she opened to her husband's love. Through continuously deepening the practice, she eventually found that she could be present in her marriage, feel herself being trustworthy, and go beyond her old survival mechanism.

Practicing meditation has been compared to exploring a castle—the castle of the mind. As a result of this exploration, the mind of the meditator holds fewer surprises than that of one who has not yet explored the inner depths and heights. Consequently, the meditator is more reliable over a greater range of unexpected events.

Trust requires honesty and reciprocity. We don't trust someone who doesn't trust us. Where does it start? It starts with someone who has found something in himself or herself that is trustworthy and who looks for the same in others. Such a person is often a "deep" person, who thinks about things deeply. This quality is developed by meditation.

ONE EXAMPLE OF *a man who was trusted is Nicholas of Flüe, a Swiss meditation master. In 1481 he was approached by both the French-speaking and the German-speaking factions in Switzerland, who were on the brink of civil war. Nicholas suggested that they form a federation, which not only resolved their conflict but left a model that has been used by many governments since, including the United States. Nicholas was asked to serve be-*

cause both sides trusted him. He was known to be wise and fair, and he had nothing to gain personally.

Who is trusted today? In Latin America, Roman Catholic cardinals sometimes mediate in peace negotiations because they are respected by both sides. What qualities and qualifications would one need to be widely respected and trusted in this country, at this time? Integrity is the world's most highly prized quality; those who want integrity must be willing to sacrifice their selfishness for it. We prove that we are fair by being able to decide against our self-interest, in the short term.

EVERYONE IN THE *corporation wanted to be seen as having integrity, and no one was ready to give the title to anyone else. It was an ideal, like a god, that all the employees coveted. Yet the attainment of this ideal was elusive because no one could define integrity, and no one had a method for developing it. Yet they all could sense it, and they could easily find its lack. Anyone who had the quality even slightly became a confidant and mentor for others.*

Self-Knowledge (EARTH)

To be honest with others, you must be thoroughly honest with yourself. But what is the self? Self-knowledge comes from many sources: experience, self-inquiry, relationships with others, accomplishing goals, meeting challenges, and so on. Yet meditation offers a method of obtaining self-knowledge that is so rapid and efficient that it is a quantum leap ahead of these other ways of learning about the self.

One model of the self that has evolved from meditation is this: You are actually an organization of sub-personalities, and the self is the one who leads the organization.

2. The Benefits and the Elements

YOU'RE IN CHARGE *of making a project happen, and there is lots to do: people to see, events to coordinate. The hardest work, however, is the coordination of your own internal team of specialists. The writer in you wants satisfaction and sees an opportunity to spend a few days in charge. The social part of you wants to go talk to people, and this project is a good excuse. The child in you just wants to play with the model. Your body wants attention too and might succeed in pulling a work stoppage for a snack or some exercise. The financial planner in you, however, is usually scared and works only when pressured, so his important job may get overlooked.*

All your sub-personalities can make a contribution, but they need to be coordinated to accomplish your purpose. If the body were not coordinated by the brain, it couldn't walk, even though the parts are capable on their own. The self is actually the coordinating function of the whole team, but we usually identify with only one part of our capability at a time. The part that we identify with is the part that is in control at that time. So we might say, "I'm a writer," when we are writing something.

By identifying with the coordinator, and no single part, we maintain our integrity and accomplish our purpose. When we lack integrity, it is because different parts of our internal team have gone in different directions, with the consequence that other people see no consistency in our actions. It is the job of the self to coordinate and direct the team to work as one, without hidden agendas, cross-purposes, conflicting motivations, and so on. A coordinator that is strong from self-mastery and smart from self-knowledge can make the team work together.

In meditation, you can identify each member of your inner team and strengthen the coordinator, which is your real self. This concept of the self is an ancient one, and it has enabled great men and women throughout history to learn the combination of respect and control that is needed with one's self. This balance is the great art, the art that we need in order to be what we can be.

2. The Benefits and the Elements

Being Natural (All Elements)

There are many paths to success. What works for one person will not work for another. You will be successful if you follow your own way. There are many kinds of meditation. Each person needs a meditation that is appropriate to his or her path and that provides the right kind of challenge. Whether you are advancing in a career or in your personal development, your practice must be customized to your type and your current level of self-awareness.

Your self-understanding will be enhanced by your experience of the Elements through the four Element Breaths in Part 3. Everyone has an element that they have already developed well and another element that they are trying to develop now. An element that is not so visible in your behavior, attitude, and abilities may be eclipsed by a more prominent element. To see what is latent in yourself, you need a non-rational process of discovery so that the critical and logical mind doesn't react out of habit, overpowering the subtle but growing aspects of yourself. This is the benefit of using meditation to explore yourself.

You might ask why a developing trait is important if it's so hard to find within the complexity and richness of your psyche. The answer is that consciously or unconsciously, your growing edge receives priority in your attention and interest, so it is most compelling and influential in making choices. You are drawn to those people who already demonstrate that element you are trying to develop in yourself. You will make choices that place you in situations that need, and therefore develop, those elements that you want to develop in yourself.

BILL IS A MANAGER *for a major international corporation. When I talked to him about the elements, he emphasized the fire in himself. Coincidentally, the corporation clearly valued fire qualities in its managers: risk taking was admired, superhuman efforts were expected, and goals were set high but nothing less was acceptable. Bill had learned a managerial style of "kicking butt" that pushed the competition and aggressiveness at his level down to his subordinates. In meditation Bill rediscovered a set of Water qualities that he had repressed in his career but that actually felt more natural to him than his adopted style. I advised him that the key to management is to manage in a way that is true to your nature. He became inspired to discover what managerial style would fit his Water Element and also meet his goals. Bill made a deliberate decision to change the way he managed his unit, emphasizing teamwork, mutual support, attention and praise, no-fault problem solving, and customer satisfaction. His manager gave him a chance to invest in the process and see if it would produce results. Not only did his unit become a star performer, Bill's own level of job satisfaction soared. There is no implied judgment of water-good, fire-bad in this story. Other managers have found the Fire Breath to be validating, rejuvenating, exciting, and fun. They sharpened their focus and made productive use of the energy boosts they got from it. At another time, they will come to value the way of water, and Bill will truly learn the way of fire, not as a tactic but as a natural experience of his fire aspect. Success comes when the inner reality matches the outer reality: behavior expresses understanding that expresses feeling.*

You will ultimately unfold within yourself all four of the elements, but the sequence and timing of that development will be unique for you.

Goals for Heart Rhythm Meditation

Now that you've read these stories of how Heart Rhythm Meditation can be applied, and you have some notes of your reactions, consider which Element—Air, Fire, Water, or Earth—you would like to develop in yourself, and how, specifically, that might help you. If you can form a goal for yourself, meditation will go much more easily than if you simply "try it out" with no particular need or expectation. Here are some examples of meditation goals.

They too are grouped by Element: Air, Fire, Water, and Earth. The more specific you can be about why you want to learn Heart Rhythm Meditation, the more motivation you will have. Consider the following goals that can be accomplished with Heart Rhythm Meditation, and choose one for yourself, modify one, or make up one of your own.

Vision (Air)

• Sharpen and intensify your concentration
• Be able to shift from linear to holistic thinking, and back
• See more of the latent potential in others
• Consciously use your inner signals for decision making
• See the meaningfulness of your present life situations
• Pick up future trends by intuition
• Develop a personal vision of your life's purpose

Energy (Fire)

• Recover from stress more rapidly
• Increase your capacity for stress through the power of your heart
• Sleep less, using the time for reflection and planning
• Face everyday situations with more courage

Emotional Capacity (Water)

• Use your subtle feelings as a "sixth sense"
• Become capable of a deeper involvement with others
• Have a better sense of the emotional state of others
• Be more creative
• Be a more magnetic leader

Integrity (Earth)

- Increase your self-discipline and mastery
- Have a deliberate positive effect on your physical health
- Be disciplined and purposeful about time management
- Say what you mean and mean what you say
- Be more patient with others
- Be more trustworthy and trusting
- Manage your many traits and skills toward a purpose

Part 2

THE
PRACTICE

3. POSTURE AND ENVIRONMENT (PREPARATION)

Part 2 describes seven steps of Heart Rhythm Meditation in both theory and technique. When one learns meditation from a teacher—the easiest and most effective way to learn meditation—the teacher provides the student with ongoing feedback. In learning meditation from a book, considerably more background must be presented so as to include the particular advice a teacher would have given.

The worst problems you will encounter with meditation are those you are not aware of. If you don't breathe out sufficiently, you probably won't know it. If you breathe erratically, you won't realize you're doing it. If you go to sleep, you won't see it coming. Once you have learned Heart Rhythm Meditation, doing it alone is sublime. We all need some help in getting started, however, and in getting through some of the well-known tough spots along the way. The instructions here are designed for you to use alone or with a group. (See Chapter 16 for instructions on solo and group practice.) If you're starting out alone, I hope you can soon find a group with whom you can practice.

If you encounter a problem with one of these steps in the practice of meditation, another tactic (besides getting help) is to go on to the next step. The process of learning meditation is actually not as sequential as we describe it here. Sometimes a later step is easier than an earlier step. Attempting a more challenging experience may foster an easier one. The future pulls upon the present. Conversely, when you have completed these steps, start over at the beginning, and let each step unfold in a new and deeper way. Once these practices have helped you to find and strengthen your heart, then the four Elements of the Heart (in Part 3) become tools for operating your heart.

Straightness

It is first necessary to relax the body, to be comfortable, but not to sit in too soft a chair or to lie down, for while the body is resting in meditation it is not in the same condition as in sleep. As mystical training is to make the body the temple of God, the body must not be neglected.

In order to meditate, attention is first given to the body, to see that it is relaxed, yet comfortable. Sitting in too soft a chair may make one too drowsy, while too hard a chair may make one uneasy. A moderate degree of composure is desirable whether one is seated or in posture. The room should be neither too hot nor too cold, and it is generally best if one is not too hungry, although meditation after a full meal is not so easy nor always so advantageous.[1]

Lying down, however, is not satisfactory for then the heart currents change in direction and besides, it is easier to fall asleep, which would destroy the purpose of the meditation.[2]

For you to listen to your heartbeat, your torso has to be upright, not bent. If you slouch, you put pressure on the chest and on the heart. That pressure will dampen the heartbeat, making it very difficult to feel. When you sit up straight with your shoulders back, you take the pressure off the heart, and its beat can resound throughout the chest. If you have trouble listening to your heart, then, the first consideration is your posture.

A second reason for sitting up straight is that it gives the diaphragm the most room to expand as you breathe in. Slouching

---

1 Khan, I (1989, 223-4)

2 Khan, I (1989, 287)

folds the stomach area and prevents it from expanding. (More details about this are in Chapter 6.)

A third reason is that the spine must be straight to optimize its efficiency as a channel for energy. One researcher has found that a low-frequency vibration resonates in the spinal cord during meditation.[3] To allow this vibration, the spine must be relaxed. As with a vibrating string, if the spine is tightened, its resonant frequency will increase. The way to relax the spine is to make it straight; any bending tightens the spinal cord. Bending forward, slouching, and pulling the legs up all tighten the spinal cord and, therefore, raise its resonant frequency, which makes it more difficult to attain the low-frequency vibration of meditation.

Of course, the spine has a natural curve in it, which the spinal cord accommodates. A "straight" spine means a spine that is not curved in any other way besides this natural curve. The scientific reason that having a low-resonant frequency in the spinal cord is beneficial is speculative. It may be that the low-frequency brain waves that occur in meditation are able to propagate down the spine and thereby spread this literal vibration throughout the body. It may be that the spine acts like an antenna and is able to draw energy from the universe by resonance at some low frequencies. The spinal column behaves like an electrical cable in some situations, conducting energy and transforming energy from one kind to another.

---

3 Bentov (1977, 42)

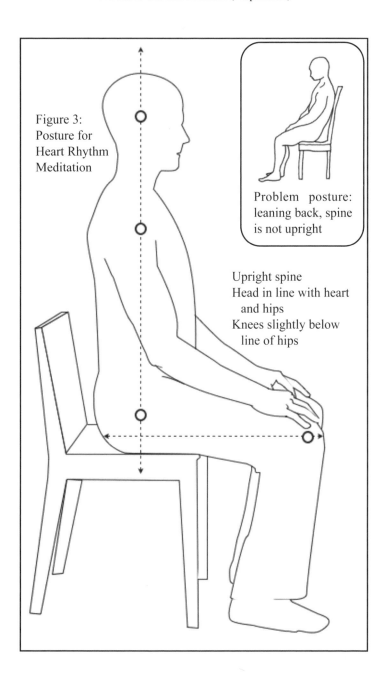

Figure 3:
Posture for
Heart Rhythm
Meditation

Problem posture:
leaning back, spine
is not upright

Upright spine
Head in line with heart
 and hips
Knees slightly below
 line of hips

Sitting

Sit up straight, without leaning back against a support. The thighs must be either level or angled down so that the bottom of the spine can be vertical. (When the thighs make an acute angle with the torso, the bottom of the spine curves.) The spine is further straightened by relaxing the shoulders.

Stretch your shoulders upward, as if you are trying to touch your ears. Now, while the shoulders are up, pull them back so that the shoulder blades meet in the back. Keeping the shoulders back, bring them down again, and then relax. You will be in a royal pose, with the chest out but not forced.

Place the hands one over the other in the lap, or one hand on each thigh.

Remember that you can't relax a muscle—in this case, the shoulder muscles—by keeping it still. Relaxation comes after tension. If you stretch, tensing a muscle, you can then relax it much more than before.

The purpose of poise or position is to keep the body in equilibrium, so that one will not sway nor have to exert a force to retain this position, to keep steady.[4]

The easiest way to get the posture right is to sit on a simple chair, with your feet on the floor, your knees and your hips making right-angles. This is the majestic position of the pharaohs and kings, and you'll feel majestic too.

Most chairs tilt the hips backward, so you may need a small pillow under your sitting bones to ensure that your knees are below your hips so your thighs are level or pointing downward. Or you can sit on the edge of your chair without leaning back, as shown in Figure 3. Your back should be like an antenna tower connecting

---

4 Khan, I (1989, 233)

heaven to earth. A meditation posture should be comfortable, stable, and straight.

Once you learn to meditate, posture becomes less important, but only slightly less. Even twenty-year meditators find that results are best when the fundamentals *aid* their concentration. At the beginning of meditation, good posture has such a powerful effect that it's not worthwhile to try meditation without it. Rather than trying to overcome the effects of a poor posture by concentration, take a few minutes and get the posture right, then ride the currents of energy that result.

Stillness

Even though you may start out comfortable, you will soon become uncomfortable if you don't make the leap from regular consciousness to meditation consciousness. The body likes to move; it was made for movement, and movement draws energy to it. It is hard to hold the body still, but if you do, the energy concentrated in the muscles is dispersed throughout the body by the arteries and nerves into a brilliant energy in the mind.

As you sit very still, you will soon notice an impulse to move. If you look at that impulse without acting on it, it will recede, and more energy will pass from your physical body to your mind. Let your body feel as if it is sinking. Its weight is an attraction to the earth, which pulls your body into itself. The human body is made of the earth, so let it feel like a rock, a wonderfully strong and dense rock, a rock that is very happy to be a rock.

I want to point out here an important concept of Heart Rhythm Meditation: The physical reality is not denied. The early Eastern pioneers of meditation found that an effective technique for learning meditation was to deny that one's body is one's own. (This is the true self-denial, which has been misunderstood by non-meditators. Self-denial means to deny that you are what you think you are.) In Heart Rhythm Meditation, we affirm that there is a body-mind connection, that your physical body is a creation of your mind, and conversely, that the state of your physical body affects your mind.

Two quotes below show this interaction between the mind and the body, the inner and the outer. First, Rumi points out that our physical senses can awaken us to what we then sense inwardly.

A feeling of fullness comes,
but usually it takes some bread to bring it.

Beauty surrounds us, but
usually we need to be walking in a garden to know it.

The body itself is a screen to shield and partially reveal
the light that's blazing inside your presence.

Water, stories, the body, all the things we do,
are mediums that hide and show what's hidden.

Study them, and enjoy this being washed with a secret
we sometimes know, and then not.[5]

The other side is that we need our inner feeling to activate our outer perception.

There were bells, all around,
But I never heard them ringing,
No, I never heard them at all,
Till there was you.[6]

The Vedantic and Buddhist traditions advise one to say, "This is not my body," or, "I am not this body." This philosophy is effective as a step to upward meditation, but it is not really true; we are our bodies. Far from having any disregard for the body, people in our time are more and more amazed by the innate intelligence within even a single cell of the body. We know that the mind alters the physical substance of the body and that the body forms the "wiring" of the mind. We see in the genetic code a fantastic accu-

---

5 Barks (1995)

6 "Till There Was You", song

mulation of experience over the life of our species and beyond into the life of all life.

I can say that there is much more to that which I am than what appears in physical form. But the physical form is a representation of all the nonphysical layers of being.

SHEILA IS A BEAUTIFUL *woman, intelligent and aware. She likes to decorate her skin with colors and her body with perfumes, fabrics, and jewelry. Beatrice, who shuns makeup, criticized her for being vain and foolish. "You're an ignorant victim of the fashion and advertising industries," Beatrice told her. "The time you spend on your appearance is an exploitation by others who have created an image of what is beautiful and expect you to adhere to it. Your susceptibility to the images of advertising shows your ignorance of who you really are, and your need to artificially augment your image shows your lack of confidence in your own natural beauty."*

"On the contrary," Sheila said, "I have a vision of my soul and that vision is exquisitely beautiful. All that I see as beautiful in the physical world—harmony of color, symmetry of form, gracefulness of line—is still nothing compared with the luminous beauty of what I feel within. It is natural that I should want to express the beauty I feel."

"You are deluded by your culture into thinking that you have to make yourself beautiful to be attractive. Actually, it's the one who sees beauty who becomes beautiful," said Beatrice.

"I agree with that," said Sheila, "and the one who expresses beauty makes it easier for others to see beauty."

"But your body is already beautiful in its natural state. You don't need to decorate it," countered Beatrice.

"I do need to. A poet may have a beautiful insight, but then she expresses it even more beautifully in rhyme. A photographer enhances the beauty of a landscape by finding just the right viewpoint from which to see it. In a similar way, I want to participate in and contribute to the beauty that God provided. It's

the job of art to enhance nature," said Sheila. "I try to bring out beauty in my personality, in my surroundings, in my children. Why not in my body as well?"

"You shouldn't encourage people to value what's superficial," retorted Beatrice. "People should learn to look deeper and appreciate the essence."

"Well then," said Sheila, "we should banish flowers and put seeds on our tables instead."

Unity is our aim on the path of the heart. The experience of unity is felt everywhere: it's not just mental; it's physical too. In Heart Rhythm Meditation, you will experience unity of your soul, heart, mind and body. Your focus on your heart will center you in your physical body, but not limit you to its confines. You are simultaneously matter, energy, light and vibration, all centered in your heart and expanding outward to infinity.

The skin has the ability to sense pressure, temperature, and pain. Through the pressure sensors in your skin, you can tell whether you are sitting or standing and where your hands are placed on the legs. But any sensation that is constant diminishes in our awareness, so in stillness your ability to feel the position of your body will diminish. Any movement, however, will cause a change in pressure somewhere, and bodily sensation will immediately return.

We begin by centering consciousness in the body in order to hold it still. At first it will feel very heavy; then it will feel monolithic, undifferentiated. If you are able to sit still for 20 minutes, what you will feel is not numbness but this "monolithic" sensation. In this sensation you can still feel your hands and your legs, but you don't feel that they touch each other. Rather, they seem to merge. It is not clear where your hands stop and your legs start, because you can't feel the pressure on the skin of your hands caused by the contact with your legs, nor the pressure on the skin of your legs caused by the weight of your hands. At first, you could feel whether your hands were palm up or palm down on your legs and where exactly they were placed. Now you can't tell by feel; you have to look at your hands to know where they are. If you move them slightly, you will then instantly be able to feel the position of your hands again.

By sitting completely still, your sense of your body will change dramatically. After about 20 minutes, the pressure sense turns off, and while you will still be aware of your body, especially the inside of it, your body will seem to be monolithic—that is, one piece without subdivisions. You won't be able to tell by feel alone, without looking, where your hands are or what posture you are sitting in.

When this happens, enjoy your freedom from physical sensation. Your mind will seem to be supercharged as the attention that it usually devotes to sensation is reallocated to creative thought. Any physical movement will immediately change this condition.

By itself, stillness is hard to achieve. It is easy if you add the concentration on breath from the next step, "Turn Within."

How still do you have to be? You can breathe, and you can swallow. If your eyes are open, try not to blink and pick a spot on the wall in front of you to focus on. (It's best to have the eyes closed or at least half-closed).

We are used to being either awake and in motion or asleep and still. To be awake and to be still is an unusual condition. After 20 minutes stillness becomes easy because the physical impulses to move die out. You know that you can move your body at will, but you don't want to. The first 20 minutes, however, are difficult as the body makes frequent demands to move. Keeping still is like wrestling with yourself. Occasionally an impulse sneaks past the conscious will and results in a movement that you notice only after it occurs. Being able to control those impulses demonstrates will-power and self-control, qualities necessary for success.

The monolithic sensation is the first dramatic evidence in the path to meditation that *something is happening*! Led by the shift in your sensory perception, your consciousness is integrating your physical and non-physical aspects, while retaining body-centeredness. It isn't meditation yet, it's concentration, but it is still a milestone to be celebrated. The skill of being able to sit still is not only necessary for the next stage in Heart Rhythm Meditation but a power in itself.

IN THE LATE *1960s, I attended a large lecture at my graduate school, the University of Pennsylvania. I arrived early to get a good seat and found that the guest lecturer was already there. He stood at the front of the lecture hall facing the audience, next to the lab table. He stood simply, not stiffly, but he was completely still. It is unusual to see anyone be still, especially when standing in front of an audience. His stillness, with his eyes open but unmoving, drew the complete and silent attention of the audience. Before he said a word, I was already tuned to him and ready to listen to anything he had to say. I knew he was the master of his body and mind.* PURAN

Therefore the mystics prescribe certain postures in order to make the body stable. And steadiness of body reacts upon the mind, making it steady also. The mind and body react on each other. So a self-mastered person who has control over his body and mind has balance and wisdom. Wisdom comes from steadiness and insight follows wisdom. [7]

One has a better possibility of controlling the mind if one can control the body. It is like developing the ability to ride a horse well before trying the jumps.

---

7 www.hazrat-inayat-khan.org: Message: Vol 13, Gathas: Insight: 1.10 Different Qualities of Mind

3. Posture and Environment (Preparation)

 SIT PERFECTLY STILL FOR 20 MINUTES OR UNTIL THE "MONOLITHIC SENSATION" OCCURS.

Turn Within

The doors of the senses should be held closed; shutting the eyes partly or entirely is beneficial. The room should not be too brightly lit nor too dark, but it is by self-control that one must shut out other disturbances. Nevertheless, especially for the beginning, a quiet place is desirable.[8]

Visual sensations are very compelling—they draw our awareness away from our selves. In meditation, we are choosing to temporarily turn our attention away from sights and sounds and toward that which interprets sights and sounds. We do this so that when we open our eyes to the world again, we will see it as it really is, as multiple representations of a single wholeness with infinite potential. How will we know that our vision is more realistic? We will be better able to operate reality if we see it correctly, so we will be better able to accomplish what we wish to accomplish and to become what we wish to become.

> Close your eyes. This quickly shifts your attention from what's around you to what's inside you. At first, the world around you will continue to dominate your attention, only it's not the world that appears around you but the world you create by the way you think.

"Surround yourself with a zone of silence"—this is an instruction of Buddha. The silence you need for meditation is self-created; it cannot be found. Use the zone of silence to create a

---

8 Khan, I (1989, 223-4)

space more quiet and peaceful than any place you could find. Do this simply by turning your attention away from sounds and toward that which interprets the sounds. Feel your ear functioning as it responds to vibrations; watch your mind associating vibrations with thoughts.

Once you see how this works, you may question whether you will continue to allow your thinking to be dominated by some waves of sound. So much more is happening in reality than the narrow spectrum of vibrations to which the ear is sensitive. With all due respect for the ears, is it right that your thinking should be so directed by the sound waves that happen to be occurring in your immediate environment? What about the cosmic rays that are striking the top of your head from their source deep in space? What about the sensations of all the other organs in the body and the thoughts they provoke?

Although you will always be aware of the sounds of the environment around you, you can shift your interest from the outside and toward the inside. When you do, you'll find that your thoughts are little affected by sounds that were once so compelling.

Over time, the world will recede and form a horizon around your inner self. Your thinking will become more deeply personal. Ultimately, at the core of "within" lies the essence of all that is "within" and "without." The journey within does not result in an isolated individual. It results in the discovery that what is most personal and most intimate is also universal.

I WAS MEDITATING IN *a cave in the French Alps on a twenty-eight-day spiritual retreat. I looked out through the mouth of the cave across the valley of Chamonix to Mont Blanc, the highest peak in Europe, which seemed to be only slightly higher than where I was. Far above the treeline and above most clouds, I looked at a heavenly world of incredible beauty. I cannot imag-*

ine a more ideal physical setting for meditation, and I go back to that place very quickly in my mind. However, it was still not quiet. There was the noise of airplanes and helicopters, the shrieking of marmots (a kind of groundhog), the dripping of water, and frequently the crash of thunder. It was not comfortable; it was cold, the rocks were hard, and the flies landed on my face. Both the beauty of the place and its noises and discomforts distracted me from meditation. I often sat facing the inside of the cave to keep from being mesmerized by Mont Blanc's grandeur. I had to create my own zone of silence.

In the end, what helped me most about the physical location was its close proximity to my teacher, Pir Vilayat Inayat Khan; the uplifting energy of the mountains; and the atmosphere of those who had meditated in the cave before me.

SIT IN A STATE OF STILLNESS AND INNER FOCUS WHERE YOU NOTICE THE DIFFERENCE BETWEEN THE PHYSICAL ACTIVITY OF HEARING AND THE MENTAL ACTIVITY OF ASSOCIATING THOUGHTS WITH SOUNDS.

Diet

We start the journey to the spiritual and to wholeness by using the physical, then the mental and the emotional levels of our being. Nothing can be omitted from the journey. Meditation is not just a mental exercise; it is physical as well, and it is aided by good health and a fine diet.

On the one hand, it's good to avoid dietary dogma; as Jesus Christ said:

It's not what you put into your mouth that defiles you, for that passes through the body and is eliminated. It's what comes out of your mouth that can defile you. [9]

However, the dietary advice of Moses and Muhammad must also be considered. These two prophets prohibited many of the same foods, especially pork.

We feel that a heart-centered way to approach diet is this: Observe what each food does to you physically, mentally, and emotionally. Then choose the food you need to accomplish your goals. Every food has benefits; many foods also have liabilities. If you can notice their effects on you, you can use them for your purpose.

The caveat in this advice is that some foods desensitize a person so much that it is very difficult to feel the effects of other foods. During the period in which you are observing the effects of foods upon yourself, abstinence from these products will be necessary: tobacco, red meat, pork, and anything fermented, including vinegar and alcohol. It may take a week or more for your body to eliminate these desensitizing foods before you'll be able to observe the effects of other foods upon you.

The effect of a food is strongest if you take it alone. Sample the most likely problem foods first: chocolate, milk, wheat, yeast, corn, shellfish, coffee, eggs. In each case, take a good helping and then meditate. As you sit quietly with your eyes closed, notice everything you can about your inner state. If you feel dizzy, dazed, sleepy, agitated, anxious, fearful, or angry; or if your face feels flushed or itchy; or if your stomach is upset or your tongue burns; or if you have to clear your throat or have difficulty swallowing, then put that food on your "suspect" list. Try other foods, and then retry the foods on your suspect list again in a few days. Finally, try the desensitizing foods listed above, the ones you've been avoiding, one at a time, to see for yourself what they do to you.

---

9 Mark 7: 18-20

You may find that you are immune to the negative reactions that most people have to some of the desensitizing foods, like vinegar. But it is very likely that some foods that are harmless to others, like milk products or wheat, will have a very negative effect on you.

When you know what meat and alcohol, for example, do to you, then you'll know what situations they are suited to, and you can use them in those situations. We are against nothing—there is nothing that doesn't have a value to someone at some time. There are occasions when being desensitized is advantageous, allowing action without consideration of the consequences. Generally, it is better to choose a food that gives you nourishment and energy without impairing your awareness, but with enough spiritual power, according to Saint Mark, even poison can be digested.[10]

Meat is a highly concentrated form of large amounts of grain and vegetables, and as such it has a powerful grounding effect. Some people need meat in their diet, especially those who are weak genetically or have been weakened through abuse or illness, so that their physical or mental stability is lessened. Unfortunately, the effects of the hormones and drugs in meat can cause unnatural physical and mental changes. Some people absorb the fear and panic of the slaughtered animal, and the animal's despair from its severely caged existence, into their own emotional state, continuing in a muted form as depression or anxiety. We can also absorb many good and natural qualities of the animals and birds we eat, especially if the animal has been treated compassionately. However, from an ecological perspective, it is clear that eating animals instead of the grains and water that the animals consume is terribly inefficient, and even wealthy nations can barely afford it.

---

10 Mark 16:18

*The Sufi takes great care in his life as to what he should
eat and what he should drink. Alcoholic drinks and drinks
made from decayed fruits naturally make the breath impure; even smoking tobacco has a bad effect on the
breath. Those who observe the mystical rules carefully
even refrain from all flesh food, even from eggs. No doubt
white meat is preferable to red meat, for red meat has
particles which block the channels of the breath. This was
the reason why the eating of pork was prohibited by the
prophets of Beni Israel. No doubt to the pure all things
are pure, but in order to become pure it is necessary to
observe the rules of purity.*

*One must not judge of another person's spiritual evolution
by seeing what he eats or drinks, because this has nothing
to do with a man's evolution, for Shiva, the great Lord of
Yogis, had fish for his food, and wine was given in the
church of Christ as a sacrament. Therefore no one has the
power to estimate his fellow-man from what he eats or
drinks. But everyone who wishes to tread the spiritual
path may observe the mystical law, which certainly enables one to progress speedily. It must be remembered
that it is the spiritual ideal which is the first thing to be
held fast; what to eat and drink, and what not to eat and
drink is a secondary thing. Any dispute about this proves
to be unnecessary.*[11]

Sleep

*To anyone who has a great deal of nervousness, long
hours of sleep must be prescribed, and even if they cannot
sleep the mere fact of lying in bed would be most helpful;
for rest of the body regulates its circulation and the*

---

11 www.hazrat-inayat-khan.org: Message: Vol 13, Gathas: Everday Life:
Inner Ablutions

rhythm of pulsation and gives much of the same result which Yoga practice produces.

Those who have need and time to rest from half-an-hour to one-and-a-half hours after luncheon may take a rest then.

It is not necessary that pupils should do their meditation trying to avoid sleep. If by doing meditation they can sleep, so much the better, for the meditation continues through sleep in the subconscious. If a pupil does a certain meditation at night before going to sleep and through that meditation goes to sleep, it would still make a hundred times greater effect than if the pupil engaged himself in doing different things between his meditation and sleep.

It must be prescribed to the pupil to do his exercises in bed immediately as he wakes in the morning, and just before he goes to bed. The importance of the process is in engraving all he practices in his subconscious mind, for that is where the phenomenon is hidden. [12]

Meditation is very different from sleep, but meditation can lead to a wonderful sleep. Going to sleep is making an abrupt transition in consciousness, as is meditating; the third great transition is death. Of these three, the most deliberate transition is meditation, and the least intentional is death. One can avoid meditation, but one cannot avoid sleep for long. One can learn to make the transition to the meditative state almost at will, but sleep is less willful. Practice in meditation makes transitions in consciousness easier, so a meditator gains more control over the onset of sleep.

Sleeping is one of the great pleasures of life, and suffering from a sleep disorder is a terrible deprival. Learning how to improve the hours we spend sleeping is a great benefit. The following are some points that may help you sleep better:

---

12 Hazrat Inayat Khan, Sangatha 2, Riyazat, *Esoteric papers* (unpublished).

1. Late at night, just before getting ready for bed or just after, remember your objective in life at this time.
2. Just before falling asleep, meditate for a few minutes. Do this by sitting up in bed, on your pillow. You could do the Air Breath (described in Chapter 14). Until you have learned that technique, just listen to your heartbeat.
3. Immediately after meditating, lie down on your right side. This will cause your breathing to shift to your left nostril, which will cause right-hemisphere dominance in your brain. This is the most receptive condition and is ideal for going to sleep.
4. In the middle of the night, turn over to the left side. Then you will breathe through your right nostril, causing left hemisphere dominance, which will cause a focusing of your mind. This will prepare you for the coming day.
5. If you wake up in the night and can't get back to sleep, try sleeping on your right side again. If that doesn't work, try the left side again. If that doesn't work either, sit up and meditate, starting over from step 2, but perhaps meditate longer. If you still can't go to sleep, just enjoy feeling your heart beat.
6. Unless the day's schedule is especially critical, don't use an alarm to wake up. It is much better to let your unconscious wake you. (If you need an alarm clock to wake up, you're probably sleep deprived, a problem you can solve by setting your alarm to go off when it's time to go to bed, instead of time to get out of bed.) As soon as you're aware of being awake, sit up. Rising when you are awake is an act of personal mastery, and it's important to begin your day with such mastery.
7. Immediately after rising, while you are still in the transition to day consciousness, meditate for a few minutes. Get in touch with your heart and your breathing rhythms. Keep meditating until you feel fully awake.
8. Get up and get dressed. At this point I do my daily meditation practice, taking about half an hour. At the end of it, I think about my objective in life again, and what I can do today to advance it.

3. Posture and Environment (Preparation)

4. CONSCIOUS BREATH (FOCUSING ON THE HEART)

Breath is the first lesson and it is also the last. [1]

What Is Breath?

Breath is the very life in beings, and what holds the particles of the body together is the power of the breath. When this power becomes less, then the will loses its control over the body. As the power of the sun holds all the planets, so the power of the breath holds every organ. Besides this, the breath purifies the body by taking in new and fresh life and by giving out all gases that should be put out. It nourishes the body by absorbing from the space the spirit and substance that are necessary, and more necessary than all that man eats and drinks. [2]

Part of what we mean by *breath* is the flow of air through the nose and mouth and into and out of the lungs. The same word, *breath*, is also used to refer to the continuing flow of air as the blood carries it throughout the body. Breathing is the body's main mechanism for interacting with the world. Taking in and giving

---

1 www.hazrat-inayat-khan.org: Message: Vol 13, Gathas: Breath: 1.3 Prana

2 www.hazrat-inayat-khan.org: Message: Vol 13, Gathas: Breath: 1.1 The Power of Breath

out, we exchange breath with the environment. Breath is the vehicle that allows us to exchange energy with the world and especially with others.

Breath also refers to the flow of energy between one's self and another, or nature, whose energy "rides" on the stream of air. The exchange of energy is synchronous with the exchange of air.

Breath is a link through which one individual is connected with another individual, and space does not make a difference once connection of breath is established. The communication will be sure and clear, if only the wire is tied to sympathetic hearts. There is much that is common to the science of electricity and the science of breath. The day is not very far off when science and mysticism both will meet on the same ground in the realization of the electricity which is hidden in the breath. [3]

To draw breath is literally to take the air and atmosphere of a place and draw it deeply into the fragile pink tissues of your inner body, absorbing it into your own bloodstream and circulating it to every cell of your body. Breathing out gathers up the dissolved gases that have been produced by every cell as a result of their functioning, concentrates this product in your lungs, and then offers it to the world, where it is eagerly received by the plants and other beings around you. Breathing is an intimate exchange. When you are in a room with others, you recycle their exhalations through your lungs many times. We literally absorb each other's breath.

Olfaction is said to be 10,000 times more sensitive than taste. A human threshold value for such a well-known odorant as ethyl mercaptan (found in rotten meat) has

---

3 www.hazrat-inayat-khan.org: Message: Vol 13, Gathas: Breath: 2.10 Communication Through Breath

*been cited in the range of 1/400,000,000th of a milligram
per liter of air.* [4]

Not only is our sense of smell extremely sensitive, but chemicals can affect us even when we cannot sense them consciously. The brain cells, triggered chemically, give off other chemicals in their respiration. These chemical products of thought go into the bloodstream, are transported to the lungs, are exported on the breath, and are carried to the nasal linings and lungs of others. The chemicals in the bloodstream of one person are thus continued through the breath and its channels to the bloodstream of others. This exchange accounts for part of the richness we experience in each other's presence.

The breath conveys the chemical products of cognition that have entered the bloodstream of one person through the medium of air—which disperses the chemical products but does not destroy or distort them—into the bloodstream of another. So the breath interconnects our individual bloodstreams into one large circulatory system.

Breath is life, and its work is to take the inner condition out externally, and to take the external conditions into one's inner being. When exhaling, the harmony or inharmony of the soul is brought out, its influence first working on one's mind, then one's feelings and thoughts working on the body, then on the surroundings. When inhaling, the conditions of the external plane, harmony or inharmony, together with the thoughts and feelings from the external plane, are drawn into the body, then into the mind, then into the soul, which sets the soul either in calmness or in disturbance. [5]

---

4 "smell", *Encyclopedia Britannica,* www.eb.com
5 Khan, I. Githa 1, Asrar ul-Ansar 6, *Esoteric papers.*

Air has content, so inhalation draws that content in and then adds to it on exhalation. This process is not much noticed, apparently because in most situations the exchange is unremarkable. But sometimes a group of people experience an inspiration that passes among them and infects all of them in their own way. One person may become witty, another insightful; another will recall a song, another will find a solution to a problem, and so on. In such an atmosphere, the mind seems to sparkle. Perhaps the word *inspire* points to a truth: that inspiration is something we breathe in.

in•spire \ in-'sp_+(e)r \ *vb* in•spired; in•spir-ing
[ME *inspiren,* fr. MF & L; MF *inspirer,* fr. L *inspirare,* fr. *in-*
+spirare to breathe—more at SPIRIT] *vt* (14c)
1a: to influence, move or guide by divine or supernatural
inspiration
b: to exert an animating, enlivening, or exalting influence on
(was particularly *inspired* by the Romanticists)
c: to spur on: IMPEL, MOTIVATE (threats don't necessarily *inspire*
people to work)
d: AFFECT (seeing the old room again *inspired* him with nostal-
gia)
2a: *archaic:* to breathe or blow into or upon
b: *archaic:* to infuse (as life) by breathing
3a: to communicate to an agent supernaturally
b: to draw forth or bring out (thoughts *inspired* by his visit to
the cathedral)
4: INHALE [6]

Besides carrying the content of the air, the breath carries another exchange between people. Breath is the medium that fills the
space between everything else. If we were fish, we would call the
ocean "breath." We are sensitive to very subtle changes in the
pressure of this all-surrounding fluid, and so low barometric pres-

---

[6] *Webster's Ninth Collegiate Dictionary*

sure has a depressing effect while high barometric pressure brings exhilaration. Anything that moves the air somewhere in our vicinity moves the air that is in contact with us. Like sleeping with someone on a waterbed, we experience a more subtle but similar connection with others through air pressure. Through this subtle sense of air pressure, one can sense when a person comes up behind one, and one can sense the graceful movements of a dancer as opposed to the threatening movements of an attacker. The pressure differential of a breath can reach across a room as easily as a sound wave, which is also a pressure differential. A breath wave is exactly like a very loud, very-low-frequency sound.

Usually your breath is calm, so its effect on the pressure of the surrounding atmosphere is slight; and usually your breath is unconscious, so it rises and falls on the waves of the breath of others like a cork on the ocean. However, a few kinds of breaths are sudden or strong, and they have a telepathic effect on others. Yawning, sighing, gasping in fright, and laughing are examples of very influential breaths that are quickly picked up by others.

There is an even subtler way in which breath acts as a medium for communication between people: it affects the body's magnetic field. The physical body has a substantial magnetic field, produced largely by the electrical currents of the nervous system and the muscles. The heart muscle is triggered electrically, like all muscles, and it produces such a strong magnetic field that in a person at rest, it is the center of the magnetic field. The field pulsates with the heart rate, and it can be made to expand and contract with the exhalation and inhalation of the breath. The human body is quite sensitive to magnetic fields, and we will experiment with that in Chapter 9.

The last aspect of breath is even more significant than these physical characteristics. In Latin, the word for "breath," *spiritus,* also means "spirit", a sign of the understanding that breath is a current of spirit that carries life to all life, interconnecting and sustaining all organisms.

Making Conscious That Which Was Unconscious

Normal breathing is usually unconscious, so the smooth muscles used in breathing are controlled by the unconscious mind, and the breathing rhythm is automatic. But breathing is the only bodily function that can be controlled by two sets of muscles, one smooth and one striated. In meditation, we shift the control of breathing from the unconscious to the conscious mind, which controls the striated muscles. This frees up that portion of the unconscious mind that had been controlling the breathing to take on a different function. It becomes a kind of gateway between the conscious and the unconscious mind, shuttling thoughts back and forth. As a result, some of what was unconscious becomes conscious, and conscious thought illuminates the unconscious.

The muscles of the heart are controlled by the unconscious mind. Consequently, the conscious mind cannot control the heartbeat to the same extent that it can control the breath. For example, you can deliberately breathe very fast or very slow. You can stop breathing anytime you want to, for a limited period. You cannot exert such control over your heartbeat, but you do have indirect control over your heartbeat. If you want to speed it up, you can recall an anxious moment or imagine a fantasy that will stimulate emotions, and these emotions will stimulate your heart rate. If you want to slow down your heartbeat, you can use a relaxation technique, like Heart Rhythm Meditation, to create a calm emotion, and that emotion will calm your heart rate.

So while you cannot control the contractions of your heart muscle, you can influence your heart-rate controller. In Heart Rhythm Meditation, even if you make no deliberate effort to change your heart rate, your awareness of your heart rate will cause some change in it. Your nervous system, too, will change, as the signal that controls heartbeat changes course and travels through a different, more efficient, conscious pathway. This is a second way that Heart Rhythm Meditation makes the unconscious conscious.

The practical benefit of making the unconscious conscious is that the experiences of life are processed more quickly and efficiently, resulting in a greater understanding of life and less unresolved emotion. This keeps the heart clear and develops wisdom. Most of us aren't as wise as we could be, despite our life experiences, because we don't draw the lessons from those experiences. Sometimes we deny that life teaches any lessons at all, and sometimes we're sure we've already learned whatever lessons it offers. Oftentimes we have the feeling that learning life lessons would raise painful feelings, require difficult changes, and pose uncomfortable questions. It is inconvenient to have to change the way we see things, but making such changes is how we get wiser.

During the course of a day, some of the events that you see or experience cannot be easily accommodated by your present mental construct, your mental view of the world. A picture of a catastrophe on television, the sight of an automobile wreck, a painful story about a friend, a fearful encounter—you may not be able to admit or accept that these things can happen. They do not support your understanding of your self and the world. So you repress it, or you review it again and again until you can reinterpret it to fit into your model, or you modify the model to accommodate it.

WHEN I FIRST MET *my teacher, I didn't know how to relate to him because I had never met anyone remotely like him. There was no category for him in my model of reality. He wasn't like my father or any old friends, or like a schoolteacher, nor was he like my idea of what Christ was like, which was my way of understanding a spiritual teacher. Since I had no construct that held him, I projected onto him different models I had already built up. I found that he was whatever I imagined him to be. Whatever image I used would stick, which was quite extraordinary. Over time, I built up a new model of a spiritual teacher, one characteristic of which is that the heart is mirrorlike, allowing the teacher to appear as whatever the student needs. But still, whenever I think I've fully understood him, my teacher bursts out of the box my construct has made for him, by showing me a part of himself I hadn't seen before.* PURAN

When you breathe consciously, the unconscious mind easily projects images onto the conscious mind. The unconscious mind can use this function to sort through unresolved experiences at high speed and save one experience after another. Clarity emerges from the jumble of impressions, memories, and undercurrents as integration occurs.

This work of incorporating new experiences into your view of reality requires considerable effort, but it produces growth. When everything you see and do affirms your current model of reality, life becomes predictable and boring. One of the goals of any life is to take in more and more of the bewildering complexities of reality and integrate them into one understanding. Thus perplexity becomes simplicity. If we repress the richness of reality, it only delays the onset of wisdom, and wisdom is our goal.

If you do not want to understand, you will not understand.

The man who will not take in the idea of unity, will be taken in by unity some day. [7]

---

7 www.hazrat-inayat-khan.org: Message: Sayings: Vadan: Boulas

Sorting and filing: that is the work of the unconscious, to fit the perceptions, emotions, and interpretations into a whole called realization. When something is realized, it is beyond doubt, beyond argument, beyond faith. Every cell of the body knows it. It is reality.

There is always a further realization, until

When we go more deeply into the phenomena of life,
we shall come to a place where the whole nature of Being
will unveil itself, and we shall be able to say,
"There is nothing but God." [Hazrat Inayat Khan][8]

Settle into a posture, as described in Chapter 3. Now begin to "watch your breath." Be conscious of every inhalation and exhalation. This will create a subtle but important shift in the nervous system. Make no effort to change the way you breathe; just notice the breath as it is, with the rhythm that is set by the unconscious.

Do not expect your mind to be free of thoughts. Your mind will continue to function and generate images and memories as it normally does. Do not fight your thoughts; rather, notice the thoughts that arise. You will see the nature of your thinking change as you continue to watch your breath. Your thoughts will have less to do with the present environment, although you can continue to be aware of your surroundings if you so choose.

Memories may arise that surprise you. Your mind uses this time to "clean off the desk" by sorting and filing. Before your mind can discard or re-file a memory from your stack of unprocessed experiences, that memory must be presented on the screen of your mind, where you can see it. The concentration on the breath keeps you awake, but the images that come are similar to dreaming. This is not yet meditation, but it is helpful and healing.

---

8 www.hazrat-inayat-khan.org: Message: Sayings: Nirtan: Aphorisms

Breath Rhythms

Breathing is usually performed automatically by the unconscious. Many things affect the breath rhythm: the emotions, the need for oxygen by the muscles, digestion, sleepiness, and so on. You should not meditate immediately after a meal, but you should do so before sleepiness occurs. After a period of sitting still, the breath rhythm is accounted for almost entirely by the emotional state. Therefore the breath becomes a barometer for the emotions. By observing your breath rhythm, you can learn a great deal about your own feelings. Every emotion has its breath.

Continuing the practice, observe four phases of your breath:

• Your breath rises in an inhalation.
• Observe whether you hold your breath at the top.
• Your breath descends in an exhalation.
• Observe whether you hold your breath at the bottom.

Also observe three characteristics of your breath:

• Length, the amount of time you take for each phase
• Depth, the volume of air moved during inhaling or exhaling
• Direction, through the nose or the mouth

Through the breath rhythms, the unconscious mind conveys a great deal of information to the conscious mind. The unconscious underlies all of our thoughts, attitudes, and nondeliberate behavior. We usually see our unconscious expressed in our dreams, which thereby give us some view into our desires, needs, unresolved dilemmas, and wounds. The breath is another immediate and conscious entrance to the unconscious. In their complexity, the breath rhythms contain signals from the unconscious. Furthermore, the conscious mind can send signals to the unconscious by deliberately breathing in certain specific rhythms. Thus breath carries a two-way communication between the conscious and the unconscious. One only has to know the coded language in order to use it.

The very act of keeping the breath conscious prevents sleepiness and promotes deep relaxation. The conscious breath also stirs the unconscious, which will yield psychological benefits.

As you continue to observe your breath, notice the relative lengths of the four phases of the breath cycle. Here are some possibilities:

- A long pause at the top or the bottom, when the breath is still (If you find you are holding your breath after the exhalation, it is important to note it. But this is dangerous; don't try to do it.)
- Short inhalation and exhalation, with no pauses
- Even breath, inhalation and exhalation the same length
- Inhalation through the mouth, shorter than the exhalation, or vice versa
- Breathing always through the mouth
- Irregular breathing cycle
- An imperceptible (light) or audible (heavy) sound of the breath

Trying to categorize your breath rhythm will help you concentrate on the breath. Again, do not try to change your natural breath in any way. Just observe its characteristics as signals that reveal the condition of the unconscious mind.

As you are sitting, your breath will change. When you need more breath, the inhalation will come through the mouth. Breathing through the mouth causes a jump to a higher energy level, like electrons jumping to a higher energy shell. Occasionally you will sigh, making an exhalation through the mouth. The sigh indicates a greater relaxation, shedding resistance to settle into the practice. Breathing through the mouth accelerates change, while breathing through the nose is stabilizing.

A breath of surprise is a sudden inhalation. A laugh is a series of short exhalations. A yawn is a strong and sustained inhalation through the mouth, followed by a short exhalation. A cry of alarm is a quick and short exhalation. A panic-stricken breath is a rapid inhalation and exhalation. An excited breath is a series of strong inhalations. A sigh is a strong exhalation. Each of these breaths has an effect on the air in the space, spreading waves of air pressure changes in all directions. The shorter the breath, the greater its effect on the surrounding air, for the same reason that a short pulse of sound contains a very wide spectrum of fundamental frequencies. These pulses of breath reach others and cause a similar breath to emerge in them.

When two people meet, they initially have their own breath rhythms. Perhaps one comes with an excited breath, the other with a stable, conservative breath. During the course of the meeting, their rhythms will change so that the resulting breath rhythm is shared. Perhaps they both become excited, or both become cautious. The breath that is more conscious will be the one that wins out, and that person will be the more influential. The other person's unconscious breath will adjust to the conscious breath.

THE ABILITY TO WATCH YOUR BREATH AND CATEGORIZE ITS RHYTHM.

Watching Your Mind, Feeling Your Emotions

Observe your breath as dispassionately as possible. Your conscious breath will cause a stream of thoughts to emerge from the depth of your heart and appear on the surface of your mind.

Some of your thoughts will be interesting, even compelling. If you direct your attention to one of them individually, however, the stream of inspiration will be broken. At this stage, you can have either the stream or a droplet from the stream. When you focus on one image, memory, thought, or experience from the dynamic flow, you stop the flow and go into the emotion of that moment. Then the breath takes on the rhythm of that emotion, and the emotion builds and immerses you. Many unresolved emotional experiences need your attention. As you touch each one, it rises into your conscious mind. Making a suppressed memory conscious once again brings it a step closer to being resolved.

To handle the emotionally charged thoughts and memories that occur in Heart Rhythm Meditation, you can take one of two approaches.

One approach is to temporarily stop the practice and go into the memory intensely, re-experiencing the feelings you had in the past and seeing the situation and yourself as you did then. You can further explore the emotions through journal writing, dream monitoring, and therapy. If you use this approach, then Heart Rhythm Meditation will greatly aid your ability to resurface and confront unresolved experiences and worries. But Heart Rhythm Meditation used this way can quickly become an undesirable chore. You may become wary of its high emotional cost and discontinue it long before you have healed your heart's wounds.

The second approach is to look for the theme underlying the emotional thoughts. The theme will not be obvious, so finding it requires insight and practice. Fortunately, insight comes from practice and practice is less emotionally wearing in this approach than in the first one. The first time an emotionally charged thought comes up for you, you will find yourself going into it, as in the first approach. When you realize this is happening, go back to the Heart Rhythm Meditation. Soon another thought will arise that creates the same emotion as the first thought. Now you have a theme to work with.

A thought may arise that is so compelling, it takes over your Heart Rhythm Meditation. It could be a leftover from the past, an anxiety about the future, or a dilemma of the present. Its dominance over the practice is signaled by a change in your breath. Your breath takes on the rhythm corresponding to the emotion that has generated the thought.

When this happens, do not be disappointed that you have failed to keep all thoughts away. The compelling thought is the surface manifestation of an unresolved experience that is lying in your unconscious, waiting for a time when it can be re-experienced as part of the process of being integrated. By exposing it and giving it an avenue to your conscious mind, you are contributing to the health of both your heart and your mind.

Use Heart Rhythm Meditation to touch as many of these emotional experiences as you can, without sinking too far into any single one of them. You might notice that they come in "themes." For example:

- Your parents, your children
- Your purpose in life
- Your fears
- Traumatic events beyond your understanding
- Your regrets, resentments, and guilt
- Your poor self-image

You can continue to do the Heart Rhythm Meditation through the emotionally disturbing thoughts by observing them as points in a continuity, connected by a theme. You cannot change the events

---

that caused the thought, but you can resolve the theme so that it stops creating more events.

FRANK'S FATHER DIED *when he was young; ten years ago, Frank got fired from his job. Being fired not only hurt his confidence, as it would for anyone, it reinforced his theme of abandonment. Now, much later, Frank sees that he does not recover from rejection as easily as others do, and he still suffers from the effects of being fired because of the existence of this theme. Often, when he does his Heart Rhythm Meditation, he finds this abandonment theme and its emotions waiting for him. But he now can go through it consciously, and every time he does, some healing happens.*

In Greek mythology, the gateway to hell—representing the unconscious depths of the heart—is guarded by a monstrous two-headed dog, Cerberus. This dog represents the unresolved memories of the past, like wounds, and the anxiety they create in the present. In order to go farther into your heart, you will have to find a way through this passage. You must make peace with the guard dog. The only alternative is to turn away from your heart, letting it become hard and bitter, its power inaccessible to you. To make peace with the dog, you have to know its name.

What is it that causes you anxiety? Don't lament that you have anxiety; rather, discover what it's about, and then celebrate the discovery. But you can't figure it out with your mind. To determine how your heart has been wounded, you need the guidance of your heart itself. Your heart will tell you, while you're listening to it beat.

WHEN I STARTED TO *meditate in my twenties without much instruction and with no feedback, I was astonished at how difficult it was to calm the anxieties that came up whenever I sat down. Gradually I was able to trace a legion of my anxieties to a single event: my separation from my baby daughter, who now lived with her mother. My various anxieties didn't blatantly announce that this was the issue to which they were connected; they seemed instead to be about a million different complaints. For example, I noticed some anger that I had toward my mother for a slight thing she did at my wedding reception. It was nothing by itself, but as it was connected to my wedding, which was connected to my marriage and then to my daughter, it had acquired a powerful emotional charge. I worked at forgiving my mother and made what seemed to be great progress, until I realized my arrogant error. I wasn't angry with my mother, I was grieving over my daughter. When I recognized this theme, I knew that before my heart would open in peace and compassion, I would have to take action to express the love that lay beneath my despair. I sent half my income to my daughter and her mother, which helped me. I hitchhiked six hundred miles to visit her, which helped my heart a lot. Over time, by staying engaged in my relationship with her, helping her mother, meditating on my heart, and trying to help others, my heart began to heal and to open. As I gained more access to my heart, it had more of an influence in my life. Then my heart no longer fought me in meditation; rather, it lifted me and carried me in a powerful stream of its own making. My Heart Rhythm Meditation then led me to deal with yet another source of anxiety. More than twenty years later, this process hasn't ended, but it has deepened. The constant peace I experience now is greater than the best moments of peace I experienced then.* PURAN

Bring peace into the practice by keeping your breath fine: inaudible, constant, gentle motion without abrupt changes. A fine breath cannot be captured by an emotion because it is already the product of the strongest emotion: peace. Peacefulness creates the fine breath, and adopting a fine breath creates peace.

As memories suddenly escape from the unconscious and recreate the emotional states that imprisoned them, you maintain peace through your ability to accept and forgive. These natural qualities of the heart will be strengthened by Heart Rhythm Meditation.

CALM YOUR EMOTIONS BY USING YOUR FINE BREATH SO THAT YOU CAN MAINTAIN YOUR CONCENTRATION ON THE HEART RHYTHM MEDITATION FOR 20 MINUTES.

Happy experiences are much easier to integrate than anxious ones, so fewer of them will surface as you watch your breath. But what seems to be unfortunate now may turn out to be very fortunate in the end.

One must be able to see the pain in pleasure and the pleasure in pain; the gain in the loss and the loss in the gain. [9]

We are not good judges of what is good for us; we only know whether something is what we wanted or expected, or its short-term effect on our financial net worth. But what we want changes. Do you remember wanting something that you didn't get, and now you're glad you didn't get it? Or something you wanted that you did get and now you're sorry you did?

Does something someone did to you in the past seem unforgivable? You don't have to condone what happened in order to forgive the person for doing it. Like putting a drop of ink into an

---

9 www.hazrat-inayat-khan.org: Message: Sayings: Aphorisms

ocean, the ocean of life's experiences can absorb all the drops of our disappointments and resentments. How many breaths have you drawn in anger, hatred, or humiliation because of that event? How many breaths have you drawn in love, joy, peace, beauty, before and since?

Can you still not forgive? Did the one who hurt you intend to do so? Or is it just that you were the one who was there to receive their anger? Did any good come from the incident, in later events in life or in the inner development or strengthening of your qualities? All that you have been through has brought you to this place of spiritual development, with your eyes lifted to the horizon of fulfillment. Even though your past may have been a very undesirable journey, now, having arrived at the present, can you complain so much about the driver who brought you? Who is the driver anyway? Is it not the same One who you seek?

At this point you have a choice about how to proceed on the path. You can take a slower path, a faster path, a safer path, an exciting path, a path alone, or a path with a caravan of travelers, and so on. Can you see that you make this choice by your attitude? The choice you make now will affect the kinds of problems you have on the next leg of the journey of your life.

Advancing in insight, in self-mastery, in love, and in peacefulness is all that matters. The problems of life are exercises to develop these qualities. The attainments of life are valuable because of what they build up within yourself; they have no other value. You are yourself the product of your life; you are the proof of your approach. If you don't like what you've become, you can decide now to modify your attitude, and that will change you, as surely as the wagon follows the horse.

Did you hurt someone else? Then that hurt must be compensated. Make a resolution now to carry it out immediately after the meditation. Get in touch with the person you wronged, and ask their forgiveness. By letter or in person, ask in all sincerity that the person forgive you this very specific event you now recall. Even after many years, it's still possible to find people. If the person has died or really can't be found, you can make a contribution in some way to recompense others who have suffered from similar acts. If your resolution is firm, clear, and sincere, then your conscience will allow you to put that emotion and memory aside and regain the peace of meditation even more deeply.

You can't fool your unconscious. Either you deal with the emotions that meditation brings up, or you will have to stop meditating. Any progress you make here will have lasting benefits. Start with the little hurts, guilts, and resentments, so you can build up your ability to face yourself and take responsibility for your life. Others will have to deal with their own consciences, but if you see yourself as their victim, you give them the power over your life, and then self-pity, powerlessness, and poor self-image will continue the damage.

When a difficulty arises, whether in meditation or in life, you can soothe your tender feelings by doing this especially soothing meditation:

As you breathe in and out, think of your stomach area—the area starting below your rib cage, just below the diaphragm muscle that moves your lungs, and extending down to the navel.

As you breathe in, fill this stomach area with breath. As you breathe out, let your breath sink down deeply. As you breathe in, be aware of the feelings you have in this area of your body. As you exhale, breathe gently, and let your concerns and anxieties dissolve into a pool of contentment.

There is no other instruction—just keep thinking of sending your breath into your stomach area.

This practice is a little gem. Even if you don't go any further with meditation than this, you will benefit from the Stomach Breath. Some people find this breath to be a deeply moving, emotional experience, producing tears. It's not sad; it's deep, like being a child held by your mother. We have such a need to be comforted, and this simple practice gives rise to a profound sense of comforting. You can do this as often as you like.

Now that the Stomach Breath has consoled the heart's pain, we can return to the fine breath that heals the heart's wounds.

Come back to the breath. Take a sigh, and let all that has disturbed your peace drain out of you. The sighing breath will lift the burden from your heart, making your heart lighter than ever. This lightness is the physical equivalent of the state of peace. Now the breath is fine—inaudible, slow, moving easily, and changing gently from inhalation to exhalation. It is not labored, noisy, quick, or changing suddenly.

Breath is categorized by Sufis as dense or fine. Dense breath is that which is noisy and labored, which strains the nerves and the lungs. The exercises of dense breath are useful for developing the muscles and for gaining control over the nerves; they are helpful also to the lungs and useful to the physical health. But in spiritual development, unless the breath be made fine, it cannot penetrate through the important contours in the body, and it cannot reach far enough into the innermost parts of one's life.

Breath, to a Sufi, is a bridge between himself and God; it is a rope for him, hanging down to earth, attached to the heavens. The Sufi climbs up by the help of this rope. [10]

Become Passive to Breath

The watching over the breath is important both in meditation and out of it. By guarding the breath one learns to control the ego, and from a practical point of view one develops efficiency in action.

---

10 www.hazrat-inayat-khan.org: Message: Healing Papers: 2,1 Breath: Lesson 7

In meditation one should observe the rhythm of the breath until one is able to get the mind quiet. If the mind cannot be quieted, one may just watch the rhythm of the breath continually. After a while there may be a tendency for the breath to become more and more refined. Then one will find that it is difficult to watch and indeed there is no need to observe breath when one enters the real silence. [11]

As man enters the silence, so does the silence enter into him. As he unites with the universe, so does the universe manifest in him. This is true, no matter what be his path or his training. Ultimately he arrives at his destination. This is the silence of all life, which without containing anything may be said to contain all things. [12]

As you watch your breath, it will change. As you watch your mind, it will change. These cases are applications of a general principle:

Whatever is observed is changed by the act of observation. [13]

So one cannot be completely passive with respect to the breath and at the same time be aware of breathing. The consciousness that observes the breath will influence the unconscious control of it. It's no loss—we can make much better use of the time spent in meditation than simple observation. While it is valuable to see the workings of the unconscious reflected in the breath rhythm, it is even more valuable to provide some guidance to the unconscious. How can we do that?

In a state of inspiration, poets get poems, musicians get music, architects get buildings, lovers get their beloved. So it must be possible to steer the unconscious according to one's interest or desire.

---

11 Khan, I. (1989, 283)

12 Khan, I. (1989, 287)

13 This rule is similar to the Heisenberg uncertainty principle in physics.

At this stage of Heart Rhythm Meditation, you are not trying to change your breath, and neither are you trying to force your thoughts into a direction. Your unconscious desire will guide the thoughts that come to you in meditation.

Remember that the time you have to meditate is extremely valuable. Now the doors between heaven and earth and the conscious and the unconscious are open. How do you want to use this time? Why are you meditating?

Remember that you want to:

• heal the wounds of the heart

• integrate the parts of your life

• advance in understanding and in power so that you can be all that you potentially are.

 BE PASSIVE TO BREATH, ALLOWING YOURSELF TO BE BREATHED, WHILE STAYING INTENSELY AWAKE.

5. RHYTHMIC BREATH (DIRECTING THE HEART'S ENERGY)

One [who has] constantly changing breath can neither meditate nor perform any other function.[1]

There are three different kinds of rhythm in the breath: the rhythm which cannot be distinguished in the continuation of aspiration and expiration [fine breathing]; the second kind, the rhythm that can be distinguished by the two distinct swings of inhaling and exhaling [conscious breathing]; the third rhythm, evenness in breathing [rhythmic breathing].

Those who have not mastered their breath are under the influence of these three rhythms, their health, their mood, and their condition in life. But those who master the breath can put their breath in any of these rhythms, and when mastery is acquired, then the healer has the key to wind any clock [Hazrat Inayat Khan][2]

Passive, conscious breathing is beautiful and self-revealing. It allows the unconscious to speak to us. Having discovered its bliss, we now move on to rhythmic breathing, where we add a small amount of control to our breath. In this way, we develop an inner dialogue, not only listening to but also speaking to our unconscious.

---

[1] Khan, I. (1989, 229)

[2] www.hazrat-inayat-khan.org: Message: Githas: Healing: 4, Rhythm

5. Rhythmic Breath (Directing the Heart's Energy)

Concentration

Nothing in this world can be thoroughly accomplished without concentration, whether in one's business or profession, or in spiritual work. Those who cannot make a success in their business or profession are the ones whose concentration is not right. And many of those who have succeeded in life owe this to the fact that their concentration is good. If one is an artist, with the help of concentration one can produce wonderful works; if one is a scientist, one can achieve great results in science; if one is a poet, poetry will be easy to write; if one is a mystic, mystical inspiration will flow; but without concentration, however qualified a person may be, he will not be able to make the best use of his qualifications; he can hardly be called qualified at all. [Hazrat Inayat Khan] [3]

In this step, we are concentrating on the breath, as practice for concentrating on the heartbeat later. The breath is easy to observe; the heartbeat is harder to find. Concentration requires effort, yet it produces relaxation, a greater relaxation than one obtains by just sitting quietly with no particular focus. This result may be surprising, but it makes sense if you compare mental exercise with physical exercise.

How does one relax the mind? The method for relaxation of the mind is first to make the mind tired. He who does not know the exercise for making the mind tired, can never relax his mind. Concentration is the greatest action one can give to one's mind, because the mind is held in position on a certain thing. After that it will relax naturally, and when it relaxes it will gain all power. [Hazrat Inayat Khan] [4]

To work with your mind, you must begin with concentration. It may seem that your mind is already too full, too busy, and too tired

---

[3] www.hazrat-inayat-khan.org: Message: Vol 4, Mental Purification: 12. Mystic Relaxation (1)

[4] *Ibid.* (2)

to be able to concentrate, with a load of things that need attention. What you want, you may think, is some relaxation for your mind, some peaceful bliss, and cosmic love, not another effort. All that shall be received, but first you have to give your concentration. Why? Because relaxation follows tension.

To relax your arm, first tighten it as hard as you can, turning on every muscle in opposition to make the arm like steel. Then relax it suddenly. It will flip into a state of profound relaxation. The mind works the same way.

"But I've been concentrating all day," you may say. "Doesn't that count?" Probably you've had a little concentration, which is naturally followed by a little relaxation. But neither is satisfying. You can learn much greater focus of mind and apply it readily to your work, then be rewarded with a much more profound relaxation. The practice of meditation develops and enhances concentration. With greater mental power and clarity, much of what was once stressful for you will no longer be stressful. It's the same with any kind of self-development: running will wear you out until you get in shape, then running will invigorate you instead.

In this practice, we concentrate on the breath more intently than ever before. The breath becomes rhythmic from this concentration, and the rhythmic breath holds the mind in focus, making intense concentration easy. It seems that all you have to do is breathe, and then the breath does everything else.

Sometimes one becomes so absorbed in the mental plane that for the moment the physical body does not exist for one. [Hazrat Inayat Khan] [5]

---

[5] www.hazrat-inayat-khan.org: Message: Githas: Esotericism

5. Rhythmic Breath (Directing the Heart's Energy)

Without rhythmic breath, concentration is very difficult, but with rhythmic breath, concentration is easy. This is why music that has a steady rhythm can speed up learning and make work more efficient. If the rhythm changes often or is not steady at all, it creates chaos and disorder. If the rhythm is steadily increasing, as in Ravel's *Bolero*, it brings the audience into a frenzy. The same is true for the heart rhythm.

> In meditation the control over mind is exerted through breath and mind. The breath is kept rhythmical and refined and it becomes ever more refined as the consciousness is turned upon it and the light of man's inner being manifests thereon. If the breath is not kept in rhythm, thoughts will enter and this battle against thought, especially against ego thought, is that battle that every saint and sage has to combat continually. For this also will-power is needed. [Hazrat Inayat Khan] [6]

Free from Disturbances

The effort of keeping the breath in a rhythm and listening to the heartbeat, which holds the mind in focus, yields an immediate benefit: liberation from self-imposed obstacles.

> The path of freedom leads to the goal of captivity; it is the path of discipline which leads to the goal of liberty. [Hazrat Inayat Khan] [7]

The cycle of the breath becomes so strong that it operates like an ocean liner cutting through the waves of life rather than like a buoy bobbing up and down on them; or it is like a steamroller that rolls over surface bumps and depressions. The steady breath produces its own inertia, the ability to keep going, despite obstacles, on the direction one has chosen. As you widen and smooth the path, the resistance falls in behind and follows along. Freedom

---

[6] Khan, I. (1989, 227)

[7] www.hazrat-inayat-khan.org: Message: Sayings: Gayan: Talas

results from this immunity to that which would otherwise trip you or stop you from pursuing your goal.

> Additionally, become aware of your heartbeat, which will turn your attention away from the disturbances around you and toward the personal experience of a presence in your chest. When you feel reassured and recharged, you can then turn your attention outward again. Then note the change in what you see and the way you see it.

When a person allows himself to be disturbed, that shows that his concentration is not good; and if his concentration is not good, that shows that his will-power fails him. The best way, therefore, to protect oneself from disturbance is to develop the power of concentration, so that the will-power develops naturally and one is able to withstand all the disturbances which arise when one has to live in the midst of the crowd.

The best remedy for a wandering mind is natural concentration; that means not forcing the mind. One should at first let the mind work naturally, thinking of things it is inclined to think about. Why should the mind think of something toward which it has no inclination? It is unnatural; it is like eating something one does not like; it will not be assimilated, nor give good results. One should think about anything one loves, then one can learn to concentrate. [Hazrat Inayat Khan][8]

Don't try to shut out the environment. Just concentrate on your breath, and later your heartbeat, with great interest and fascination. The breath is telling you so much that you don't want to miss any part of it. You may well be affected by others around you—you're not a stone. But what's interesting is the *way* you are affected, and by *what* stimulus. Watching the small changes in your breath pattern gives you a measure of your degree of disturbance. When you

---

[8] www.hazrat-inayat-khan.org: Message: Vol 4, Mental Purification: 12. Mystic Relaxation (2)

watch yourself this way, the intensity of your reaction diminishes. In this way you can be sensitive and peaceful at the same time.

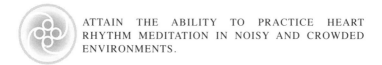 ATTAIN THE ABILITY TO PRACTICE HEART RHYTHM MEDITATION IN NOISY AND CROWDED ENVIRONMENTS.

The Rhythm of Life

A thoughtful person will easily see that in all of life there are cycles of change. Those that experience life most fully by experiencing it as a whole, have emphasized two different rhythms in life. The first is a rising-and-falling rhythm: building up and dispersal, acquiring and disposing, achievement and renunciation, acting and planning. The second is a give-and-take rhythm: buying and selling, teaching and learning, loving and being loved. The interplay of these two rhythms with various periods makes for the variety and diversity in life.

All these cycles of life can be used for benefit. We can be successful by doing those things that are in harmony with our life's rhythm at a given time, or by changing our life's rhythm to match the task we have chosen. Upward meditation is well suited for discovering what one's rhythm is, whereas downward meditation is a tool for changing one's rhythm.

We are all aware of mood swings, and sometimes we just aren't in the mood to do something we should or must do. But we seldom make good use of our inactive moods. Perpetual activity is not natural; we must have periods of reflection as well, and if we deny that part of life's cycle, we may develop cynicism, a self-defeating attitude, alienation, or illness. Likewise, it is not natural to be always reflective; we must have periods of active accomplishment as well, and if we deny that part of life's cycle, it causes jealousy, envy, resentment, or rebellion.

Life cannot always involve building up; there must also be breaking down. But that which was built up is not necessarily that which is dismantled. The descent after a rise, the taking away after a gain, separates the false from the true, the nonessential from the essential. The lesson of accomplishment is retained, though the object of accomplishment may be lost. Conscious breathing is a lesson repeated over and over: life is a cycle. Every step up is followed by a step down, every defeat by a success. It is not wise to mourn the exhaled air or try to hold it; another inhalation will be coming. Why wish for exhaling when one is inhaling? Why think of inhaling when one is exhaling? Do each in its own time, and nothing else.

A KING ONCE *assembled his wise men and women and said to them, "I find that at times I am depressed, feeling as if the whole world has gone wrong, and at other times I am so happy that in my giddiness I myself go wrong. I ask you to make me a potion that will lift my sadness with happiness and temper my happiness with sadness." They labored together and finally presented the king with a "magic ring." Whenever he felt too happy or too sad, he was to look at the ring. On it were inscribed the words, "This too shall pass."*

Some people become anxious as a result of conscious breathing. Their anxiety is caused by a fear that the cycle will stop, that at some point they won't be able to get enough breath.

Watching many breaths come and go is a therapy that builds faith. There are endless waves in life, rising and falling. And there is something that is unmoved by the waves, and something too that floats on top of the waves.

Meditators are not immune to life's cycles; rather they are more aware of them and better able to make use of the rhythm of life.

You can be successful both when life's energy is building up and when it is dispersing, if you act appropriately in each phase. Some rhythms have a daily cycle, so that different activities are appropriate for the morning and for the evening. Some rhythms have an even shorter cycle, occurring many times within one day, like the shift in the dominant hemisphere of the brain from left to right and back again. Many other rhythms are slower, corresponding to our current challenges and our long-term development cycle. Meditators are keenly aware of these different rhythms because they have a simple way to monitor them. Observing your breath and heart rhythms through the day and over time reveals the rhythms of your life reflected within yourself.

> [By breathing practices,] the Sufi sets his breath to the proper rhythm and when it becomes a habit, by a practice done every day, the Sufi's whole life becomes orderly and regular, because the rhythm in time becomes a habit of the breath, and while awake or asleep the breath goes on rhythmically, keeping all pulsations in rhythm, on which the health entirely depends. The rhythm so produced by the breath keeps the thoughts in order, the will powerful, the memory in order, the feelings normal, and thereby all one's affairs in life come into perfect and proper order. [Hazrat Inayat Khan][9]

At an advanced stage, you can alter your life's rhythms to suit your purpose, rather than modify your activities to suit the rhythms. This is the practical equivalent of the miracle that Christ performed when he calmed a storm. The first step is to learn how to live in harmony with the rising and falling rhythms of life, to use both cycles like left and right steps in order to make progress toward your goal. This harmony contrasts with the usual way of working, which is to develop a certain style and then to apply that style to all the conditions of life, all the time.

---

[9] www.hazrat-inayat-khan.org: Message: Githas: Esotericism: 2, Rhythm in Fikr

PETER, A CREATIVE *and courageous man, had an inspired idea for a product that would be very helpful to many people. After expending a tremendous effort, he raised enough money to start a company to develop his idea. Shortly after the company got going, however, his life's rhythm took a turn, shifting from an active building-up phase to a reflective taking-apart phase. This shift affected his whole life, not just his business, and led him into an intense re-evaluation of all he believed in. His energy turned from outer-directed to inward-directed. Meanwhile the new company proceeded with research and development in a nonlogical, intuitive fashion that allowed it to make many important discoveries in a short time. The product that emerged was very innovative and useful; but the company failed because it didn't have the strength to bring it to market. In the descending cycle, research can be very successful, like the development of an embryo into a fetus, but it is not the right time for a birth. In business, as in life, timing is everything.*

Unaware of the rhythms of life, Peter started another company while in the same descending phase. Again, he excelled in research and developed an innovative product. But this time his rhythm turned again to building up, and his company brought the product to market and was successful. If a person is persistent in applying the same method time and again, the rhythm of life will eventually be in favor and success will follow. Even better than persistence is sensitivity to one's natural rhythm and choosing the action that is appropriate at the time.

If Peter had been aware of his rhythms in his first company, he could have dispensed with the cover of bravado and the driving force of greed and taken a low-budget approach to prolonged research. Then when his energy cycled upward again, he would have been ready to harness it. His company failed because the company was in one phase when he was in another.

5. Rhythmic Breath (Directing the Heart's Energy)

In his book *Seasons of a Man's Life,* psychologist and researcher Daniel Levinson documents the long-term rhythms of life that create several distinct periods from childhood to old age. For shorter-term rhythms, Chinese doctors can feel five types of pulses produced by the heartbeat and attribute meanings and effects to each.

Meditators of many different cultures have discovered that their inner state corresponds to their life situations and have carefully studied the relationship of the two. Some of these inner states can be measured in the heartbeat, some in the breath rate, and others in the endocrine and nervous systems. There is a delight in looking upon the phases of one's life as revelations of the phases of one's inner condition and in seeing one's inner states projected onto the screen of life's phases.

It might appear at first that life events and situations have a stronger effect upon our inner state than the other way around. When we receive a promotion at work, see our child make a breakthrough, have our car break down on the highway, or are rejected by a friend, the resulting emotional, mental, and physical state is easily recognizable. We are very aware of the effects that life's events have on us. But to mystics, the opposite effect is even stronger—so much stronger that they consider it dominant. Our inner state has a way of creating our lives. Before each event in Peter's story, a shift in Peter's inner condition took place that was likely responsible for it.

The rate at which we breathe affects the metabolism of the body, which in turn affects our physical and mental rhythms alike. The breath rate is one of the two clocks in the body; the other is the heart rate.

By observing your breath and heart beat, you become aware of your inner condition. Many people don't know what they are feeling emotionally until they notice the *effects* of their feelings. They may deny that they are depressed, don't know when they are out of touch, and even start to enjoy their isolation. But living without emotion is an illness of the heart.

5. Rhythmic Breath (Directing the Heart's Energy)

 BECOME SO ACCUSTOMED TO OBSERVING THE RHYTHM OF THE BREATH THAT YOU NOTICE THE SHIFTS IN YOUR EMOTIONS AND ENERGY DURING THE DAY, AS THEY OCCUR.

Using the Rhythm of Breath

The one who is led by the breath is the slave of life, and the one who controls breath is the master of life. The words "led by breath" mean that it is the breath, its speed and its change into different elements and into different directions, which conducts all the affairs of man's life. Man, ignorant of this fact, is led by the breath and experiences conditions in life as they happen to come, and therefore life becomes not his kingdom but a prison.

When man becomes aware of this truth he wishes to gain control of his thoughts, feelings, emotions, passions, and of his affairs. [Hazrat Inayat Khan][10]

Realize that you are a participant in all the situations of your life, and that your participation changes the outcome of everything that happens. Nothing is happening "to" you; everything is happening "with" you. You are fully involved, and your every breath, especially the *way* you breathe, is one of the forces that determines what happens. Keep your breath flowing evenly to dispel feelings of anxiety, powerlessness, and fear.

You can be too sensitive and too insensitive. Life is a flow, like a river. There must be taking in and giving out. This cycle works best when the inflow and outflow are even. Consider which half of the breath is easier for you: inhalation (taking in) or exhalation (giving out). Thinking all the time of one half and not the other causes stress.

[10] *Ibid.*

Can you listen and take in what others contribute without dominating? Are you distressed by the opinions or actions of others to the point that you can't act creatively?

Send the exhalation out of your chest, forward, giving silent inspiration to others, anonymously. Bring the inhalation straight into your chest, and accept into yourself all that rides on the breath from the hearts of others.

Swinging the Breath

As a model of rhythmic motion, consider the pendulum, specifically its form as a swing. When you push someone on a swing, you have to deliver the push at precisely the right time. If you push too soon, you catch the swing on the rise and your push actually slows it down. If you push too late, the swing's descent has already begun. A small push at the right moment, regularly, is all it takes to keep the swing going.

Imagine a swing in front of you. As you breathe out, the breath carries the swing away from you, and as you breathe in, the breath draws the swing back to you again. By this swing, you can communicate with your unconscious.

As you breathe out, put a question on the swing of your breath as it moves away from you. The thought you have placed on the swing will be delivered to your unconscious. The swing carries your thought down and away and disappears in the mist at the far end of its arc. When you breathe in, the swing returns to you. Eventually, it will carry a reply from your unconscious, which you can then draw into your conscious mind.

> You can send messages from your conscious to your unconscious mind by repetition. So you must hold the exact same thought and send it out with every exhalation.

When your unconscious mind sends a reply to your conscious mind, it happens unexpectedly. The message appears in a thought that arises spontaneously, with compelling force and clarity. You do not imagine or reason; the thought is always surprising. The thinking of the unconscious is different from logical thinking. It may confirm or deny logical thinking, but even when it confirms, it does so from a different point of view.

> That's how you recognize the message from your unconscious: it comes suddenly, and it has a different point of view. Sometime, without warning, while you're swinging your breath and repeating your question, the answer will come. Don't look for it; that will lead your mind to imagine what the answer might be. Just keep swinging in an even rhythm, holding your concentration steady on your exhaled question. When the answer comes, it will grab your attention so strongly that you will not be able to miss it. It will come not as a voice from outside but in your own mind. It will be just like a thought, but with more force. Whatever it is, accept it, and let your breath impress it deeply into your memory.

You can carry this practice further and apply it to communicating with others:

> As you exhale, place on the swing a thought you would like to send to the world.

Let each swing reach out farther and farther until the swing of your exhalation carries your message to the horizon and beyond, communicating with the whole world through the swing of the breath.

The distance the breath reaches is unlimited. If you can think of a farther place, the breath reaches there too. As far as you send it, the breath goes farther still.

This practice may seem elementary, but it's not. The master teachers use the breath to carry blessings and inspiration to their disciples. You can use this practice to reach those who are at a distance, either physically or emotionally, as long as you feel closely connected to them within.

By exerting only a slight amount of control, you can direct the tremendous power of the breath. As Hercules redirected a river to clean out the Augean stables, by a simple concentration we can direct the powerful stream of breath that passes through us.

 COMMUNICATE WITH YOUR UNCONSCIOUS THROUGH YOUR BREATH—SENDING A QUESTION, RECEIVING AN ANSWER—WITH A RESULT THAT PROVES TO YOU THAT THE UNCONSCIOUS KNOWS WHAT THE CONSCIOUS MIND DOES NOT.

6. FULL EXHALATION (ACCOMPLISHMENT)

There are some [students] who have no capacity of breathing deeply, and there are some whose breathing organs are affected. In those cases, the rhythm of breathing must be changed. No doubt for those whose breathing is not good or whose organs of breathing are not in a good condition, the practice of breath is most essential; but it must be done very slowly, and to begin with, they must take a few breaths. [Hazrat Inayat Khan][1]

Confronting Fear

Our breath is generally shallow, and much of the capacity of our lungs is unused. Partly, we breathe in a shallow way out of convenience: it takes an extra effort to breathe fully. But we also do it because of an unconscious fear. Breathing out all the way leaves us vulnerable for a moment. If no air were available for inhaling, the body would go into oxygen debt immediately. Our fear even of the possibility of airlessness causes us to carry around a "cushion" of reserve air, which becomes stale. It is this fear that makes changing the breath pattern so difficult for some people. But facing this fear and conquering it unleashes power that can be applied to one's goals in life.

Note that "to expire" means both "to die" and "to breathe out."

ex•pire \ik-'sp_+(e)r, *oftenest for vi 3 and vt 2* ek-\ *vb* **ex•pired; ex•pir•ing**
[ME *expiren,* fr. MF or L; MF *expirer,* fr. L *exspirare,* fr. *ex-* + *spirare* to breathe - more at SPIRIT] *vi* (15c)
1: to breathe one's last breath: DIE
2: to come to an end

---

1 Khan, I. (1989, 229)

3: to emit the breath
~*vt*
1 *obs:* CONCLUDE
2: to breathe out from or as if from the lungs[2]

Some students have difficulty following the instruction to breathe out all the way and empty their lungs. They strongly resist extending the exhalation by more than a token amount. At first, such students may have the feeling that they are doing it right, that they *are* at the empty point, when actually they may still be retaining twenty-five percent to fifty percent of their lungs' capacity.

The fear that lies at the bottom of the breath is exactly the fear of death. At this point in the breath cycle lies one of the main conditions of a dead body—no breath. Breath is life. When a body dies, it finally gives up its reservoir of breath. It is not an exaggeration to say that a full exhalation brings a (very short) simulation of death.

We experience death by playing life, and we experience life by playing death. [Hazrat Inayat Khan][3]

This practice is a vaccine against the fear of death. Our goal is to be more fully *alive*, and we cannot realize how much our life is restricted and limited by death's fear until we can experience expiration.

Many meditators stop at this point; either they retreat back to the pleasant, relaxing, rhythmic breath without experiencing full exhalation, or they cease the practice altogether. Seldom, if ever, do they name fear as the reason they don't meditate anymore. They name time pressures, or say they have so many other things to do. When fear is in the heart, the mind races to find some distraction from the fear and some excuse for the distraction.

---

2 *Webster's Ninth Collegiate Dictionary*

3 www.hazrat-inayat-khan.org: Message: Vol 6, The Alchemy of Happiness: The Continuity of Life

Not until one gets through this fear can meditation really begin. The full exhalation is the only way to get to the full inhalation. The full inhalation is required to power the leap in consciousness that defines meditation. With full inhalation, meditation develops a power that transforms life.

You do not vanquish the fear of death at this level of Heart Rhythm Meditation. That will come with an accumulation of experiences of the absorption of the individual self into the Universal Heart. But this experience of the state of no-breath is essential; it begins the process of overcoming fear, and builds the power of the breath to achieve the state of meditation on the Universal Heart.

The First Intervention

The first intervention is to breathe all the way *out*. So far, you have made your breath intensely conscious, but you have not intervened in its rhythm. Now, for the first time, you will deliberately make a small change in the way you breathe. This will require practice, for you will be retraining the breath.

Let your breath come around to the usual end point of your exhalation. Now extend the exhalation for three seconds longer, and use that time to empty your lungs. Limit your intervention to these few seconds, once per breath, and let the rest of your breath cycle proceed normally. Never hold your breath at the end of the exhalation.

You can easily breathe out much longer than you normally do. (You may need help here, because those who hold on to a reservoir of breath are not aware of doing it.) But avoid an extreme effort that would make your breath audible or strained.

You might do this practice lying down. (Meditation lying down is not recommended because it is too easy to fall asleep, but this preparatory practice is an exception.) Lie on your back and place one hand lightly on your stomach area. Feel how your hand goes up and down as you breathe in and out. On your exhalation, you should feel your hand sink down below the level of your rib cage. On your inhalation, your hand should rise above the level of your rib cage. It is just like having a balloon there that fills and empties with air.

For inspiration, observe the breath of an infant or small child in sleep. The range of motion in the diaphragm area is very large.

Now sit up again and use the full exhalation to make your breath be rhythmic. That single intervention, in the last few seconds of the exhalation, is enough force to keep the breath going all the way around, as the push of the foot on the spinning wheel turns it around, as the steam piston turns the wheels of the locomotive, or as an explosion drives the pistons down to spin the crankcase in the automobile engine.

Limit the number of breaths you take this way to about ten. It is very important in meditation to learn to breathe all the way out, but this is only part of the process. A second intervention, introduced in the next chapter, complements this full exhalation. For now, practice full exhalation for only a limited number of breaths.

Rush of Energy

Inhaling is energizing; it creates a "rush" in the nervous system that you can feel emotionally. Note that the word *inspire* also means "to breathe in." An inhalation following a complete exhalation is especially powerful. It seems to *rise,* as opposed to the exhalation, which seems to *descend.*

Always begin the inhalation as soon as the exhalation is complete. Do not stop the breath at the "bottom," after exhaling; that is exhausting. Let the inhalation rise naturally, without trying to speed it up or slow it down, to a complete breath. Then it gently turns into an exhalation. The breath should always be smooth and silent.

You'll know you have the exhalation right if the inhalation causes a powerful rush of energy. It is like diving to the bottom of a pool and touching the bottom at the end of the exhalation, then springing off the bottom and rising rapidly on the inhalation. Don't stay at the bottom—just touch it—then let the inhalation spring off from there.

This way of breathing is invigorating and refreshing. It makes everything look new and fresh. A full breath will give a full life, in contrast to the half-life that a shallow breath allows. If this stage is the furthest you reach in your practice, you will still benefit immensely from the positive and powerful impact of breathing all the way out and all the way in. Transitions will become pleasant; change will not be avoided.

Start each breath with the abdominal muscles; then in the last few seconds use the chest muscles. With each inhalation, the stomach area should move visibly out. Then to maximize the inhalation, you expand your chest. Exhaling also starts with the diaphragm muscle. Compress the chest slightly only at the end of the exhalation cycle.

If you keep your breath in this rhythm, with a consciously complete exhalation, you will not get sleepy in meditation. The energy of the breath will keep you awake. Sleep needs a breath that doesn't touch the "bottom"; if it did, the resulting inhalation would wake you up.

Meditation is one way to make the breath conscious. Another way is exercise. The benefit of exercise is the attention it draws to the breath. Consequently, exercise produces some of the benefits of meditation, especially the stirring of the unconscious to bring the unresolved to the light of consciousness. But the exertion of exercise limits the effect by placing physical demands on the breath.

I USED TO WONDER *why I got so much enjoyment out of exercising and playing sports and yet got so exhausted from mowing the lawn. I liked the gym and I hated the lawn mower, but how did those feelings affect my stamina and endurance to such a great extent? One day I noticed my breath as I was mowing. I was breathing out, then pausing a long time before breathing in. So there were two differences between my mowing breath and my exercising breath. First, my mowing breath was unconscious, whereas my exercising breath was coordinated with my movements so it was both conscious and rhythmic. Secondly, because I disliked mowing so much, I had unconsciously adopted the "death breath," which is sure to cause exhaustion in anyone. The "death breath" is to breathe out and then pause before breathing in.*

Exhalation is also called exhaustion. To be without breath is exhausting. It is a simulation of the death state, where there is no more breath at all. Staying in that condition takes the life out of us. Having noticed this, I changed my breath so that the inhalation started immediately when the exhalation was over, without a pause. Then mowing became exercise instead of drudgery.

PURAN

Full Rhythmic Breath With Movement

Another way to practice the full breath is to coordinate your movement with your breathing, making your breath both conscious and rhythmic. Puran's son, Dr. Asatar Bair, has made an extensive study of rhythmic breathing and movement, so we will let him share his experience here with two forms of movement: walking and running.

Walking Breath Practice

DR. ASATAR BAIR: Spiritual seekers throughout history have spent a good deal of time walking, and have developed many meditative practices which can be done while walking. To apply Heart Rhythm Meditation to walking, you'll become conscious of your breathing by coordinating the rhythm of your steps with your breath. You may already do this naturally while you walk, without being aware of it, but this method uses a slower breathing rhythm, which allows for a full, deep breath. The average breath you take unconsciously uses only about 10 to 20% of your lung capacity. By extending the length of your breathing, you allow for a more efficient use of the oxygen that you inhale. Longer breaths are also calming, while providing a great deal of energy. To make the breath full, you'll be using your abdominal muscles to squeeze your diaphragm. Don't be surprised if you're using your abdominal muscles much more than you ordinarily would while walking—this means you're doing it right!

You will also make the inhalation and the exhalation the same duration. It is often the case that your unconscious breath is uneven—either the inhale or the exhale is longer, making the other side more forceful. By balancing the breath, you will smooth out energetic imbalances which may have accumulated due to unconscious habits.

So when you're ready to walk, breathe all the way out, and as you breathe in, take a step with your right foot, and count 8 steps as you walk. The eighth step will be your left foot, so when you take the ninth step, exhale, again for 8 steps (8-8). You'll find this easier to do if you're walking at a moderate pace on flat ground. If this rhythm doesn't work for you, try starting with 4 steps on the inhalation, and 4 on the exhalation, but try to work your way up to 8-8. If you're walking very slowly, 4-4 may be a good rhythm, but you'll find that 8-8 is a better match for the pace of walking in most activities. The main thing is that there must be time for you to completely empty the air from your lungs, and then completely fill them. Practice walking with this rhythm for a while, then see if you can maintain 8-8 on a moderate hill. This is more difficult, but it builds up control over the breath as it develops the abdominal muscles, the ability to relax the diaphragm while maintaining the tension in your core, and opens up the muscles surrounding the ribcage. Also, see if you can maintain a rhythm of 10-10, or even 12-12 on flat ground.

It's best to breathe in and out through your nose while doing this practice. If you find you cannot maintain the breath in and out of your nose, perhaps you are walking too quickly. Take a break; then resume at a more manageable pace.

Once you've mastered the breathing rhythm, you can add to it by imagining that your breath is a stream of energy, which comes into your heart on your inhalation, and goes out from your heart on your exhalation. Feel the breath coming into your heart from the back as you breathe in, sweeping you along like a powerful current, and pouring out from your chest as you breathe out, moving you forward.

When you begin, you'll be in the concentration phase: focusing your attention on your breathing to match up with your steps.

As you get used to the practice, it will become automatic, and you'll enter the contemplation phase; you'll feel a sense of flow, that your breath is driving you forward and moving your legs. As you continue to practice, you may enter the state of meditation, in which you experience the breath as an infinite current of energy flowing through you. It is no longer you that walks, but the Universal Heart, which powers your motion effortlessly with unlimited energy.

Try this method of Heart Rhythm Meditation next time you go for a walk—it can be practiced at any time, walking around your neighborhood in the morning, or walking to the car during the day. I think you'll find it adds a new dimension to your walking experience, by combining meditation with gentle exercise.

 MAINTAIN THE BREATHING RHYTHM OF 8 STEPS IN, 8 STEPS OUT AS YOU WALK FOR ONE MILE (1.6 K), OR 20 MINUTES.

ONCE A SUFI *went to the city, and on his return he said, "Oh, I am filled with joy. There was such an exaltation in the city." His student thought, "How wonderful! I must go and see this!" He went to the city, and when he came back, he said, "Horrible! How terrible the world is! Everyone seems to be at one another's throats. That was the picture I saw. I felt nothing but depression, as if my whole being were torn to pieces." "Yes," the Sufi said, "you are right." "But explain to me," the student said, "why you were so exalted and I was torn to pieces." The Sufi said, "You did not walk in the rhythm that I walked through the city.[4]*

4 www.hazrat-inayat-khan.org: Message: Vol 2, The Cosmic Language: 9. Reason

Running Breath Practice

DR. ASATAR BAIR: Once you have mastered the Walking Breath Practice of Heart Rhythm Meditation, you can then begin to practice the Running Breath Practice. As the above quote suggests, shifting from walking to running changes your rhythm quite a bit. The rhythm of your steps will be faster, your breathing will be faster, and of course, the demands on your lungs and musculature will be greater.

Nonetheless, the Running Breath Practice is basically the same as the Walking Breath Practice described above; you'll maintain the rhythm of 8 steps in, 8 steps out. I recommend starting this practice on a completely flat, predictable surface, like a field or running track. Take a deep breath in, then begin running with the right foot as you exhale, continue exhaling for 8 steps, then inhale as your right foot takes the ninth step. Continue to inhale as you take the rest of the steps, finishing your inhalation on the 16th step with your left foot.

When you walk at an ordinary pace, the rhythm of your steps tends to be somewhere between 15 and 18 steps every 10 seconds. When you run, the rhythm of your steps will be faster, more like 25 to 30 steps in 10 seconds. To maintain the same pattern of breathing and steps means you'll be taking more breaths per minute than when you were walking, yet you'll be breathing at a much slower rate than is the case for most runners, who tend to maintain a rhythm of 2 steps in, 2 steps out. You'll be taking only one-quarter the number of breaths of the average runner running the same speed.

It may seem impossible to run at all when you are taking fewer breaths, yet remember that the lungs require time to absorb oxygen from the air. Simply breathing more rapidly does not always result in greater absorption, because the muscular demands of breathing also require energy, and breathing rapidly causes a physiological stress reaction, activating adrenaline and stress hormones, resulting in another energetic drain. The average runner may take as many as 45 breaths per minute, or a breath every 1.33 seconds. At this rate, the lungs simply do not have enough time to absorb the oxygen, so the runner ends up breathing out much of the oxygen, an obvious inefficiency.

We want to retrain the lungs so that we can run and use the lungs more efficiently, taking fewer breaths per minute (about 11 to 14) yet extracting more of the oxygen and energy from each breath.

I have used this breathing rhythm to run all kinds of terrain, at many different speeds, and over all kinds of distances. I've climbed the steepest hills in San Francisco, and run distances ranging from 200m to 1 mile on the track at racing speeds, all while assiduously maintaining the 8-8 breathing rhythm. I've found this method gives me more strength and alertness, and speeds the recovery time between runs. On the spiritual level, I feel that running with this method has strengthened my faith, by continually bringing me in touch with a place of no breath, testing my ability to maintain the rhythm even when I want to shorten it. I've found that the times I said, "I just can't stick to this rhythm!" and allowed my breathing to become rapid and uncontrolled, I did not feel better, I felt worse. Overall, the Running Breath Practice has strengthened my breath, as well as my concentration and determination. [Dr. Asatar Bair]

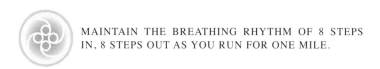

MAINTAIN THE BREATHING RHYTHM OF 8 STEPS IN, 8 STEPS OUT AS YOU RUN FOR ONE MILE.

Accomplishment

It is not enough to subdue thought, it is to raise the pitch, and although it may be said that to overcome one's thoughts, to become master of one's mind, is most difficult, one must face that battle. If one passes into sleep or into a dream or musing state, the mind is relaxed, but it is not properly relaxed. This is running away from the battle, thinking one has won it. One may think one has won the battle, but what has one won? The answer is easily seen when one looks at the great tasks which have been accomplished after meditations, which show that meditation is a positive action, not merely a relaxation. [Hazrat Inayat Khan] [5]

There is a connection between your ability to breathe out fully and your ability to accomplish things in life.

As a meditation *teacher, I observed people's varying ability to exhale fully, and I grew accustomed to the common difficulty in breathing out, their fear of being out of breath even for a moment. When I was teaching meditation in corporations, I expected the same problem to be present among executives. But I did not find it among those who had both responsibility for business and an interest in meditation. This group knew that they had to take risks and face fears, and that they could not hold back from making a complete effort. Hence, they could make a complete breath. But among older executives, the story was different; the risk taking was earlier in their career, and a conservative attitude had set in since then. Their attitude was to hold on*

---

5 Khan, I. Sangatha 2, Riyazat. *Esoteric Papers.*

rather than to expand. So the tendency to retain breath resur-faced in them, and they were less interested in meditation.

PURAN

Breathing out fully is necessary, but not sufficient, if you are to accomplish your desires. Every accomplishment requires you, at some point, to give much more than you had planned, to extend yourself. You can do this if you are familiar with the power in reserve at the end of each exhalation. People who have done extraordinary things have found this reserve and used it—exhaled it into their work.

In retrospect, the effort required to achieve a goal always looks greater than the result would seem to need. Before it is gained, the result seems worth the effort, but afterward it seems to have cost too much. By accomplishment of one's desire, more is gained than the resulting object, position, or recognition. The invisible but most valuable gain is the ability to accomplish, called mastery, that is built up with every accomplishment. Mastery leads to self-confidence, which is the mystics' definition of faith.

The comedian says, "You know the definition of an atheist? Someone with no *invisible* means of support."

When our breath is fully exhausted, we've given our all, expended our resources without reserve. Why does this effort produce results? Where do the results come from? They come because the pendulum we pushed away has swung back to us.

Put thy trust in God for support, and see His hidden hand working through all sources.
Give all you have, and take all that is given to you.
[Hazrat Inayat Khan][6]

---

6 Khan, I. (1989, 227)

> Take this breath as the model of an approach to life: take it all in, resisting nothing; give out all you can, holding back nothing. Maximize the flow; increase involvement.

Simply put, the inhalation affects the inner world, ourselves; and the exhalation affects the outer world, our circumstances and environment. Breath is an exchange between the two worlds. When you realize this, you see why the exhalation is necessary in accomplishment.

The most powerful part of the exhalation is its end, the completion. But most people don't use that part of their breath, except when they become angry and allow themselves to scream. The scream empties the lungs, completes the exhalation, and carries the feeling behind it to a complete expression, in accomplishment. The one who screams develops the experience that "nothing gets done until I yell about it!" Actually, something got done due to the full exhalation, not to the emotion. The full exhalation brought the desire from within and projected it into the world.

Howard wanted *to be a gentler father, and he was resentful that his wife and children wouldn't let him be one. His wife took the kind and gentle role, so Howard felt forced to be the heavy when things went wrong.*

"I don't like to get mad," he said, "but nothing happens until I do. Nothing gets done until I yell about it. I don't know any other way to move things." The problem was that he didn't know any way to fully exhale other than by screaming. His full exhalation was so powerful that it worked in spite of all the negative reactions provoked by his temper tantrum. His power and influence came from his breath, not from his anger.

Howard came to a meditation class, where he told this story. Besides his ignorance of his breath's power, he had to overcome a behavioral habit and give up the satisfaction of exercising a strong emotion. But he was committed to trying because of his kids—they were being traumatized by his outbursts. "It works as you said," Howard told me later. "It's breath that makes things move." SUSANNA

BECOME COMFORTABLE WITH FULL EXHALATION SO THAT YOU CAN TOUCH THE POINT OF NO RE-TAINED BREATH WITH LITTLE EFFORT FOR TEN BREATHS IN A ROW.

Causing Change

Some people say that no one can really change. Others say that since change is inevitable, no one can really remain the same. Still others say that "the more things change, the more they remain the same." One reason to avoid dogma is that a truth has to be allowed to change if it is to remain the same truth.

The interesting question is "Can *I* change?" All of the above statements apply to this question. Can you change your behavior? You can learn to act differently, but unless your basic attitude and identity are changed, you will not be able to maintain your new behavior in all situations.

A WOMAN HAD *a dog that she dressed up in clothes and treated like a person. She even taught it to sit in a chair and eat delicately from a plate on the table. She told everyone that her dog was really a prince in a dog's body and should be treated as such, not as an animal. A Sufi heard this story and went to investigate. As she walked to the woman's home, a cat followed her, and when she arrived, the cat was beside her at the door. When the woman opened the door, her dog saw the cat and immediately jumped from its chair and chased the cat into the street. The Sufi said to the woman, "Excuse me, I was looking for the dog who has the nature of a prince, but I see that your prince has the nature of a dog."*

169

Even a dog can be taught to act like a nobleman, until a cat comes along.

On the other hand, change is inevitable; all of life is changing. You can't help but change.

A TEACHER WAS SHOWING *an ax once owned by George Washington. "Did this ax really belong to President Washington?" his skeptical student asked him. "Of course," said the teacher, "although I admit it's had three new heads and four new handles since then."*

"You can't call it 'Washington's ax' if there's not one piece of it that is the same as when Washington had it," declared the student. "Why not?" said his teacher. "There's not one cell in your body now that was there when you were born. They've all died and been replaced by others. Yet you claim to be the same person."

While change is continual, it also has a continuity. The change you truly desire is to become more like what you have always been. As you develop a sense of what that is—your fundamental identity—you will be willing, even eager, to change everything else.

A RABBI PROUDLY ANNOUNCED *that the eternal flame in the synagogue had been lit continuously for 215 years. His student asked, "Since you periodically supply new oil, and since a flame is a part of the substance that burns, the flame is not the same, isn't that true? And since you use a different kind of oil now than you did a century ago, not even the kind of flame is the same. There are times that you've replaced the lamp, so the base hasn't been constant either. What is there about this eternal flame that hasn't changed?"*
"Its light," said the Rabbi.

When you realize your light nature, you will be happy to change anything about yourself that would allow you to become more luminous. It is ecstatic to realize that no matter how compromised, wounded, or dysfunctional you have become, you can still change to become the happy and radiant person you would like to be, because this is the person you've always been. If you can remember it or envision it, you can become it, because that memory or vision results from an inner reality. People have very different visions of the ideal person that they would be if they could, which shows that each person's ideal expresses their own real being.

"MASTER," THE STUDENT *blurted out, "I have received a vision of myself becoming a spiritual teacher." "Silence!" said the teacher, who was meditating. The force with which his teacher delivered this command took the student's breath away. He was literally dumbstruck. The student, a very intellectual and articulate man, often lectured to hundreds of people who were enraptured by his talks. Suddenly he felt no need to speak, and from that moment he became silent. The power of his mind and his speech welled up inside him and became incomparably greater because it was reserved. He continued to meet with his audience, but now instead of speaking, he only looked at them. People said that they benefited more from his glance than from his words. The glance of his eyes became a spiritual power, and thousands of people came to be seen by him, which allowed them to see themselves.*

Change may be either conscious or unconscious. To make change conscious, you need a vision of what you would like to become, and a catalyst to make the change occur. The catalyst for change is the full exhalation, the breath where nothing has been retained. To stimulate, to encourage, and to cause change in yourself, breathe out fully. The inhalation that follows a full exhalation is so powerful that it can make whatever change you envision. These two requirements, vision and exhalation, are present in the story above.

You have protective mechanisms that prevent change, and you have adaptive mechanisms that stimulate change. When you feel threatened, you take protective measures to encourage stability and survival. When you feel safe, you take adaptive measures to improve yourself. (The opposite might also be true: you might adapt under pressure and stabilize when unchallenged.)

The method of conscious heartbeat and conscious breath, Heart Rhythm Meditation, enables conscious change. This change is neither random change like the wind, nor periodic change like the seasons. The change you choose is change with a purpose, toward a direction, so that you can become more fully what you would like to be and fulfill the inner vision of yourself, the vision that reveals your eternal soul.

7. RETAINED BREATH (CONSERVING ENERGY)

The Second Intervention

The inhalation is like a rising fountain of energy; the exhalation is like a descending waterfall. In between, the breath has a "bottom" and a "top." The top of the breath is the period after the inhalation and before the exhalation. The normal breath looks like an ellipse, and the first intervention lengthened the breath into a longer ellipse, as shown here in Figure 4.

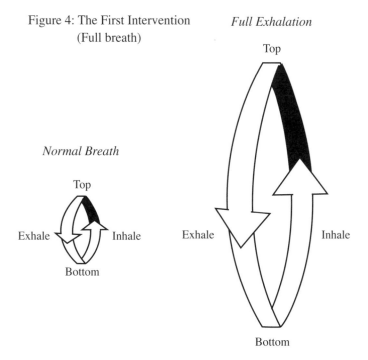

Figure 4: The First Intervention
(Full breath)

Now we need to make another intervention in our breathing rhythm: to hold the breath at the top of the cycle. The practical reason is to prevent hyperventilation, which can be caused by taking in too much oxygen during the powerful in-breath. The full exhalation causes the inhalation to start from the depth of the lungs, so one may get as much oxygen in one breath as one normally gets with two or three breaths. Initially, the brain and nervous system make good use of the extra oxygen, but after a while the need for oxygen, even at a higher level of awareness and vitality, diminishes again.

Holding the breath balances the supply with the need, without reverting to a shallow breath and its many limitations.

The picture of the breath is now like an ellipse with a top, as in Figure 5. The length of each side of the triangle represents the length of each part of the breath. Never hold breath at the bottom, after the exhalation, only at the top, after the inhalation.

Figure 5: The Second Intervention
Full Breath with Retention at the Top of the Inhalation

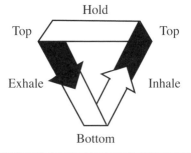

After breathing *in* all the way, hold the breath for a time, without straining. The longer you breathe out, the longer you can hold your breath.

Holding the inhalation slows down the breathing cycle and prevents hyperventilation. The combination of breathing all the way out and then holding the inhalation makes a breath that can be repeated indefinitely.

At first, holding the breath may give you a sense of urgency rather than peace, if you feel anxious about needing to breathe. You may overcome this by extending the exhalation a little longer so it's easier to hold the breath. Practice will give familiarity with the retained breath.

DEVELOP STABLE BREATH USING FULL EXHALATION AND RETENTION OF THE INHALATION. BECOME COMFORTABLE WITH THE STILL BREATH SO IT BECOMES A PERIOD OF PEACE.

Energy Is Conserved

The effect of holding the breath is to stop all expression and suspend all activities. Consequently, all one's energy is conserved. The first step in conservation was achieving stillness of the body; the second step is stopping the movement of the breath. The inner processes continue, but all actions and interactions with the outer world are paused. The power within builds rapidly and is not depleted by the subsequent exhalation. It is like charging a battery.

> If one needs magnetism or desires it, there is no better manner of obtaining it than through meditation. For then it is that the battery is recharged which had been giving out so much energy in thought, speech and action. [Hazrat Inayat Khan][1]

Notice the contrast between this retained breath in meditation and the breath of sleep. During sleep, the pause occurs at the bottom of the breath, never at the top. This has a very different effect and

---

1 Khan, I. (1989, 231)

demonstrates that sleep involves conserving energy less than re-processing mental events, like the second digestion of a cow chewing its cud. The conservation of energy from retained breath, resulting in a powerful energy buildup, is unique to meditation. The meditator who has not previously tried full exhalation followed by a retained inhalation will be surprised at the power of this simple technique.

> In whatever we do and in all our thinking and imagining, we consume energy. This consumption of energy brings on old age and weakness. Contrariwise, meditation of itself may cure man's evils, whatsoever they be.
>   When the breath is kept in rhythm and is refined, the magnetism which is ordinarily wasted or consumed is preserved and absorbed into one's personal atmosphere. This makes one a battery of life. . . . By silence and stilling the mind one draws upon endless resources of space. [Hazrat Inayat Khan] [2]

Take this breath now as a model for life: you cannot persevere, you cannot be successful over time, you cannot sustain growth, you cannot continue to expend energy, unless you also conserve energy. You conserve energy with a retained breath.

Time Stands Still

The power of the inhalation has given us the opportunity to experience the timeless aspect of a still breath. Holding the breath seems to slow down the passage of time. You now begin to sense another aspect of yourself, an aspect that does not change or that changes very little.

The rate at which you breathe affects the metabolism of your body, which in turn affects both your physical and your mental rhythms. The breath rate is one of the two clocks in the body; the

---

2 *Ibid.,* 227

other one is the heart rate. When we breathe slowly, we slow down our perception of time and assume a long-term outlook.

The experience of holding the breath demonstrates how much our perception of ourselves and the world is affected by our perception of the passage of time. Albert Einstein discovered the principle of relativity by imagining that he was riding on a photon traveling at the speed of light.

When one is moving, other moving things appear to be stationary. When one is stationary, everything else appears to be moving. When one is very still, one can sense the motion of the sun, the growth of a tree, the dance of a flower, even the evolution of a rock.

The moment is short, when our breath is very fast;
Long gone is the past, and next day's future's unknown.
With very slow breath, the present becomes so vast,
Present holds the past, and the future present owns.

Can't know the river, from a small raft swept downstream.
Get off time's river, let the water pass under
A bridge we stand on, to view the flowing present.
Each drop of the past, becomes drop of the future,
We look at them all, and we call them a river.

But how can we see, the length of the river Time?
The sight is too short, on this bridge of the moment.
The bridge doesn't see—where river's drops have come from,
In hues of earth's ore, how their past has colored them!
It doesn't see drops, evaporate in the sun,
Drops pass out of sight, though the bridge counts every one.

What can see and know, the nature of the river?
The bed and the banks, the arms of earth that hold her.
Still and eternal, stretching from the mountain source,
To the ocean goal, carrying her every mile.

They *make the river, water just fills their vessel.*

Under the river, the endless river of Time,
There is ageless earth, who knows her eternally.

As a meditator advances, his or her personality begins to change. First the personality takes on some of the pure qualities of animals. Later it becomes enriched by the qualities of plants, then rocks, and then the sun and moon.

The deer stands perfectly still in the forest. As its eyes are optimized for seeing movement, it sees potential predators best when it is still. (It sees still objects when it is moving.) As the deer stands, it becomes part of the forest because of its stillness, and it sees its environment in a way that few animals and even fewer people see theirs. But the tree sees the forest even more clearly, for it grew up with the other trees and stands with them, their roots intertwined for decades, through the lifetimes of many deer. The deer see the forest as it is; the trees saw how the forest developed.

Even more still are the rocks. They have seen the forests come and go. They live in geological time measured in millennia.

The more one knows, the less one says.

The silence of the rocks covers their wisdom, but each stone is fully the whole of the earth and carries within itself the record of the birth and development of the planet. To read its knowledge, one has to enter its time scale. The rock speaks softly, without expending energy, by storing its experience in the arrangement of its molecules, altering its composition, resonant frequency, and opaqueness. Over time, a rock evolves into a crystal that has purity, transparency, and a single defining frequency of vibration, the crystallization of its whole existence.

As you hold your breath, think of yourself as a being in a slower time scale, like that of a tree or a rock.

> With every breath, time passes more and more slowly; eventually time seems to stop completely. Consequently, you become aware of your eternal component.

The Enhancement of Memory

We do not perceive time as a uniform continuum. That is, some minutes seem longer than others. Nor is memory allocated to life's events uniformly; some moments are given large amounts of memory, while some whole days may hardly register. The degree of awakening is a multiplier applied to memory. When our consciousness is enhanced, an event that may have been only a moment long occupies a large space in our memory, as if it had been recorded in slow motion. In stillness, time passes slowly, so that the perceptions and thoughts that occur are magnified in our memory, and we can recall them in great detail.

This accounts for why a half hour of meditation can affect our whole day. The wakefulness of the meditation time makes that time appear much longer in our memory. The rhythm of the meditation state is impressed strongly upon our unconscious, which then echoes the same rhythm all day.

This enhancement of memory by meditation, together with the extraordinary closeness that a group feels from doing Heart Rhythm Meditation together, results in participants assigning great importance to their meditation group. The experiences in meditation are quite profound, and with the multiplier effect that meditation has on memory, these experiences become major life events.

Rise Above

Man can train his ego by being patient with all around him that has a jarring effect upon him. For every jar upon the soul irritates the ego. When man expresses his irritation he develops a disagreeable nature; when he controls it and does not express it, then his ego becomes crushed inwardly. The idea is to rise above all such irritations. [Hazrat Inayat Khan] [3]

The retained breath lets us hold the sense of "height" in meditation that is inspired by the rising inhalation. To stay in the height requires breathing out fully, because it is the length of the exhalation that gives length to the retention. The second intervention allows us to fully benefit from the inhalation by pausing in the elevated and rarefied condition to which the inhalation lifts us.

Now we find literal meaning in the phrase "to rise above." It comes from understanding the inhalation as an *ascent*. Holding the inhalation is actually "staying high." This is why heaven is pictured metaphysically as "on high" or above. Gravity pulls things down, so "down" becomes the default condition. "Down" takes no effort and is undistinguished. Gravity attracts everything that is matter; the buoyancy of the spirit is alone immune to gravity and gives an opposite direction: rising. [4]

A further discovery is that "rising above" things is exactly how one feels when one is on high with the breath. It is like seeing the world from an airplane: what was important on the surface is unimportant now, and what was unimportant on the surface, indeed inconceivable, is very important now. Rising above allows one to see what is really important and what is not, what needs attract your involvement, how to be best involved, and how to help people most. To truly help someone requires having great insight. To see into a lake, one must be above the lake, not at the edge. The view from on high allows one to see into the depth.

After this experience on high, you will follow your exhalation into a descent into the concrete, the particular, and the immediate. From the timeless, you reenter the time-critical. Your ability to

---

3 www.hazrat-inayat-khan.org: Message: Vol 13, Gathas: Morals

4 Even hot-air baloons rise by the force of gravity, just as submarines surface through gravity. If there were no gravity, neither baloons nor submarines could rise. Airplanes fly by the principle of lift, a property of a fluid in motion. Nothing material is immune to gravity.

prioritize your use of time, to remember what's important when surrounded by distractions, and to follow through on your insights are the test of your loving concern about people and proof of your sense of responsibility. Your experience with the timeless will greatly enhance your ability to manage, and master, your own time. Without the experience of height, your life would appear relatively flat, with little difference in importance between things, and the experience of your present moment would strongly dominate your reality. From above, you see that your habits of the past exercise their force on the present and drag your future toward an eventual result. The future you desire will be built up only if you reorient yourself.

W HEN PEOPLE DON'T *have an experience of the height of the heart, they have difficulty determining what is important and what is not. A major corporation, for example, debated for half an hour whether to install a bicycle rack outside their corporate center. But it agreed to acquire a new subsidiary virtually without comment. In terms of the future of the company, immediate cost, company reputation, or any other criteria, the acquisition was much more important than the bike rack.*

As another example, a man we know devotes considerable time and attention to his prioritized to-do list, which usually contains at least thirty items. He frets about the items he has to roll over to the next day. He reprioritizes them often. It would be better for him to spend a few minutes in Heart Rhythm Meditation, in order to gain the perspective to be able to discriminate between the important, the unimportant, and the urgent. Then he could better focus on those tasks that would truly advance his goals.

Draw the breath upward on the inhalation, as before. Let your center of consciousness be lifted by the ascending breath, like a rubber ball on a fountain. Hold the breath and feel your heart expand upward, and in all directions. When exhaling, keep the energy of your heart high, and let the breath descend from there.

When you have reached such an expanded state that and your personal world has disappeared from your consciousness, turn your attention downward. From the height to which you have been lifted by the breath, "look" down upon your self in the context of your life. Thinking of your current life situation from this vantage point, see how the present is the natural outcome of your whole life and at the same time a necessary stage in the development of the qualities and abilities that you need to fulfill your purpose in life.

This experience naturally leads you to reformulate your direction and priorities so that your attention in the present will nurture the seeds of the future you desire.

Warning: If this practice produces nausea, fright, or any unwanted experience of any kind, either stop the practice altogether or substitute light for the notion of breath. Light is a particularly safe form of energy. It takes considerable experience to be able to handle internal energy in its general form.

EXPERIENCE THE HOLDING OF THE INHALATION AS AN UPLIFTING INTO THE TIMELESS HEIGHT OF THE HEART, FROM WHICH YOU CAN LOOK "DOWN" AND GAIN INSIGHT INTO YOUR LIFE.

8. BREATH AND HEARTBEAT (PEACE)

It is our artificial and highly specialized intellectual life with unnecessary concern and worries which destroys the rhythm of the heartbeat and makes it difficult to place the center of gravity of the personality where it belongs. Sleep at best gives only partial relief. Meditation removes self-consciousness, the greatest obstacle to calm and peace. [Hazrat Inayat Khan][1]

Finding the Heartbeat While Retaining the Inhalation

Meditation is the task of escaping from the control of the lower mind and living in the heart. It is only when the consciousness is in the heart that the soul can be free. By "heart" is meant not only the physical heart but all that is physical that is connected with the heart, and at the same time it includes all the higher emotions, purer thoughts and deep intuitions. All of these belong to the heart. [Hazrat Inayat Khan][2]

After the *in*halation, hold your breath, and look for the sensation of your heartbeat anywhere in your body. The longer you hold your breath, the more pronounced your heartbeat will become. If you don't notice the heartbeat, hold your breath longer. To hold your breath longer, exhale longer, then inhale again. (Never hold your breath after the *ex*halation.)

---

1 Khan, I. (1989, 305-6)
2 *Ibid.,* 303

Once you have found the heartbeat, it is easy to find it again; it's just a matter of knowing how it feels and where to look. Through awareness of your heartbeat, you will become more aware of your heart and all that "heart" means.

Life in the heart comes when consciousness is centered in feeling. [Hazrat Inayat Khan][3]

A DOCTOR WE KNOW TREATS *heart ailments by having patients listen to their own hearts. He provides them with a stethoscope for this purpose. The theory is that attention from the conscious mind will stabilize and strengthen the action of the unconscious mind that controls the heartbeat. He told us that he has good results. We told him that for millennia meditators have made the heartbeat conscious, for spiritual development as well as for physical health and strength, but they don't need a stethoscope. He asked how it was possible to hear the heart. We replied that one can feel the heartbeat very clearly, both the "lub" and the "dub." He assumed that we were fantasizing a heartbeat or else describing some superpower that was irrelevant for his patients. But we explained that the ability to feel the heart is quite easily achieved if only one has practiced the two interventions in breathing: full exhalation and retained inhalation.*

When you first discover your heartbeat, it may cause you some anxiety. First, the discovery may come as a surprise. In a meditative state, your awareness is so keen that the sudden pronounced feeling of your heart, autonomously beating in your chest, is startling. Second, it can be frightening to discover the heart in action, dynamically pumping blood to preserve your life. Sometimes nonmeditators worry that their heart may suddenly stop, but then they

---

3 *Ibid.,* 309-10

forget about it again. But when you're doing Heart Rhythm Meditation, you cannot forget whatever feelings you may have about your heart and its fragility. But just as we learned to breathe out fully, in trust that air would be available for the next inhalation, you can learn to be aware of your heartbeat and trust that the pulsation will continue.

If this practice is anxiety-producing, do not blame yourself in any way but try to discover more about your anxiety. Keep up the practice. Any progress you make will result in an increase in faith and a decrease in fear. With practice, awareness of the heartbeat will become comforting and reassuring.

Heart Rhythm Meditation develops faith by developing a conscious certainty that the heart is beating and will continue to beat. Infrequent contact with your heart may be unnerving to you, but an ongoing contact will build a familiarity with your heart. Your initial anxiety about whether your heart will continue to beat will be replaced by a confidence that your heart will beat and pump for a long, long time. This confidence is based not on a theoretical probability calculation but on your experience of direct contact with your heart, repeated day after day.

Faith can be defined by two words, "self-confidence" and "certainty in expectation." The great people of the world, the greatest people, are great more by their faith than by anything else, because mostly great people have been adventurous and at the back of a venture is faith, nothing else. [Hazrat Inayat Khan][4]

Notice *where* in your body you feel your heartbeat. It could be anywhere: in your hands, in your ears, in your stomach. There is

4 www.hazrat-inayat-khan.org: Message: Vol 13, Gathas: Metaphysics: 1.2 Faith

information in this: your unconscious is directing your conscious attention to an area that needs it. Consider what message that part of your body might have for you. Why does it need your attention? What impression is stored there from the past? What advice does it have for you about how you could put that part of your body to better use in service of your purpose?

Keeping the Heartbeat Continually

When the entire mechanism of his body is working in a rhythm, the beat of the pulse, of the heart, of the head, the circulation of the blood, hunger and thirst—all show rhythm, and it is the breaking of rhythm that is called disease. [Hazrat Inayat Khan][5]

After you've found the heartbeat as you hold your inhalation, you may find that it disappears again when you exhale. As you breathe in and out, the motion of your breath can mask the heartbeat, but the heartbeat will be waiting for you when you return to the top of the breath.

Get the rhythm of the heartbeat while you can feel it, then, during the exhalation and inhalation, count off with that rhythm. This count will help you find the heartbeat underneath the breath until the breath is still again.

Breathe very lightly and slowly, and you'll be able to stay aware of your heartbeat throughout the whole breathing cycle. Even though the breath is light, finish it with a complete exhalation.

With practice, your heartbeat will become quite pronounced and a constant companion whenever you look for it.

---

5 www.hazrat-inayat-khan.org: Message: Vol 2, The Mysticism of Sound: 6. Rhythm

Notice two quite different but linked experiences in Heart Rhythm Meditation: an exquisite vulnerability of a sensitive heart that takes you into your deepest feelings, and a powerful energy charge that radiates into the space around you. The first is often accompanied by a slight ache in your heart. In the second, the power of your heartbeat may cause a subtle rocking of your body. These are landmark experiences of Heart Rhythm Meditation.

SENSE THE HEARTBEAT IN YOUR CHEST, AT LEAST WHILE YOU ARE HOLDING YOUR INHALATION.

Counting the Breath with the Heartbeat

If there is any form of concentration to be used in meditation, it consists in first getting into the rhythm of the heart, by watching the heartbeats, feeling them and harmonizing with them. [Hazrat Inayat Khan] [6]

Coordinate the two main clocks of your body by using the heartbeat to time the breath.

Using the heartbeat as a timer, count the number of heartbeats in your exhalation. Remember to extend the breath to the end, using the last few counts to do this.

At the bottom of the breath, start counting heartbeats from one as you inhale.

At the top of the breath, start counting heartbeats again from one as you hold the breath.

6 Khan, I. (1989, 307-8)

> Now you have three numbers that measure the length of the three parts of the breath. Keep counting each breath.

The Square Breath Rhythm

The first thing that is necessary in meditation is to realize that it is an act of attunement, an attunement with God. Therefore, while it is necessary to relax, while it is important to control the emotions and the functions of mind and body, it is also important to raise, so to speak, the pitch of the heart, so that this attunement can be accomplished. [Hazrat Inayat Khan][7]

At this point we introduce the third and final intervention in the breath rhythm, which tunes the breath to harmonic resonance with the heart. It gives a literal meaning to the above quotation, which opens its metaphysical meaning. By meditation practice you have, by now, developed an awareness of both the breath and the heart rhythms. You have experienced how the breath reflects your inner state, and you know the heartbeat is regulated by the unconscious alone. Bringing these two rhythms into alignment attunes the conscious and the unconscious mind. Having experienced relaxation in meditation, you know that meditation is also much more than relaxation; it allows a balance of feeling and thinking, contemplation and action. What finally allows this attunement to be accomplished is raising the pitch, the level of intensity, of the heartbeat in your consciousness.

Rhythm is most important in [breathing practices], for there ought to be a balance in the breath. Inhaling and exhaling must be even in rhythm, but the holding of the breath should not necessarily be even with the rhythm of inhaling and exhaling, for it makes three bars of an even rhythm, but three bars make a phrase or sentence of music odd in rhythm. To make it even, four bars are required. Therefore the holding should balance

---

7 Khan, I. (1989, 225)

evenly with inhaling and exhaling both, in order to make it four bars. [Hazrat Inayat Khan][8]

The third intervention is to adjust the three parts of the breath cycle to correspond to a four-part rhythm, called the Square Breath. The cycle of breath is set by the length of the exhalation, which is one of the four equal sides of a square. The inhalation is made the same length as the exhalation, completing another side of the square. Then after the inhalation the breath is held twice as long as the exhalation, for the remaining two sides of the square, as shown in Figure 6.

This breath is balanced in two directions: the length of the inhalation equals the length of the exhalation, and the length of the moving breath equals the length of the held breath. The Square Breath is not only balanced internally, it is aligned to the heartbeat because the pulse establishes the tempo for counting. If the exhalation is six heartbeats, then one side of the square is 6, and the length of the whole breath cycle is 6 times 4, or 24 heartbeats. That makes the frequency of the heart equal to the twenty-fourth harmonic of the frequency of the breath. The two main clocks of the body are now synchronized with each other. The square could be

---

8 Khan, I. Githa 2, Ryazat. *Esoteric Papers.*

based on longer cycles as well; it is the shape of the square that is important, not the length of the sides.[9]

Figure 6: *The Square Breath*

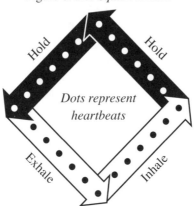

Dots represent heartbeats

---

9 Note that there is another version of the Square Breath practice which emerges from the Vedanta tradition, and is sometimes taught in Yogic breathing classes. In this version, you have two periods of holding, each of equal length; for example: inhale 6, hold 6, exhale 6, hold 6. This practice is not generally done with the heartbeat but with a mental count.

We don't recommend this practice, and it's not part of Heart Rhythm Meditation, because this way of breathing isn't compatible with a full breath. If you've taken a full exhalation, you'll find it impossible to hold the breath, as there is no breath in the lungs, and there is a physiological reflex which prevents the holding of the breath when the lungs are truly empty.

Holding the breath after the exhalation weakens the heart as well as the body. The Vedantic square breath practice is clearly not intended for long-term use, but rather as an introductory exercise to gain control over the breath; Vedantic practices are designed to free the consciousness from the body, to facilitate the realization that your consciousness is not bound by your body. That's a worthy goal but, in our view, a better way to achieve it is to realize that your heart contains the entire universe. The Square Breath from within Heart Rhythm Meditation will strengthen and energize the heart with a rich, full breath.

The Square Breath: Set a length for the exhalation equal to six heartbeats. Use the last three beats to complete the exhalation. Count six heartbeats for the inhalation as well. Then hold the breath for twelve heartbeats.

If that breath is too long, take four heartbeats for the exhalation, for the inhalation, and eight for the holding. If six heartbeats made the breath cycle too short, use eight heartbeats for the exhalation and the same proportions from there. A short breath is four heartbeats. Six is average. Eight beats is moderately long.

The inhalation doesn't have to be linear over time. Most of the inhalation will come in the first few counts, but keep the breath coming, if only in feeling, to the end of the count. Only when the inhalation count is finished do you start the holding count. In the exhalation, too, most of the breath will pass in the first few counts, but the finishing counts are very important.

The breath should be regular. Change its length only very gradually. The breath should also be smooth. Avoid sudden changes, gasps, and heavy breathing; keep the breath silent.

MAINTAIN THE SQUARE BREATH FOR 15 MINUTES.

Control of the Heartbeat

One must accustom oneself to get power over, or to have influence on, one's circulation and pulsation, and one can do that with the power of thought and with the power of will together with breath. By will-power one can bring about a certain condition in one's body so that one's circulation takes a certain rhythm. It is decreased according to will. One can do the same in regulating one's pulsation by the power of will.

Therefore, to have relaxation does not mean to sit quietly. It is to be able to remove tension from one's system, from one's circulation, one's pulsation, and one's nervous and muscular system. [Hazrat Inayat Khan][10]

Once your heartbeat and your breath are in rhythm, the tension in your body will begin to dissipate. A powerful sense of peace will come over you. This peace is not just an emotion, it is a power. One of its effects is to slow down your heartbeat. As this happens, you will need to adjust your breath.

As you continue the Square Breath you will notice that your breath, which is now tied to your heartbeats, is too short. With relaxation, your need for breath is less, which contributes to the feeling that you want your breath to be even longer. Consequently, you should increase the number of heartbeats per breath. If you are counting eight heartbeats for the exhalation, go to ten. Ten beats makes a long breath; a full cycle is forty heartbeats. If you're already at ten, go to twelve beats.

Increase the length of your breath slowly, and only when necessary. You want to be able to sustain the new pace without strain. As your heart rate and breath rate lengthen, your sense of a minute of time will also lengthen.

No sooner has the will taken in hand the circulation and the pulsation of the body, than the will has in hand a meditation of hours. It is for this reason that sages can meditate for hours on end, because they have mastered their circulation. They can breathe at will, slower or quicker. And when there is no tension on one's nervous or one's muscular system, then one gets a repose that ten days sleep can not bring about. [Hazrat Inayat Khan][11]

---

10 www.hazrat-inayat-khan.org: Message: Vol 4, Mental Purification: 11. Mystic Relaxation

11 *Ibid.*

Radiating Peace

Peace comes when self is in harmony with the rhythm of the heart. This is accomplished in two ways. In silent meditation all vibrations are stopped and one enters into the life-stream in the heart. In music, the rhythm and harmony are directed to and through the heart so that it takes up the proper pulsation. [Hazrat Inayat Khan] [12]

Synchronizing the heart and breath rhythms creates a powerful radiance: the radiance of peace. Peace radiates with the pulsation of the heart into the atmosphere around you. It affects the space and can be sensed at a great distance. (In Chapter 11, the magnetic field of the heart is described.)

As you breathe out in the Square Breath, let the coordinated rhythm that you experience internally extend outward into the space around you as peace. This peace is a powerful, stable wave of vibration that brings everything it reaches into rhythm with itself.

It starts within you when the rhythm of the heartbeat, in harmony with the breath rate, creates a peace that extends throughout your body as a single pulsing wave. Then it expands outward without effort, without "pushing" the breath outward.

Every person whom this breath of peace reaches becomes more harmonized internally as the source of it is rhythm. Peace has the power to create peace in others by bringing everyone into alignment, or attunement.

We mentioned in Chapter 4 that when two people meet, their breaths become coordinated. The strongest—that is, the most conscious—breath sets the rhythm, and the other person's breath adapts to it. The Square Breath is the strongest breath of all; it sets

---

12 Khan, I. (1989, 307-8)

all other breaths to its rhythm, which is peace. The way it does this is not mysterious—it does it the way the beat of a drum establishes the rhythm of an ensemble, or a clear voice establishes the pitch of the choir. The reason the Square Breath is the strongest breath is that its rhythm is extremely stable, since it is tied to the heart rate, which in meditation is itself quite stable.

Your breath sends out waves of pressure, exactly like very low-frequency sound waves, that fill the space around you. Simultaneously, you send your waves of magnetism on the heartbeat. The coordination of these two rhythms is evident to everyone, albeit unconsciously.

To be influential, a breath has to transmit energy at a frequency that can be matched to the receiver. A quick breath, like a gasp, has little influence. If you gasp, other people do not take it up. The energy of one person's quick breath doesn't couple to the breathing of others, unless it is repeated, as in laughter or chanting. (A laughing breath will spread over a group of people, producing a tickling sensation in the mind that evokes more laughter.)

The slowest rhythms are the most influential. A yawn, for example, is a very infectious breath. Even a single yawn reproduces its rhythm in the breaths of others.

These examples may help to explain why the Square Breath has so much power to influence others. It is a repeated breath of a single low frequency within the breath range, slower and more stable than any other breath. Its effect is to slow and stabilize the breath of others. Consequently, it produces in others all those emotions and experiences that correspond to that kind of breath, primarily peace.

EXPERIENCE EXTRAORDINARY PEACE, BOTH WITHIN YOURSELF AND EXTENDING AS A POWER INTO THE SPACE AROUND YOU.

9. DIRECTED BREATH (HEALING)

Pulse Everywhere

Each time the heart contracts, it sends out a wave of blood to course through the arteries. Like a miniature wave machine, the pump turns the smooth flow of blood entering the heart through the veins into waves. These waves of blood branch out through the tree-like structure of the arteries, being pushed down smaller and smaller channels until at last the waves reach the capillaries. The capillaries are so narrow that only a single blood cell can pass through them at one time. A wave of blood hits this constriction like a wave at sea hits a sea wall. It crashes into it, and the crash registers as a pressure differential in the tissue around the capillary. Consequently, one can feel the pulse in any part of the body that one chooses, just by directing attention there.

During the Square Breath, think of your fingertips. By your concentration, you make the pressure sensors in your fingertips very sensitive. Consequently, you will be able to feel the pulse of your heart in your fingertips.

You might find the heartbeat first in your stomach, or ears, or legs. It's very individual. Direct your attention to your feet, and look for the pulse there. When you have found it, look for the pulse in your temples. It's similar to a certain kind of headache but without the pain: just throbbing. You'll be surprised that the pulse is so strong there, and that it ever goes away. Wherever you've found your heartbeat is helpful, but keep looking in your chest for the source of the beat.

Now concentrate on both your chest and your fingertips. Look for the heartbeat in your chest and in your fingertips at the same time. With practice, you'll be able to feel that the fingertip pulse happens a fraction of a second later than the heartbeat.

Finally, try to feel the pulse in all of these places at the same time. When you can, all parts of the body will seem to be pulsing at once, especially the torso and head, with the hands and feet slightly delayed.

FEEL YOUR HEARTBEAT IN YOUR HANDS, FEET, AND TEMPLES.

Direct the Breath Within

The respiratory and circulatory systems are complementary. The circulatory system continues through the bloodstream what the respiratory system starts. Respiration is a process of exchange with the environment; circulation is an internal process. The Square Breath synchronizes these systems into a single rhythm using the heartbeat.

The bloodstream literally carries the breath throughout the body. On the exhalation you can feel a wave of breath expanding outward from the chest and sweeping through the body. You can direct this wave by your concentration, so that you can feel the breath through the hands, for example.

One of the breakthroughs of meditation is the experience of breathing in or out through some part of the body. The air component of the breath continues to flow through the mouth or nose, of course, but one can feel that the energy component of the breath passes into and through a particular part of the body, such as the chest or hands.

Illness is primarily a failure of the breath to reach the affected part of the body. By concentrating on some spot within the body or on the skin, you can make the breath pass in or out through that point. You will feel it as a flow of energy. This natural feeling, not at all strange or uncomfortable, does indeed feel like breath is passing through the area of your concentration.

Biomagnetism

The human body has a measurable magnetic field. This field is weak in relation to the earth's magnetic field, which can move a compass needle, but in relation to the body's size with respect to the earth, the body's magnetic field is enormous. The magnetic field of the earth, shown in Figure 7, is approximately 10^{-4} Tesla in strength. The field of the human heart is approximately 10^{-10} Tesla in strength, so the earth's field is one million times stronger. But the human heart weighs just 10 ounces, while the earth weighs $1.3 \times 10^{+25}$ pounds. Pound-for-pound, the heart's magnetic field is $5 \times 10^{+18}$ stronger than the earth's.

The earth's magnetic field is a result of its iron core, but the human body's magnetic field is a result of its electrical currents. Any electrical current generates a magnetic field along the direction of its flow, and the body has many electrical currents flowing through it in the muscles and nerves.

Notice the similarities between the pattern of the

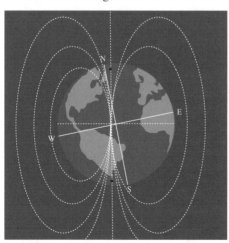

Figure 7: The Earth's Magnetic Field

Earth's magnetic field and the heart's magnetic field, shown in Figure 8.

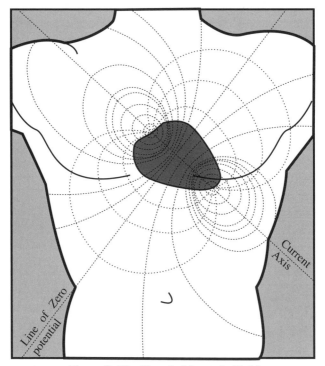

Figure 8: The Heart's Magnetic Field

THE BODY'S MAGNETIC *field is easy to observe if other fields are screened out. The Harold Bitter Magnetic Laboratory, at the Massachusetts Institute of Technology, has a Faraday cage, an enclosed room that shields the interior from external magnetic fields. Within that room, the magnetic field of a person can be readily detected at a distance of ten feet by conventional instruments. A demonstration we saw there affirmed our inner experience about the poles of the magnetic field of the body and the direction of the magnetic flux: the body has two magnetic poles, one in the heart and one in the head, and the magnetic flux turns around the heart.*

The human body is considerably more sensitive to magnetic fields than are conventional instruments. It is at least as sensitive as a plant. Research has shown that plants have an acute sensitivity to the magnetism of humans which the plant can indicate by changing the electrical resistance across the surface of its leaves. This reaction is called Electrical Skin Resistance (ESR) in humans and is a key component of a lie detector test. By measuring the ESR of the plant, the plant's perception of a person's magnetism can be deduced.[1]

The following meditation demonstrates quite dramatically the reality of the body's magnetic field.

While meditating with the Square Breath, concentrate on your hands. Look for two feelings there: the first is the pulse, the second is an energy like an electric field, a life force, a buzz, or a light pressure, throughout your hands.

If this feeling doesn't come immediately, be patient.
Once you get it the first time, you can regain it easily. It's a breakthrough experience, like riding a bicycle. Remember how hard that was to learn?

Open your eyes, and look at your hands. Then bring one hand up in front of your chin, palm up, fingers pointing straight ahead and curved slightly upward. Now blow gently across that hand, sending your breath over the heel, across the palm, and onto your fingertips. Direct your eyes to the target of your breath: the fingertips. After a few breaths, change hands.

---

1 Tompkins (1973)

After several minutes, lower your hands and look at them. You will likely feel a great sensitivity develop in your hands, a sensitivity to magnetism.

Now hold your hands in front of your chest, a foot or so apart, palms facing each other. Slowly push your hands closer together, stopping before they touch. Notice the feeling of pressure between them, as if you were trying to compress a rubber ball. As you push through the resistance, the force drops suddenly, then builds up again at a closer distance, as if you encountered a smaller ball within the larger ball.

Now slowly pull your hands apart, even to a distance of three feet, and push them toward each other again. Repeat. Try it a little faster; that can help you feel the pressure differential.

This energy that you feel in your hands is the breath. Because you're concentrating your mind and your glance on your hands, you bring the breath there more intensely. The breath makes the hands more sensitive to magnetism.

Everything has some magnetic field around it, and when the hands are sensitive, they can feel the layers of that field, especially around the edges of things. Each hand is feeling the magnetic field of the other hand. The magnetic field has layers, which accounts for the levels of resistance one feels at different distances.

 FEEL YOUR BODY'S MAGNETIC ENERGY IN YOUR HANDS.

Self-Healing

When you can feel the breath passing through some part of your body, then you are ready to use your breath for healing yourself. By directing breath into a part of your body that is weak, you can bring it health and strength. When you can feel your breath in some specific area, you are increasing circulation there, focusing the immune system there, then expelling toxins on the exhalation.

Sitting in a meditation posture, breathing the Square Breath, scan the body for areas that feel uncomfortable or painful. In meditation, you may feel pain in some part of your body where you don't ordinarily feel pain. The pain you feel, while physical at the moment, may be nonphysical in origin, a signal of emotional anguish, mental conflict, opposing pressures, or existential pain; in other words, mental or emotional stress.

When you find a painful or uncomfortable area, gently send your breath into that area. Begin by visualizing the area. Direct your thoughts to the appropriate depth, corresponding to the skin, muscle, organ, or bone. If you have a clear feeling of pain, then you know exactly where to put the breath. If not, then you won't know what kind of tissue is hurting, so send breath to the general area. The effect of the breath will be to clarify the feelings there. If the feeling goes away, then go on to another area.

If you can't find an area of your body that needs breath, you should be suspicious. Look between your shoulder blades, or in the back of your throat, or just above the stomach. These are all very sensitive areas.

People in different professions can adapt the Heart Rhythm Meditation to their special needs.

Athletes: Heart Rhythm Meditation can benefit physical strength, timing, endurance, and coordination if physical exercises are done with the rhythm of the breath and heart, and particularly with the use of the full breath. (Refer back to the Walking Breath and Running Breath practices in Chapter 6.) Use Heart Rhythm Meditation to focus on muscles that need strengthening or flexibility. The inhalation brings rejuvenation, while the exhalation cleanses the muscles of toxin buildup. Muscle cells, like all cells, have a memory. Their strength can be sapped by some memories, or boosted by others. They respond instantly to your emotional condition. Muscles have a high demand for oxygen, yet few athletes learn how to breathe. A continuous flow of breath through the muscle tissue feeds it and purifies it on the physical, mental, and emotional levels.

Scholars: The brain develops unevenly without meditation. Send breath into the front of your head (behind the forehead), the top (crown), the back of the head just above the neck (the atlas), and the left and right temples. Do any of these areas feel different in their openness to breath? By sending breath there, you will balance the hemispheres and help your mind to absorb both concepts and details.

Artists: The left side of the heart is moved by harmony and beauty, while the right side expresses what you feel. The left side receives inspiration; the right side creates. Do you feel the passion for art deeply enough? Can you portray your passion so that others receive from your art what you feel as you create? Send your breath through the left side of the center of your chest, above the breasts. Then send breath through the right side of center. Spend more time on whichever side responds less. Repeat until you feel a pressure inside your rib cage, expanding your chest outward on both sides, indicating enhanced heart qualities.

Managers: Breathe in through the solar plexus, just below the rib cage in the center. Then breathe out into your stomach area, just below the solar plexus. This will increase the power of your control and your centered presence. The inhalation will sensitize you to the subtle but clear signals of your "gut" intuition—the internal compass that says "right direction" or "wrong direction." The exhalation will extend, or broadcast, your internal mastery and order into the world around you. Since your outer world is created from your inner world, it strengthens that natural process that makes your life a projection of yourself. (It is also quite pleasant to direct the exhalation into the stomach area.)

Helping Professionals: Without the left side of the heart, you would become a bureaucrat who is unable to empathize with the people you serve. Without the right side, you would suffer emotional burnout, and perhaps physical burnout as well. You need to disentangle yourself from your patients, clients, or students, but do it in such a way that you can reattach again easily. You also need to develop your insight, because if you do not see what they do not see, you can't help them, and if they succeed in making you see the way they see, you can't help them. This facility of compassionate insight is developed by breathing through heart. Breathe in and take in the hearts around you deeply, holding nothing away from you; as you breathe out through the chest. Repeat until what you know intuitively you also feel, and what you feel in your heart makes sense to your understanding.

FEEL AS THOUGH YOU ARE BREATHING IN AND OUT THROUGH SOME PART OF YOUR BODY, NOT YOUR MOUTH OR NOSE. FOR EXAMPLE, BREATHE THROUGH YOUR HANDS OR YOUR CHEST.

Healing

The whole mechanism of the body works by the power of breath, and every disorder in the working of the mechanism is caused by some irregularity in the breath. Therefore physicians feel disorder in the health of a patient by feeling his pulse or the beats of his heart. The physician will say that it is the physical illness of the body that has caused the change in the pulsation and in the beats of the heart, but the mystic knows it is caused by the breath. [Hazrat Inayat Khan][2]

---

2 www.hazrat-inayat-khan.org: Message: Vol 13, Gathas: Breath

Your breath can be directed so as to help speed the healing of another. You can add your breath to their breath, making their breath stronger, more rhythmic, and more balanced.

If the patient who is ill had the ability to direct his or her breath into the affected area, and had a developed breath that was conscious, rhythmic, and full, and had remembered the need to use breath for personal healing, then perhaps the illness would not have occurred. In any case, your combined breath is strong and may be able to reach the illness, where the other person's breath alone could not.

You can use the healing effect of breath for the benefit of another by directing your breath through your hands. After the hands are energized, place your fingertips over the patient's affected area.

Instruct the patient to breathe in when you breathe out, and out when you breathe in. Then take a rhythmic breath that is not too long, so the patient can match your rhythm. Don't use the Square Breath here; and don't hold your breath at all. You can signal the rhythm of your breath by, for example, pulling your hands slightly away from the patient as you breathe in, and pushing them closer again as you exhale. If the patient can't see your hands, then use a word or sound when you change direction so that the patient can coordinate with you.

When you breathe out, direct your exhalation out through your fingertips as a cool spray of healing energy. When you breathe in, draw your breath in through your fingertips, absorbing the polluted energy of the patient. Keep your breath silent. (A breath that is audible is restricted somewhere.)

An enhancement of this practice is to concentrate more on one half of the breath than on the other. Your exhalation will give energy; your inhalation will absorb pollution. When the affected area of the patient is weak and needs to be strengthened, your exhalation is best. But some illnesses, like a headache, a swelling, or a tumor, result from an energy overload. In such cases, your inhalation is needed most.

Of course, your breath has to have a full cycle, so even though you're concentrating most on the inhalations, for example, you're still breathing out between them.

This practice works because your hands are emitting real energy. The existence of this energy has been documented by Kirlian photography which shows that long streams of energy extend out from the fingers of a healer. (Figure 9 shows the energy of the human hand) Science hasn't yet discovered how this energy affects the body, but mystics say it is the energy of life itself. Some have called it biomagnetic energy because it behaves for biological objects somewhat as magnetism behaves for ferrous objects.

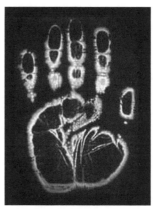

Figure 9:
Kirlian photography showing the energy of the hand

It would be a mistake to think that "healers" are specially gifted people. Healing is a natural power that everyone has innately by virtue of their breath. Some people have developed their concentration, their breath, and the openness of the channel from the heart to the hand so that they can give the natural healing effect of breath to others.

Anyone who has a child, parent, lover, or friend has both the need and the incentive to develop their healing ability.

Direct the Breath Beyond the Body

The body's magnetic field is not limited to the space inside the skin—it can be effectively directed beyond the body's confines into the surrounding space. In fact, the magnetic field easily transcends this boundary to form a very large body of magnetism.

It is a scientific fact that the body has a magnetic field, and that this field pulsates with the heartbeat. The magnetic field of a body at rest has two primary points of concentration, or poles: the heart and the brain. The magnetic field of the heart is a hundred times stronger than that of the brain. The magnetic field of the body is created largely by electricity moving through the muscles. The heart muscle is the only muscle that is continuously contracting and relaxing, so it dominates the magnetic field of a person at rest.

The magnetic field is not the product of the physical body, but its source. Instead of seeing the energy, magnetism, or "vibrations" that a person gives off, become aware of the energy, magnetism, or vibrations that are continually *becoming* that person. This is the "downward" view of Heart Rhythm Meditation: the body is continually created out of thought, which is continually created out of emotion, which is continually created out of energy or magnetism, which is continually created out of consciousness. Instead of thinking that you feel the magnetic field of your body coming out of your fingers, you could think that you experience in your fingers an intensification of the magnetic energy that is becoming your body. The magnetic body is not an extension of the physical body; rather, the physical body is a concentration of the magnetic body.

This subtlety is important at a more advanced stage because it leads directly to the state of contemplation. At the beginner level, the idea helps to overcome any notion that this magnetic energy is "mine."

Here is the next meditation about the magnetic body:

Start with the Square Breath, using the heartbeat to count the breath cycles. Then look for the heartbeat everywhere in the body at the same time: the chest, hands, feet, temples, everywhere.

Next, look for the heartbeat in the skin, throughout your body. Hold that experience.

Now notice that your "skin" doesn't feel like the surface of your physical body; instead it's the skin or surface of a very much larger "puffy" body. This is the magnetic body. Your physical body is inside this magnetic body as the earth is inside its magnetic body. The magnetism doesn't just surround the physical; it interpenetrates it.

As you breathe out, let the magnetic body expand outward, becoming very much larger but more diffuse. As you breathe in, draw the magnetic body inward again, becoming continually more intense as it concentrates, until it materializes as your heart (not *in* your heart; *as* your heart).

FEEL YOUR HEARTBEART IN THE SKIN OF YOUR MAGNETIC BODY.

Meditating with Plants

In order to send energy, we need a receiver. Thus, we can go further with the magnetic practice of sending energy if we have someone to whom we are sending it. As you experienced in the section on healing, the energy that you feel is intensified when it has a purpose. In that practice, you used only the energy in your hands. Now you'll use the whole magnetic field, having just discovered where to look for it.

In the practice below, you use plants as receivers of your magnetic energy.

Place a live potted plant at a distance of six feet from where you sit.

Repeat the practice immediately above to feel your magnetic body.

Extend your magnetic field outward toward the plant as you breathe out; then draw on its magnetic field as you breathe in again.

In a second meditation, place the plant on the other side of the room, or face a plant just outside your window. Extend your magnetic field toward the plant as you breathe out, and draw the magnetism of the plant into your heart as you breathe in.

In experiments that we've conducted with meditators and plants, the meditators were able to sense whether the plants needed water or not.

As you exchange magnetism with the plant, your identity merges with it and you begin to feel what the plant feels. Notice if you feel dry and thirsty, or if you salivate easily. Then notice if you feel weak and lifeless or vigorous and abundant. Do you have any feelings like itchy skin or sore limbs?

After the meditation, check the condition of the plant, and try to correlate your experience with what you observed.

Part 3

THE ELEMENTS OF THE HEART

10 . THE FOUR ELEMENTS

Now that you know how to coordinate your breath and your heart-beat, your objective is to develop the qualities of the heart. To do so, we have found it useful to draw upon the four fundamental kinds of energy in the universe, which have been called the four Elements: Air, Fire, Water, and Earth. These energies are not elements in the scientific sense of a particle that cannot be subdivided (to our knowledge science is still searching for this fundamental particle); rather, the four Elements represent four kinds of energy, each with different characteristics.

The four Elements correspond to the four states of matter: solid is earth, liquid is water, gas is air, and the fourth, fire, is plasma, which is rare on earth, but common in the universe, as it is the stuff of which stars are made.

In our book *Energize Your Heart in Four Dimensions,* we discuss the development of the heart in four dimensions: vertical (height and depth), width (left and right), forward (front and back) and inner (expanding and contracting), as shown in Figure 10.[1]

The four dimensions of the heart are the outcome of the heart's growth. In our experience, the heart doesn't grow in all dimensions evenly and at the same time, but it grows in one or two dimensions at a time. Our hearts are always growing and developing, so this process never ends.

Because the heart grows in different ways, we've found it useful to work with the development of the heart using different kinds of energy, using the different breathing patterns that give us the

---

1 Bair and Bair (2007, 49)

Element Breaths. Table 1 summarizes the effects of each element on the heart.

Each Element first performs a particular type of purification upon the heart: filtering (Earth), washing (Water), melting (Fire), or expanding (Air). Then the Elements have a further effect on the heart: to develop it in one of the four ways it can be developed. For example, to develop the water qualities of the heart—creativity, generosity, and empathy—the Water Element is used. This application of the Elements to human development was a breakthrough discovery, expressed in the mystical art of alchemy, the process of transformation of leaden hearts into golden ones.

Figure 10: The Four Dimensions of the Heart

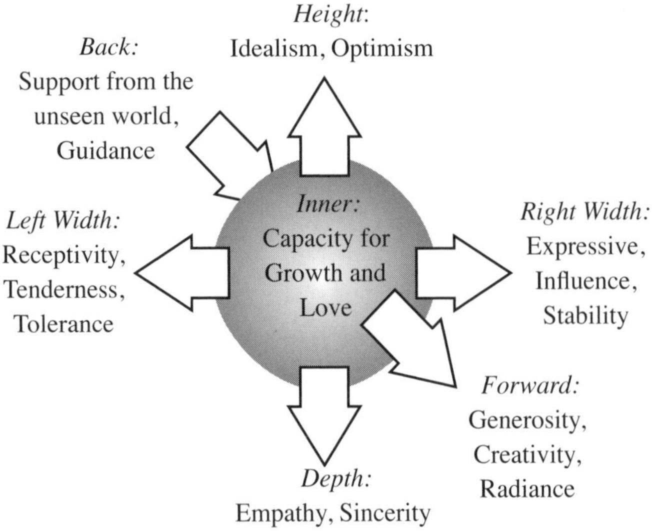

Height:
Idealism, Optimism

Back:
Support from the
unseen world,
Guidance

Left Width:
Receptivity,
Tenderness,
Tolerance

Inner:
Capacity for
Growth and
Love

Right Width:
Expressive,
Influence,
Stability

Forward:
Generosity,
Creativity,
Radiance

Depth:
Empathy, Sincerity

Table 1: The Four Elements and the Four Dimensions

Element	Dimension	Effect on the Heart
Air	Inner, Height	Listening with the heart, expression of heart in words, opening the capacity for growth, discovering the ideal
Fire	Height, Forward	Building power, courage, and radiance in the heart, reaching upward toward perfection
Water	Forward, Depth	Developing creativity, generosity, empathy, love, deep emotion
Earth	Width	Expanding influence, stability, tolerance[2]

By expanding the Heart Rhythm Meditation to include the four Elements of the Heart, we gain an even more powerful tool that we can use to bring ourselves into the awareness of our hearts, to bring out the qualities of the heart, and to live from the heart. The way to apply the Elements is to modify the breathing and visualization during Heart Rhythm Meditation. There are four basic ways of breathing, and these breaths correspond to the four Elements:

Element	Breathe In	Breathe Out
Air	mouth	mouth
Fire	mouth	nose
Water	nose	mouth
Earth	nose	nose

---

2 The Element Breaths are described in slightly different terms in our book *Energize Your Heart.* The Air Breath is described as the Rising Breath, p. 175; the Fire Breath is described as the Streaming Breath, p. 201; the Water Breath is described as the Downward Breath, p. 147; the Earth Breath is described as the Widening Breath, p. 124.

Each person tends to breathe in one of these four ways all the time, and the way that you breathe produces the energy of that Element in your mind and your heart. [3]

> At every change of the element in the breath—which takes place often in the day and night—the mood of man changes; his desires, his inclinations, his expression, even his atmosphere changes. And not only that, every Element that he breathes has its effect upon every affair that he does. [Hazrat Inayat Khan][4]

- The Earth Breath is the form of breathing that you do when you're sitting quietly by yourself. It is very calming. You also use this breath in a crisis; it gets you through. When you are scared, or to avoid being noticed, you breathe in and out through both nostrils, with the mouth closed.
- The Water Breath comes spontaneously in the sigh: you cast off burdens by a short exhalation with emphasis, through the mouth. The Water Breath is also used in healing. It is good for putting children to sleep, for it is the breath they use while sleeping.
- The Fire Breath gives you a needed boost, such as the breath of surprise—a very quick inhalation through the mouth. The Fire Breath is the breath a weightlifter uses just before the lift, or the football player just before the play. It gives a sudden surge of energy.
- The Air Breath is often used by computer programmers, who tend to be mouth breathers. It directs energy into the mind, which is the surface of the heart. When one is disoriented, trying to get one's bearings, one breathes with the mouth open, perhaps more quickly than usual.

---

3 There is also the Ether Breath (in and out through both the nose and mouth). The Ether Breath is sometimes called a 'fifth element', but it is better thought of as a more refined and abstract form of energy, a 'meta-element' which has the potential to become any of the four elements at any time.

4 Khan, I. Githa 1, Mysticism, The Direction of the Elements. *Esoteric Papers.*

We use different breaths in the course of a day, and each of them expresses a different condition. These breaths differ not only in length (rhythm) and depth (the degree of exhalation) but in their emphasis on inhalation or exhalation. There are four possible combinations of emphasis: on the inhalation, on the exhalation, on both, and on neither. The emphasized breath is shorter and through the mouth. When you watch yourself breathing, you will notice these and other examples of the four breath rhythms.

Each of these breaths also intensifies the heartbeat in different areas of the body:

Element	Breath Rhythm	Heartbeat
Air	No pause, light breath	beyond skin
Fire	Emphasize inhalation, then pause	head
Water	No pause, emphasize exhalation	hands
Earth	Square breath	in chest

We will start with the Square Breath, in the chest, as we have been doing it, then add a concentration to the Square Breath to bring out the Earth Element. Secondly, we will change the breath rhythm to breathe out through the mouth to introduce the Water Element. Third is the Fire Element, and last is the Air Element.

The type of breath you use changes throughout the day, corresponding to changes in your mood and attention. It indicates how you feel, how you are "tuned" at the moment. It therefore tells you what kinds of activities are appropriate at that time. Inappropriate activities are not likely to be successful. With sighs, you don't climb mountains, but you do relax, even to the point of sleep. With quick inhalations, you don't sit still, you act! By meditation with the Elements, you will become more familiar with the breathing rhythms we all use every day. They contain vital information that you need to judge the right time for doing things. By recognizing the Elements in your breath, you can choose activities that are best suited to your inner state or condition.

The details of each Element and the path it defines are given in the following chapters.

The Practice

In essence, the Element Breaths are done as follows:

> By inhaling, think that you receive; by exhaling, that you radiate. What does one exhale and spread? The divine power of the space, which purifies and revivifies one's life, which inspires one and enables the soul to unfold. This thought must constantly be kept in mind during the exercise. There exist many other forms of this experience, but this is the general prescription. [Hazrat Inayat Khan][5]

Hazrat Inayat Khan recommended that every student of meditation do these practices every day. In their shortest form, the four Element Breaths are each practiced five times.

It is necessary for the beginner and for the most advanced to do the twenty breaths of the Elements. [Hazrat Inayat Khan][6]

The Elements of Health

Purification of the breath not only gives sound health of mind and body, but it gives perpetual youth and long life. [Hazrat Inayat Khan][7]

The first effects of the Elements are to purify the physical and emotional heart, in order to enhance health.

---

5 *Ibid.,* Sangatha 1.

6 *Ibid.*

7 Khan, I. Githa 2, Esotericism, Purification of the Breath. *Esoteric Papers.*

Physically, the Elements enhance health both to heal physical illness and to promote the wellness that prevents disease from occurring.

> There are germs and impurities, but there are also elements to purify them. Those four elements, earth, water, fire and air, as spoken of by the mystics, do not only compose germs, but can also destroy them, if one only knew how one could make use of those four elements to purify one's body with them and also one's mind. [Hazrat Inayat Khan][8]

In the emotional and mental realm, the short explanation is that the Elements are natural properties of the mind, but if one of the Elements is too weak, a mental illness will result. The longer explanation is that if the various capabilities and functions of the mind are categorized according to the Elements, then a treatment plan for the mind's dysfunctions emerges from that model. If you look at life through the lens of the Elements, you begin to see ailments as deficiencies of the Elements. Then if you have a therapy that develops the Elements, you can create a treatment plan. Fortunately, Heart Rhythm Meditation is especially effective in developing the Elements, both in your body and in your thinking.

> As there is need of sun and water for plants to grow, so there is need of the four Elements for a person to keep in perfect health. A person who knows how to breathe perfectly can keep the body free from every kind of impurity. Even the mind derives benefit from this. For the mind too is composed of four Elements, the Elements in their finest condition. [Hazrat Inayat Khan][9]

Some common mental and emotional disorders that can be helped by meditating with the elements in Heart Rhythm Meditation are the following:

---

8 www.hazrat-inayat-khan.org: Message: Vol 4, Healing and the Mind World: Part 1, Health

9 *Ibid.*

Element	Effective Against
Air	Guilt, confusion, despair, grief, denial
Fire	Depression, lack of discrimination, pessimism
Water	Rigidity, stubbornness, resentment, withdrawal
Earth	Spacing out, fear, lack of purpose

Part of what makes good health so difficult to attain is the lack of a model by which we can recognize health and notice the beginning of our deviation from it. Health is typically thought of as an absence of physical ailments. This is looking backward, at the effect instead of the cause. When the mind has an unhealthy attitude, the physical body will eventually suffer the effects, but it will take so long that one will probably not notice the cause-and-effect relationship. What we need is a forward-looking view, a leading indicator, an ideal of a healthy attitude against which we can compare ourselves. Then when we notice the onset of any unhealthy conditions like those in the table, we will recognize it as an early-warning symptom of what ultimately will lead to illness, and we can immediately address that condition before the illness develops.

We see that a person who ponders often upon inharmonious thoughts is very easily offended, it does not take long for him to get offended; a little thing here and there makes him feel irritated, because irritation is already there, it wants just a little touch to make it a deeper irritation. [Hazrat Inayat Khan] [10]

One advantage of Heart Rhythm Meditation is that it gives a model of what health is. This model is developed in Part 3, as the Elements are described in greater detail. For example, optimism is a natural part of a healthy psyche. When things look bad, the optimist knows that there is much that he or she can do, personally and immediately, to keep the bad outcome from happening. We lose

---

10 *Ibid.*

that spirit only when we are beaten; as long as we have optimism, we are still winning. When we lose our optimism, cynicism, resentment, frustration, and self-destructive behavior take over. Physical illness follows these mental disorders. Heart Rhythm Meditation can restore the optimism of the human spirit and the clarity of vision on which it depends. On the other hand, denial is another kind of illness. What allows a person to remain optimistic without going into denial? The power of the heart.

Another advantage of Heart Rhythm Meditation is that it nurtures the development of emotional depth.

> To the scientist the emotional side of man is not of interest; if the body is perfect according to his idea, he thinks the man is healthy. But from a mystical point of view if, bodily, man is strong, but his emotional nature is buried beneath, he is not healthy, there is something wrong with him. [Hazrat Inayat Khan] [11]

I'm sure you know many people who seem to have abundant energy and mental agility but who bury their feelings beneath a personality shell. Despite their conviction that they are "fine," such people have no idea what they're missing. For one thing, they are hard to get close to.

The natural condition of human beings is to have an open heart that allows us to be easily moved, touched by commonplace beauty, responsive to simple human kindness, vulnerable rather than defensive, deep in feeling, and magnanimous toward others. This natural quality is shut down when the pain that the sensitive, open heart feels becomes overwhelming. Heart Rhythm Meditation can strengthen your heart so that it stays open and still functions in the world. Some wonder if they could have a truly open and sensitive heart and still function in a competitive world. Because the open heart is also a source of great power as well as sensitivity, opening your heart gives you a great advantage in every

---

11 www.hazrat-inayat-khan.org: Message: Vol 13, Gathas: Everyday Life: 2.1 The Purity of the Body

field from art, science, research, teaching, communication, sports, and business.

11. THE EARTH ELEMENT

[By the color] yellow you will know that it is the Earth Element, which suggests benefit, for earth is productive, solid and substantial. [Hazrat Inayat Khan] [1]

What Earth Is

As wetland scientists and organic gardeners know, the Earth has the capacity to purify wastes by absorption and filtration. In this step of Heart Rhythm Meditation, we apply this capacity to the purification and development of the heart. Every cubic centimeter of the soil of the planet Earth contains billions of microorganisms. The bodies of these microorganisms are an integral part of what we call soil. They create new soil, and they also bind soil together by their activities. The entire biosphere, including our own bodies, is saturated with microorganisms. Microorganisms create the foods we eat and even digest our food for us. They will eventually digest our bodies and return us to the soil when we die. The Earth Element is represented as the mass of all the microorganisms in us and around us, making up the soil and all that is living.

While the Earth can be polluted in the short term by human activity, it can purify itself by absorbing the pollution and turning the impurities into itself, Earth. This is the principle of composting, by which garbage and sewage, for example, are transformed into soil.

The Earth can effect this transformation because it is alive. The microorganisms that constitute Earth ingest all the carbon-based matter with which they come in contact and digest it to build their own bodies and thereby the one body of Earth. Even as the Earth is literally digesting our bodies, it is also providing our bodies with

---

1 Khan, I. Githa 3, Mysticism, The Universe in Man. *Esoteric Papers.*

the substance, nutrients, and biological elements they need. Your physical existence is the result of an equilibrium of these two activities: Earth's providence to you balances its digestion of you.

The Earth Element practice is an experience of the biblical phrase "From the Earth Element [dust] you came, and to the Earth Element you will return." By doing this practice, we enhance our relationship to the Earth, our ultimate mother, and strengthen our psyches and bodies.

Sorting and Filtering

Here is the first stage of the Earth Element of Heart Rhythm Meditation:

Breathe in and out through your nose. Keep the inhalations and exhalations balanced, equal in length, emphasizing neither. Complete each exhalation.

Let your exhalation be a discarding, a casting off, a disposal of all you don't need, physically, mentally, and emotionally. Let your inhalation be a renewing, rebuilding, and redemption of all that you really *do* need.

Take several breaths, thinking of what you are discarding and what you are renewing. This is the simplification effect of the Earth Element: sorting or filtering the building materials from the refuse.

By these breaths, you develop the quality of discrimination — to know what to abandon, what to draw in. Ultimately, this simple act of discrimination creates your life. What is food to one person is poison to another; what is attractive to one is repulsive to another. What one considers exciting, another finds boring. What one takes as a curse, another receives as a blessing. So you sort and filter all of life to make your own life. You draw to yourself and absorb all that you need and find beautiful, and you expel what you can't use and don't like. Your heart does this by the process of affinity, recognizing what is like itself. When your heart is strong, it does this very well, filling your life with what is attractive and familiar to you and making life a paradise. When your heart is weak, it is not able to attract or hold what is like itself; without this cohesive power, your life loses its natural integrity and happiness.

No matter how hurt and wounded the heart has become, no matter how weak, bitter, or hardened, it can always recover. We can take inspiration from the Earth Element: the microorganisms of Earth have an uncanny ability to recover, to grow in any circumstances, to thrive wherever there is even a slight opportunity. Orchids grow where there is little soil, moss where there is little light, and cactus where there is little water, yet soil, light, and water are requirements for plant growth. When your external conditions are not ideal for your heart's healing and growth, you can still create internal conditions that will nurture your heart. To heal and develop your heart is to focus your attention on it and to direct your breath through it, as we do in Heart Rhythm Meditation.

Throughout the Earth Element of Heart Rhythm Meditation, maintain the rhythm of the Square Breath (Chapter 8), and be aware of your heart beating in your chest.

To be aware of your heartbeat, you have to open the unconscious. Once you've done that, you feel your heartbeat. You may not notice any other effect of this state besides the heartbeat, but at some point you will notice that your thinking is different. Admittedly, it is hard to notice your thinking process since those thoughts become part of your thinking process too. But you can look back on the stream of thoughts you have produced and see that you're thinking of things you don't normally think of, and what's more, that you're thinking from a different point of view. When you have more experience with Heart Rhythm Meditation, you will find many more indications and results of this state.

Exchange with Earth

The next step is to consider the process of discarding and renewing as an exchange that you have with the Earth. All that you discard the Earth absorbs, and all that you take into yourself is a gift from the Earth's abundance. What you no longer need can be used somewhere else; what you need is available as a by-product of other processes.

Your breath controls the direction of the exchange; your heartbeat drives it.

Beyond this metaphor for expansive consciousness, what is really being exchanged here? Is something actually passing between yourself and the Earth? The Earth has a distinctive smell. Much of what we notice about the land is its odor. Our breath carries this odor into our bodies and circulates it there. This odor is produced primarily by the microorganisms that are carried into the air from the ground. Your inhalation is literally an intake of the substance of the Earth Element, since Earth includes the bacteria, fungi, molds, and so on, that interpenetrate it and whose bodies are a major ingredient in its soil. Some of these microorganisms, within our bodies, are responsible for our digestion. What we discard from our bodies in our waste streams is a rich source of nitrogen for the microorganisms that create new Earth. After our waste is digested by the Earth, it becomes water, carbon dioxide for plants, and soil.

Our intake of the Earth is most obvious in our food supply. The wonder of a carrot, for me, is that its seed somehow caused the microorganisms in the soil to rearrange the chemical elements in the soil so as to create molecules that weren't there before, like beta-carotene, and to build up living cells in a characteristic orange shape. There is very little in the carrot that wasn't already in the soil of the Earth.

So we are feeding the Earth and eating the Earth. Here, in meditation, you can be aware that these processes are continual and ongoing. Not just every meal you eat but very breath you take is an exchange with the substance of the Earth, our biosphere.

SAINT FRANCIS WAS *sitting in the woods, surrounded by animals, with birds on his shoulders and hands, as a man from the village approached. Immediately, all the animals and birds fled. "Why were they content to sit with you but afraid of me?" the man asked. "What did you have for lunch?" Saint Francis inquired.*

Earth's Magnetism

The next step in the practice is to think of the size of the Earth upon which we live. Think of places you have been on Earth, other places you've heard of, and still more vast spaces you have not even heard of. Think also of the numbers of people, animals, fish, insects, and plants that share the Earth.

As you exhale, think of yourself as but one of uncountably many beings in a very large biosphere. As you inhale, see yourself as the embodiment of the Earth and all that is contained in its scope. The Earth has contributed its own substance to form your body. Your cells contain its proteins, which have been evolved and organized into DNA over aeons of time. You are the direct beneficiary of the Earth's experience, and you are part of the Earth's mechanism for passing on its experience.

Realizing the immensity of the Earth brings you to the threshold of the shift from matter to energy. Beyond the huge mass that forms its physical body, the Earth has an even larger magnetism that forms its magnetic body. The interchange between yourself and the planet is magnetic as well as chemical and biological, and making this magnetic exchange conscious will benefit you.

If you take a bar of iron and rub it repeatedly in one direction over a magnet, it will become magnetized. In this process, the magnetism of the original magnet is not diminished. Magnetism is the result of a physical alignment of the molecules of a substance. The magnetism of one piece of iron is able to align the molecules of another piece of iron, so that magnetism is increased overall. A magnet can lose its magnetism by vigorous shaking.

We already know from Chapter 9 that the human body has a magnetic field. The correlation between one's magnetic field and one's health and influence has not been the subject of scientific research, but we intuitively associate the magnetic field with charisma, as we call charismatic people "magnetic."

Whenever a conductor, like a wire, is placed in a moving magnetic field, a current flows in the wire. Whenever a current flows in a conductor, a magnetic field is produced around the conductor. These are the principles of electromagnetism that are applied in all electric generators and motors. These principles show how magnetism can be exchanged. The magnetic field of the Earth is steady in its direction but slowly fluctuating in its strength. The magnetic field of a human is also relatively constant in orientation, but it fluctuates with the heartbeat. So both the Earth and the human create moving magnetic fields. In any fixed conductor with the proper orientation, an electric current will be created. The human spine has that vertical orientation, and the spinal column conducts electricity. Even microvolts are significant at the cellular level.

This leads to the practice:

As you breathe in, think of the magnetic field of the Earth, with its lines of force circling the globe, perpendicular to your vertical spine. Your spine extends from an area of weaker Earth magnetism at your head to an area of relatively stronger Earth magnetism at your seat, several feet closer to the center of the Earth. Even this short distance and small magnetic differential still create a current flow in your spine, which is a biological superconductor for such energy when you are in a meditative state.

You can enhance the energy flow up your spine as you breathe in. Do this by imagining that your inhalation draws the Earth's magnetic energy up through your spine. This image seems to reduce the resistance in the spine to a minimum, allowing a greater current to flow upward. The energy flowing in your spine seems to rise directly from the Earth.

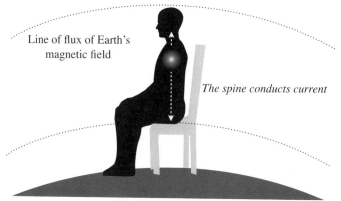

Figure 11: An Upright Spine Maximizes the Body's Magnetic Field

The energy flowing through your body intensifies your magnetic field. Consequently, absorbing the Earth's magnetism causes an increased personal magnetism.

You don't feel magnetism directly since there is no sense that perceives it. You feel it only indirectly, as pressure in several ways. First, the skin in which you feel your pulse, the skin of the magnetic body (Chapter 9), seems to be much larger than your physical body. Second, you can feel a tingling and a pressure in your hands. Third, your heartbeat seems to be "bigger," broadcasting its beat stronger and farther. Fourth, you *feel* powerful—emotionally strong—so much so that you feel a generosity toward the whole world.

As you breathe out, the rising current stops and your magnetic field weakens and contracts. This contraction is accompanied by a feeling of sinking into the Earth. This sinking is not physical, of course; it is due to the diminished magnetic field of the body. When your field is strong, you can easily experience your own magnetism as distinct from the Earth's magnetic field. But as your field shrinks, your magnetism is overwhelmed by the Earth's. This is the basis for your feeling of sinking, or surrender, or absorption by the Earth.

A moving magnetic field, or a moving conductor within a static magnetic field, is necessary to generate a current, which is a moving stream of electrons. In the human magnetic field, the movement is due to the breath. The magnetism of the Earth changes only slowly, and your spine, the conductor, is still. We conjecture that one can change the resistance of the spinal column by breathing through it, and that this accounts for the experience of a building up and collapsing of the body's magnetic field. While the physical mechanism is not known, the experience is well known.

As you breathe in, imagine that you are drawing the magnetism of the Earth upward into your own magnetic field, increasing it.

As you breathe out, imagine that your magnetic field is collapsing into the Earth's magnetism.

Through the buildup and decay of your magnetic field, you generate a current of energy between the Earth and yourself.

EXPERIENCE A CURRENT OF ENERGY FLOWING ALTERNATELY FROM THE EARTH TO YOU, AND FROM YOU TO THE EARTH, AS YOU BREATHE IN AND OUT.

The Being of Earth

The being of Earth has many names; almost every culture has a name for her. The Zoroastrians (like the three kings/priests who foretold the birth of Christ from the stars) named the being whose body is the earth *Zamiat*. Their religion, like the Native American spiritual tradition, considers all parts of nature as living beings: streams and mountains, even fire, water, air, and earth, are all great beings. Intelligence, self-awareness, self-preservation, self-expression, and the pursuit of a purpose are features of every living thing, and everything is living. I think of Zamiat as the Earth Element, the single giant organism whose cells are the microorganisms within and around the planet, forming the biosphere. Gaia is a modern name for her.

With the awareness of Zamiat, the archangel of the Earth, you can take the Earth Element of Heart Rhythm Meditation into the realms of emotion. The interchange between yourself and the Earth becomes a relationship between two beings.

Feel your exhalation as a surrender to Zamiat, and allow yourself to lie in her arms. As you continue the practice, try to eliminate any resistance you feel to her embrace. As you breathe in, your surrender turns into the desire to serve the interests of the Earth, out of love for she who gives you the substance of herself to become the substance of yourself.

As your inhalation reaches its peak, you feel her power and wisdom emerging within yourself. You become the *representative* of Zamiat and intuitively feel her concerns and priorities.

I ENCOUNTERED ZAMIAT IN *a retreat in the Alps in 1984. After meditating for many days, I reached a state in the depth of my heart that had been unknown to me. I surrendered to this experience (that is, I committed myself to going into it without interruption), however long it would take. It was like being drawn into the Earth and enveloped by it. I felt increasingly vast and immobile. Then I surrendered my body, giving up any desire to move.*

Over hours, as the experience intensified, I felt that even more surrender was necessary, and I gave up my witness and analysis. That is, I resolved that I would not think about or watch what was happening to me; I would only feel it in the present without having to know where it would lead me. Then I began to feel the presence of a vast being, around me and in me, something that was me and also more than me. More surrender was asked of me, and I gave up my future. That is, I knew that this experience could change everything about the rest of my life. Then more surrender was asked, and I gave up my notion of being a separate being. A vast emotion came over me. Still more surrender was asked, and I gave up the last vestige of my self, my sense of independent life. I didn't die, but I was willing to die; my life was replaced by a sharing of all life. It was then that I realized I had been absorbed into the consciousness of Zamiat. I thought her thoughts and felt her feelings. Later that night the feeling abated, and I mostly regained my individuality.

My life did change, dramatically, from that time. Every aspect of my external life changed significantly: my work, my relationship, my living situation, my community. My inner life improved in a deep breakthrough that finally centered me in the heart and opened my spiritual understanding. A few years later I was invited to bid on a project to build a computerized composting plant. My enthusiasm at the invitation was so great that the client took no other bids. I was immediately and completely positive that I wanted to do this project because of my experience with Zamiat. It has become the apex of my technical career as a program manager and technical designer. PURAN

Two great emotions of life are surrender and glorification. Surrender is not defeat or failure; it is simply acknowledging that you are part of a great and vast thing that humbles everyone. Through surrender of your personal pride, you can experience the glory of the whole. The child surrenders to the parent; the lover surrenders to the beloved. The CEO surrenders to the customer, or to the market. The doctor surrenders to the body's ability to heal itself.

A surrender begins as a surprise but becomes a recognition and an acceptance. It yields the uplifting emotion that you are not alone or acting alone but are part of a very great movement, or system. Surrender is a recognition of the greater force that is opposing your own effort, but it doesn't result in defeat. It leads to a reorientation and ultimately to a greater victory.

In the Earth Element of Heart Rhythm Meditation, surrender to the Earth gives you a reorientation of your purpose that then allows the power and wisdom of the Earth to support and augment your own effort. You know what it's like to work against your body, like staying up all night to write a paper, going to a job even when you have the flu, or running with a sore knee. Contrast that opposition with cooperation, of having your body support your work. Here your muscles power your run effortlessly, a shower inspires a creative thought, your good health gives you persistence, or a shared meal creates a collaboration. The principle of the Earth Element is applied in the maxim:

> Don't work against your body; let your body support your work.

Your body, an outgrowth of the Earth, has power and wisdom, as the Earth does. You can't disregard your body and succeed in the long run. Similarly, no business venture can ignore its effect on the Earth and still survive, unless it is exempted from the results of its actions by some government policy, the way laws and policies favor and protect mineral extraction and nuclear energy, to name only two examples. If executives listened to their bodies, they would benefit from the wisdom of the Earth that is conveyed to them through their bodies. Listening to your heartbeat is an important part of listening to your body, which carries the message of the larger body, the planet Earth.

Identify with the Earth itself. Then feel how the Earth "works" — its approach, attitude, understanding, and principles.

The Earth is bigger than any conflict or disturbance. It is older than any individual living on it. Those who draw upon its qualities develop its persistence and endurance. From those develop further qualities: discipline (unwasted, enduring action), ethics (principles that endure over time), and responsibility (for enduring).

Representing the Earth

As Zamiat's representative and as an embodiment of the Earth, the principles of the Earth become your principles as well. Violating them will put you at risk of being unseated, toppled, or buried. Keeping the Earth's principles makes you a person upon whom others, even the Earth, can rely.

Peter, you are the rock upon which I will build my church.[2]

Consider how your life demonstrates the Earth's principle of conservation. An ecological system reprocesses its own waste independently. What is the waste in your life? Do you pass that waste to others, exploiting and burdening them? For example:

- The costs of dealing with the waste products of our own consumerism are passed on to society as a whole.
- Our undisciplined periods are exploited by the entertainment industry, which then encourages escapism and titillation in others.

---

2 *The Holy Bible.* Matthew 16:18

- Our anxiety and fear feed the arms industry, which encourages armed conflict and feeds the fears of others.
- Our unwillingness to take responsibility for our community gives rise to government authority, which reduces personal responsibility in society.
- Our unhealthy lifestyle choices put a burden on our families or on society.

Consider how you use the wastes of others. Do you:

- Take advantage of the fear, mistakes, or ignorance of others?
- Use those who have forgotten their own purpose to serve your purpose?
- Retain in your self-concept the mental poison of those who ridicule and insult you?
- Allow your rhythm to be upset when those around you are upset?
- Lose your faith by seeing so much violence and hopelessness in society?

When your Earth Element is strengthened, you will be better able to recycle your own mental, emotional, and psychic wastes without dumping them into someone else's atmosphere. Just as we must stop wasting our physical waste, which contains valuable minerals and essential components that need to be returned to the soil, so we must stop wasting our nonphysical waste, which contains valuable lessons for our lives. If you don't take responsibility for creating your own problems and blame others for victimizing you instead, you don't learn all that life is teaching. The value of life's experience is then wasted.

Of course, you have made mistakes. I have made bad mistakes that polluted the emotional soil and the mental atmosphere of others, making life more difficult for everyone. Much of what we do in error is a result of our ignorance, of wanting to get ahead without seeing the long-term effects on ourselves or the short-term and long-term effects on others. (Herbicides kill microorganisms in the soil, pollute the water, and harm the health of farmers and consumers, but in the short term making them seemed like a good idea to the herbicide producers.)

In your Earth Element, you can reprocess your mistakes. Using an analogy to composting, you can make new soil out of the garbage you've produced. Here are some facts about composting:

- Compost is made by aerobic (oxygen-breathing) microorganisms, which produce new earth by digesting, without odor, organic wastes that have been mixed in a certain ratio.
- Where a compost pile gets cold, the composting action slows down. In the middle of the pile it generally stays warm, but the middle does not have enough air for aerobic digestion.
- Consequently, the pile must be turned periodically and protected from the cold. Since aeration and warmth are hard to achieve together, composting usually takes a long time.
- If organic waste is closed off from the air, anaerobic microorganisms digest it instead, producing terrible odors and methane.

Composting teaches us, by analogy, how to reprocess our nonphysical waste products:

- Begin by uncovering your mistakes, exposing them to your awareness (aerobic) rather than repressing or denying them (anaerobic).
- View your mistakes and failures in the perspective (mixing ratio) of your accomplishments as well. Don't try to process a single event or events in isolation from your life's pattern and history.
- View the mistakes from different points of view (turn over the pile) to assure consistent and continued attention (aeration).
- Keep up the passion (temperature), by your sincere and earnest desire to change.
- Protect the process from others' judgments and analysis (the harsh, cooling wind) by staying in the safety of your heart. That

is, stay aware of your emotions and keep your heart soft so that defensiveness and rationalization (coldness) don't occur.

- If resentment, withdrawal, guilt, or hardness of heart (bad odors) begin to occur, get help to change the process. These are symptoms of poor insight (anaerobic). They don't indicate progress. Although some psychologists feel that any reaction (digestion) is progress, the Earth Element teaches that only that reaction that is accompanied by insight (aerobic) is progressive (produces new earth). Without insight, the process (anaerobic digestion) can produce a worse result (a stinking compost pile) than the original problem (garbage).

To retain their power, everyone needs to reprocess their own waste. If we exploit the wastes of others, we deny them the value of part of their lives. For example, many people have some leisure time in the evenings after work. The television industry takes up that time for its own benefit, while fueling people's desire for further entertainment and for consumerism. But people need leisure time to process their dilemmas and challenges, to deepen their relationships, and to think about their future. Filling up this leisure time with other stimulation is like depriving a person of sleep with dreams, which will make them confused, disoriented, hopeless, and eventually mentally ill. (The entertainment business, like all human activities, has its value, especially when it expands the dreams, ideals, hopes, and faith of people, and when people deliberately choose it.) There is no better healer than peace, and anything that contributes to peace contributes to health. Spreading an atmosphere of peace with the Earth Breath will benefit your family and even your community.

The Earth has several principles to increase your wealth. First, reprocess your waste, turning it into something valuable, so that nothing will be lost. Wealth will not stay where it is wasted. Second, become more responsible; that is, either become more reliable about what you are already responsible for, or extend your scope of responsibility. Wealth will leave a place where it is not cared for; it will be attracted to the place where it is safe.

> Earthly riches, explain to me your character. "I fly from the hand that holds me, I escape from the one who pursues me, I fall into his purse who collects me, I live with him who spares me, I leave the one who does not look after me, I keep away from him who has me not. The one who does not possess me is poor indeed, but the one whom I possess is poorer still." [Hazrat Inayat Khan] [3]

Third, consider that the greatest asset of a person or a business is a good reputation. A good reputation is what a business develops and is the outcome of one's life. To enhance your worth, do that which is good for your reputation.

> A good reputation is a trust given to a man by other people, so it becomes his sacred duty to maintain it. [Hazrat Inayat Khan] [4]

The Earth is the steady platform that supports all life. As you breathe in and out, feel the continuity that strings together the events of your life like beads in a necklace. The events are numerous, but they are connected by a singular thread, an evolving direction of growth in a developing but constant interest. It is the steadiness in a life of change.

Earth's Peace

Your sense of time comes from your breath and your heartbeat. As you slow down your Square Breath, you become extended in time.

The Earth is enormous in physical size and age. We can comprehend its size because of our experience of seeing it from the moon. But the age of the Earth is still quite difficult for us to grasp. It exists in geological time measured in millions of years. Com-

---

3 www.hazrat-inayat-khan.org: Message: Sayings: Vadan: Tanas

4 www.hazrat-inayat-khan.org: Message: Sayings: Gayan: Chalas

pared with our personal experience of time, the Earth is eternal. We use this ageless, eternal property of the Earth in the final step of the Earth Element of Heart Rhythm Meditation:

As you settle into the Earth on your exhalation, you naturally adopt the Earth's feeling of space and time. Let your sense of self expand horizontally in all directions as you breathe out, so that you become spread over the Earth.

In the same way, your sense of time expands from the local to the global, from solar to geological time. It is the difference between time that is based on the Earth's rotation and orbit around the sun, and time that is based on the state of the Earth itself. From the perspective of someone who has lived a long life, time is marked not by trips around the sun but by the changes that have occurred within one's self. It is not the time of doing, but the time of being.

Your inhalation takes you into a dissolution of time, where there is only the eternal present that includes past and future. Your held breath takes you into timelessness. Your exhalation brings you back into the time that has a past, present, and future.

There is an emotion that corresponds to the timeless condition of the held breath, and that emotion is peace. As you breathe out, let peace extend outward from yourself to the four horizons. As you breathe in, let your own being be imbued with peace.

Peace is not passivity; it is an expanding atmosphere that has the power to bring people and conditions into harmony and balance, spreading peace.

As you breathe out, feel the extension of a zone of peace, bringing the world around you into the same condition. As you breathe in, feel the experience of peace intensify within yourself. As you hold your breath, let your sense of time dissolve in the timeless.

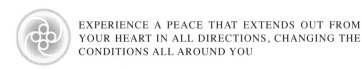 EXPERIENCE A PEACE THAT EXTENDS OUT FROM YOUR HEART IN ALL DIRECTIONS, CHANGING THE CONDITIONS ALL AROUND YOU

12. THE WATER ELEMENT

When we come to the water element, we find that it is pliable
and can be poured from one vessel to another. The course of a
river or a stream may be diverted and made to go in another
direction. [Hazrat Inayat Khan][1]

What Water Is

The Water Element is that which makes things soft, pliable, flowing, flexible, and fertile. It's the water in the earth that allows it to
support life.

The purification by water is washing. Water has the capacity to
dissolve substances and carry them away. Its flow purifies everything in its path as it deepens, smoothes, and polishes.

In the process of alchemy, the Royal Art, the first step is to take
the substance from the solid to the fluid state and from the fluid
to the volatile state, so that it can be transformed. As long as it
is solid, it cannot be transformed. In the fluid state we can be
purified more easily. [Vilayat Inayat Khan][2]

Within the body, the Water Element is seen in the circulation of
blood and lymph and in the contents and the interface of every
cell. By the action of the Water Element, nutrients are distributed
and the impurities of the body are flushed out. In the psyche, the
Water element is shown in the ability to give and accept, to create
and appreciate beauty, and to love.

Because water is (usually) a fluid, it is more responsive to the
pull of gravity than a solid. Due to the gravity of the Earth, both

---

1 www.hazrat-inayat-khan.org: Message: Vol 5, Pearls from the Ocean
Unseen: Blessed Are the Poor in Spirit

2 Khan, V. (1980, 6)

rocks and streams tumble down a hillside, but the rocks get lodged and stop where their friction resists further movement. Water has practically no friction, no particle size, and no fixed shape. Its adaptability allows it to find a way past all obstacles, eventually reaching the river at the bottom of the mountain and flowing on to the sea.

Water is also responsive to the warming rays of the sun, which lift it into the breezes. Depending on climate and geological conditions, water might be flowing fast downstream, lying in a stagnant pool, vaporized in the wind, falling as rain, absorbed by the Earth, or covering the Earth as ice. Yet water remains essentially the same.

The definition of water as a molecule of H_2O is exquisitely simple. None of the other Four Elements have such a simple and clear definition. We might say that its chemical formula is its "soul," while its manifestations are its varied forms. The soul of water is pure, and yet its manifestation quickly takes the shape and quality of anything it touches. Its soul is simple, yet it exists commonly in forms as different as snowflakes and clouds. Its beauty is seen in its beautiful effect: on a landscape, on a flower, and in a rainbow. Things that have water in them become flexible like a willow branch; things with little water become brittle like a dead limb.

Water likes to move, to flow, to circulate. Moving water tends to purify itself, whereas stagnant water becomes impure. When water has depth, it circulates naturally within itself; when it has height, it flows more quickly. Its aim is always to reach the ocean, and it accepts no obstacle. If blocked in its journey of return, it builds up until it can go around or over the obstacle. Its direction is always predictable—it does not surprise you by jumping up or by refusing to budge. It only wants to flow toward its reunion with the sea. It might disappear in the air or sink out of sight, but then you see it in the clouds or aquifers, and you know where it's going. However it moves, it moves with beauty and grace. Its fluid nature could not do otherwise.

So these are the qualities of water: purity, flexibility, adaptability, beauty, responsiveness, and generosity. Water is noticed, admired and sought after, for its qualities are attractive and highly valued. The Water Element of Heart Rhythm Meditation brings out the qualities of water in a person.

Creating Movement

Sitting in a meditation posture, having made your breath conscious, rhythmic, and full, you begin the Water Breath by changing the direction of your breath.

Breathe in through your nose and out through your mouth, creating a downward flow of breath and energy. With your mouth only slightly open, put your emphasis on the exhalation. Make the outgoing breath into a fine stream, like a very gentle, controlled blowing. Always keep your breath silent and effortless, but complete each exhalation. Relax your body.

Let the Water Element flow through you on your breath. Imagine that you stand under an ethereal waterfall of a fine spray of energy. The waterfall not only passes over you but also enters your body through the top of your head and flows through you. (We imagine a waterfall because it's really happening. There *is* a shower of rays and particles from outer space that is impacting you at every moment.)

You can do this practice standing or sitting. If you are standing, the stream of water that washes through you exits through your fingertips and the soles of your feet. If you are sitting, it exits through your fingertips with your arms hanging at your side, and through the base of the spine. Either way, the water continues to flow into the ground.

On the inhalation through the nose, concentrate very intensely on the crown center (the top of the head) and on the essence of water descending through the crown as a shower of energy. On the exhalation through the mouth, let the energy diffuse throughout the body. You are conscious of the descent of the energy of life through the center of the body, and along the arms and legs. You expel it through the soles of your feet, through your fingertips, and through your hair.[3]

The important effect of this practice is to feel a *downward* movement of energy through your body and eventually to feel that you are essentially fluid. The flow is physically downward, from your head to your feet, and it also corresponds to the downward aspect of meditation. (More on this may be found under "Transforming Energy," later in this chapter.) This fluidity can overcome any blockages in the flow of energy within yourself. Water likes to move, to flow, and in flowing, it resolves all problems. It accepts all shapes and fills all containers.

An enhanced energy flow frees the mind from its traps, overcoming anguish and negativity.

FEEL A FLOW OF ENERGY DOWN THROUGH YOUR BODY, AS A PHYSICAL SENSATION, ESPECIALLY IN YOUR FINGERTIPS.

This is the same objective as acupuncture—to move energy within your body, which will then resolve any illness.

The beating of our heart, our pulse throbbing in wrist or head, our circulation, the working of the whole mechanism of our body is rhythmic. And when this rhythm is obstructed, then disorder and illness come. [Hazrat Inayat Khan][4]

[In the Water Breath,] the energy flows throughout the body. We have to account for not just the ascending and descending

3 *Ibid.,* page 7

4 www.hazrat-inayat-khan.org: Message: Vol 11, Philosophy: 8. The Law of Rhythm

current, but also for the circulating currents permeating the body. [Vilayat Inayat Khan][5]

You will alternate between (a) feeling a stream or current flowing through you, and (b) feeling that you *are* the fluid of the stream. This is the difference between "channeling" and "being." It is easier to *channel* the current down through yourself than to *be* the water itself. But this is a fine point that you can work on later; it should not be a concern when you're learning the practice.

Try to reduce your resistance to the flow. Allow your channel to open wider, and the current will immediately increase. The only limit to the current is in your channel. A channel has two ends: it both receives and gives. You'll never be given more than you can give out. To increase the intake, increase the outflow by concentrating on the exhalation flowing out from your heart, forward from your chest, and into the world.

Examine your feelings and resentments toward and about others and any frustrations with yourself that are persistent and unchanging. Dogmatism, grudges, prejudice, and bigotry are all stuck feelings. Emotion is like water; stuck feelings are like ice. The purpose of feelings is communication between people and between the levels within a person. When your feelings become rigid, communication practically ceases, so you are cut off from others and from knowledge of your inner state.

By its rhythm and its full exhalation, your breath will loosen up your feelings. When you feel stuck in your emotions, you can also exhale with a sigh. Then you can apply the principle of Water to your relationships: an increase in the exhalation will increase the inhalation.

- If you want to be admired, admire others.
- If you want to be respected, respect others.
- If you want to be considered, consider others.

---

5 Khan, V. (1980, 6)

• If you want to be loved, then love others.

The opposite is also a Water principle: an increase in the inhalation will increase the exhalation. As you breathe in, feel the descending stream of life energy as a stream of love that is poured upon you. You are being loved continually and unconditionally; your inhalation is proof of it. As you experience the descent of love through your body and your mind, you will naturally feel that you can generously pass on the generosity you receive. The more you let love move through you, the more love you can take in.

Consider—where in your relationships is there insufficient flow? What is it that restricts your ability to love or be loved? Let the Water Element flow through your heart, taking you deep into your emotions, developing sympathy and compassion for others and the vulnerability of an open heart that allows others to reach you.

Just as it is the heart that circulates the blood, so it is the heart that circulates the Water Element within you. Be aware of your heartbeat for proof that fluid is your essence and that this essence is flowing throughout your body.

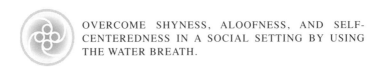

OVERCOME SHYNESS, ALOOFNESS, AND SELF-CENTEREDNESS IN A SOCIAL SETTING BY USING THE WATER BREATH.

The Being of Water

The next step in the Water Element of Heart Rhythm Meditation requires a further realization. So far we have meditated on the nature and qualities of water in its different forms. Behind these qualities of water is the being of water. As the purpose of earth is to be a living platform that supports all life, water also has a purpose, and that purpose is to open the way for and carry the Stream of descending energy.

All the manifestations of water are connected, and together they form one gigantic body of water. This is easy to see in the streams that connect to the rivers that connect to the seas that merge into the oceans. In the being of water that divides one part of its body from another, there is no boundary anywhere. The molecules of water form a continuous fluid substance. When a drop of water is added to a glass of water, the water in the glass completely assimilates the drop. In this way the Water Element is connected to the quality of love. One body of water shows such a great affection for another that the two merge without distinction.

Not only are all the tributaries that lead to the ocean connected, but all water everywhere is connected. This is because throughout the biosphere there is no place that does not have some water. Even very dry desert air and sand have some water. All the microorganisms of the body of the Earth need water, as they absorb food and oxygen only in solution. So by defining the Earth Element as the body of microorganisms, we require that Earth and Water exist together.

THIS COMMON BODY *of water is recognized by science and used as the electrical "ground," a common reference point for all electrical phenomena and one side of some electrical circuits. It is the Water Element that makes the electrical "ground," not the Earth Element, which is an electrical insulator.*

Since all water is connected, water serves as a communication network by which all life communicates globally. In large bodies of water, whales send messages over hundreds of miles, and perhaps over thousands of miles, by ultra-low-frequency sonar. It may be that fish in a river also communicate through water. We see water as something that divides land, but from the point of view of water-based creatures, water is a continuous medium that simultaneously provides food, shelter, and communication.

12. The Water Element

Representing Water

SOMEONE WHO DOESN'T *know the Tigris River exists brings the Caliph who lives near the river a jar of fresh water. The Caliph accepts, thanks him, and gives him in return a jar filled with gold coins. "Since this man has come through the desert, he should return by water," says the Caliph. Taken out by another door, the man steps into a waiting boat and sees the fresh water of the Tigris. He bows his head and says, "What wonderful kindness that he took my gift." [Rumi]*[6]

The very nature of water is generosity, to share itself, and this story is about generosity. The man who brought the jar of water was being generous with the most treasured substance in the desert. The Caliph was generous in return. Then the man was moved by generosity itself in the form of the river.

All that we give to others, all that we receive from them, all that there is to give, is water, which is love. No one makes it; no one destroys it. We just carry it and pass it around. We become loving by giving it, and we become gracious by receiving it. During the course of giving and receiving water, eventually we get wet. Then we wonder, "Whose water have I spilled on myself? The water I was giving, or the water I was receiving?" This confusion results in an insight: it doesn't matter. Either the jar of water I give you or the jar of water I receive from you may lead us both to the river of love.

As a being of water, you can contribute in many ways to the healing and unfoldment of others. Your very presence can make things grow and flourish. Like a gentle summer rain, you can affect the atmosphere in a wide space, bringing fresh life and creativity.

---

6 Jelal ud-din Rumi, in Barks (1995, 199). A Caliph is a leader in a Sufi school.

12. The Water Element

Even a desert blooms after a rain. If people are not blooming, consider it your duty to bring them the water they need.

First you have to identify with water; then you have to communicate it. Don't worry about *what* you will do. When you are identified with water, your every move will be grace, your glance will be creative, your smile will be love, and your breath will be healing.

Identify with the Water Element in your essence, and feel the nature of water as your own nature. You are water, and everyone else is water too. As water, there is no boundary between yourself and all other beings of water.

People are not as they appear to be. To appreciate someone you don't understand, or to understand someone you can't connect to, think of that person as you breathe in and out. Draw his or her atmosphere over yourself as you breathe in, and let the exhalation take you into feeling how he or she expresses his or her inner being. People are not really defined by the roles and situations in which you see them. They will eventually break free of their confinement, and they may surprise you. You can help a person develop, and receive benefit from his or her increased abilities, by recognizing the person beyond the limitations of their situation.

Consider where in your life you can bring the Water Element. Do you not make enough money? The principle of water is to increase the flow.

Money, what do you like most? "Changing hands." [Hazrat Inayat Khan][7]

In business terms, this principle translates into increasing volume or market share with less concern for profitability. Increase cus-

---

7 www.hazrat-inayat-khan.org: Message: Sayings: Gayan: Tanas

tomer contact and service. Do more, for more people. Get more involved, more deeply, with your customers. This involvement is not about being discriminating, strategic, or efficient. Water's advice is: open more stores; increase volume; hire more people; do more transactions; expand the scope of your services. Wealth will increase as surely as small streams become major rivers.

Are you involved in a project that is stuck? Do you have difficulties with your children? The Water Element will bring success and growth as long as it is in motion. When water is trapped, it stagnates or evaporates instead of flowing on into the sea.

The preceding paragraphs read like platitudes until you take them as a practice, performing them with breath and heart rhythms. The problem with platitudes is that they do not mobilize one's will enough to effect a substantial change in behavior. People act the way they do because of their experience and because of their nature. Running a business is no different—you will operate as you have learned to operate, supported and limited by your nature. You may recognize the wisdom of the principle of water, but if the Water Element is not strong within you, and the Earth Element *is* strong, your habit of saving money and building slowly and securely will overwhelm the principle of water. Using the Water Element of Heart Rhythm Meditation will activate the Water Element within you so that you can operate according to water principles easily and naturally. All four of the elements are your birthright, not just the element or two that have emerged in you so far. If you need the Water Element, it is available to you—just activate it with your breath.

With the Water Element flowing through you on your breath, consider how you can flow around your obstacles, how your continual movements can wear away even stone, and yet how your fluid nature makes pliable what is rigid. You harmonize with everyone, making difficult situations bearable. Your motion sweeps everyone along with you, overcoming objections by your flexibility and grace. Everyone wants to be a part of what you do because you are a part of everyone. The Water Element in your presence dissolves their obstacles, just as the Water Element within you dissolves your own obstacles.

One can overcome rocks by striking them and breaking them with a hammer; or one can use the method of water to go around the rocks; or if that's not possible, one can build up patiently behind them, eventually to flow right over them. The hammer has its place, but the way of water should be tried ten times before the hammer is tried even once.

A further development of the practice is to consider ourselves as the continuation of the bodies of our ancestors, as a stream of life that has flowed through our ancestry, a stream that is continually in the process of transformation. The second aspect of this is to become aware of the flow of ourselves into other people and of other people into the universe. We are continually absorbing the universe and transforming the universe into a human being. [Vilayat Inayat Khan][8]

Transforming Energy

In physics, forms of energy are categorized according to their level. Lower-frequency forms of energy, like gravity and heat, cause movement of physical matter, while higher-frequency forms of energy like X-rays and cosmic rays, pass through matter. One principle of energy that is common to both physics and inner work is that lower energy is more easily assimilated but also more easily used up; higher energy is more difficult to tap in to but is more abundant by far.

---

8 Khan, V. (1980)

12. The Water Element

The levels of energy within a person are shown in Figure 12. The physical world is actually the point of all these energy levels: the ultimate, last step of creation where the hidden potentials of the universe are proven.

Figure 12: The Descending Energy System of Manifestation

Higher Frequency, More Abstract

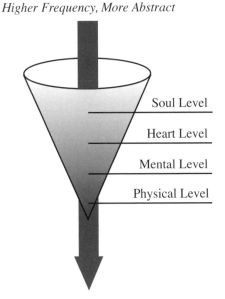

Soul Level

Heart Level

Mental Level

Physical Level

Lower Frequency, More Concentrated

Your physical body may be tired, but your mind can rejuvenate it with more energy. For example, as soon as you think you're in danger, your body will respond energetically, without fatigue. Also, by concentration you can change the state of your body: you can tell it that you're not hungry or not tired. The body tires quickly, but it also recovers quickly if the mind is helpful. What usually happens is that the mind also becomes tired, and then it cannot inspire the body. The tired mind abdicates responsibility for the body, which then slumps, while the mind restores itself by shutting out the external environment and turning its attention within. The mind actually shuts down, in a deep sleep mode, for only an hour or so a night.

During the rest of the sleep time, it is sorting and filing the impressions of the day. When it is finished, the neural pathways are clear, and the memory is restored and available again.

When your *mind* is tired, it can be reinspired by your heart's deep feelings. Your *heart* can also become tired, as in compassion fatigue among health care workers or rescuers, but it too can be recharged by what you know to be true in your essential being, your soul. Even your *soul* may become disillusioned and withdraw its interest from life—and then you will not be able to lift your heart when it falls into pessimism, depression, or pain.

Fortunately, a still greater and more remote resource of energy lies within, one that is capable of effecting a redemption of even the most cynical and disillusioned person. An undefeatable *spirit* is basic to all life. You can't say it's *your* spirit; it is *the* spirit, the spirit of all. It is the unity "behind" or "within" every bit of existence, and we can call upon it to recharge our individuality.

As you draw breath downward through your body, you are transforming the higher energy into lower energy. You are using the spirit of the universe to refresh your soul, drawing upon your soul's idealism to recharge your heart's creativity and generosity, drawing your heart's love into your nervous system's automatic reactions, and drawing your mind's awareness into all the cells of your body.

This purification and renewal infuses your body with the light, power, and consciousness of your essence. Instead of being a cover over the purity of your inner being, your body becomes an expression of your soul. This is exactly the point of downward meditation—creating a new world in real life from the world of pure potential, where the blueprint, or soul, of all things is held. This is re-creation and rebirth as a co-creation with the created.

This experience of the flow of spirit into flesh, energy into matter, happens in a downward flow that is continuous but is also composed of levels. It is like a series of billiard balls, each of which travels a short distance before striking the next one in line. It is also like an electrical current, in which electrons jump from one atom to a neighboring one in a continuous sequence. The electron that comes out of one end of a wire is not the same one that went in the other end. But unlike billiard balls and electrons, the energy of pure spirit, universal and impersonal, is transformed through several stages before it becomes materialized in the cells of your body. This process is happening continuously, but you intensify it by making it conscious.

The stream of descending energy that changes at every level from spirit to flesh has been called many things in different traditions; it is simply love. The objective of the Water Element of Heart Rhythm Meditation is to experience the stream of love descending in and through yourself.

You are a channel that passes downward and outward the energy that descends through you. But you are also more than a pipe; you are also transforming energy as it passes through you.

Considering the Stream of energy that flows from higher to lower levels, transforming its state at every transition, "reach up" in your consciousness to the highest levels of energy and tune yourself to the ethereal source "high above."

Placing the higher levels of energy physically above you is simply pragmatic. The subtle, diffuse, and limitless spiritual energy is everywhere, and so is the dense, focused energy that actually moves matter around. But there is a reason why humans link the concept of "finer" with "higher" and place that which is "higher" physically "above" themselves. Perhaps it relates to the head being above the rest of the body. Scientifically, there is an actual shower of invisible, high-energy subatomic particles, like neutrinos, that strikes the planet continually from outer space, a direction that is always "up" in relation to the center of our Earth.

This shower of cosmic energy is a physical form of the downward stream of love.

MOST LIKELY, ASTROPHYSICISTS *tell us, the water on our planet is celestial in origin, the accumulated deposits of countless meteorites of ice over aeons of time. This gives us justification for saying that the origin, the source, of the literal* waters of life *is high above us, and that water flows* down *to us.*

How we developed this notion that "higher," in the sense of "more essential," or "more original," is also "higher" spatially, is not our concern here. As long as we understand that it is just a mental device, it works, so let's use it. Actually, spirit permeates all matter, just as mind permeates all the cells of the body. All the cells, not just those in the brain, have memory and intelligence. While everything is everywhere, your senses perceive best that which is most substantial: that manifestation of energy that is matter.

You can become more aware of the energy behind matter, the thought behind action, the feeling behind thought, the archetype behind the example, and the spirit behind the form, by reaching "up" in your consciousness. This internal action is the upward, transcendental part of the water meditation. (See Chapter 1 for a discussion of upward and downward meditation.)

Be aware of a flow of signals descending from your brain down through the spinal column and into the organs and muscles, giving a coordination and rhythm to all parts of your body. As you breathe in (through your nose), think of your brain. As you breathe out (through your mouth), think of the flow of signals downward.

As you breathe out, think of the descending stream of high-energy subatomic particles and high-frequency energy radiation that constantly rains down on us from space. These particles and waves pass right through your body vertically, in alignment with your vertical spine.

Consider the abstract descent of archetypes into examples: subtle notions into specific ideas, into desires, into commitments, into actions. Connect your head (inhalation) with your hands (exhalation).

As you breathe in, think of yourself as being light, diffuse, and ethereal. Merge into the "high" energy that is impersonal, subtle, pristine, and infinite.

As you breathe out, draw this energy from its source "high above," down through your channel and into your beating heart. Your heart is the focus for the whole stream of love, and it beats in response as a dramatic demonstration of energy infusing matter.

Channeling the Stream

The next step in the Water Element of Heart Rhythm Meditation is to offer to others the downward stream of love that comes through you.

As you breathe out, direct the stream of energy descending through your body to turn forward when it reaches your heart center, and send it out through your chest into the area in front of you.

Then think of someone you know and love, placing that person right in front of yourself, and send the stream of heart energy into his or her heart. It is your love for this person and their need for the unconditional flow of heart-opening energy that opens your heart. Remember that the stream is made of love; it touches your heart, moves you deeply, expresses itself in your love for another, and reaches that person at any distance through your unconditional connection. In short, the other person feels it when you feel it.

12. The Water Element

There is a real experience called "blessing," and this is it.

Someday an electronic sensor will be developed to detect blessing, and then we will be able to measure and quantify it. There is no doubt that other people can feel this energy pouring out of your chest through your heart on your exhalation. If the receiver is in a state of meditation, he or she can feel it directly and clearly. If not, they feel it intuitively.

The effect is to recharge the person's heart, especially as you breathe out, just as your heart is being recharged as you breathe in by the energy you are channeling and transforming from spirit. From their heart, the Stream descends to their mind and body.

Water's Love

As water is the cleansing and purifying element in the physical world, so love performs the same service on the higher planes. [Hazrat Inayat Khan] [9]

Water is a metaphor for love. Love has the ability to move your heart, to make life flow, to create beauty. And your heart has the power to move the hearts of others: to soothe their distress, sweeten their bitterness, smooth their roughness, and fill their emptiness.

---

9 www.hazrat-inayat-khan.org: Message: Sayings: Gayan: Tanas

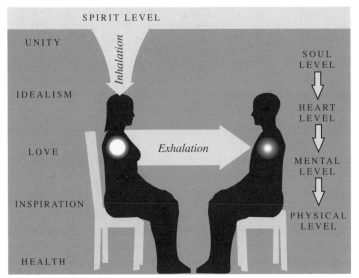

Figure 13: Using the Water Breath to Recharge the Heart of Another

Be aware of your heartbeat in your chest. As your awareness touches your heart, it brings your breath there. Think of the breath at the heart level as love. The breath flowing through your heart moves your heart deeply. Think of the unceasing beating of your heart, the only motion within you that never stops, as your essence. Then love is flowing through your essence always.

It is love in you that touches the love in others and creates the receptacle of Love, the Beloved, who receives the Lover. The Lover and Beloved annihilate each other to become Love itself, just as two drops of water unite and leave their "dropness" to become "wetness."

In this, the conclusion of the Water Breath, you meditate with your breath on the three aspects of Love: Inhale the source of Love, the Cosmic Lover. Exhale as Love expresses itself, reflecting itself as a Beloved. All the while there is Love itself, independent of form or direction. Both inhalation and exhalation strengthen the breath; both lover and beloved strengthen the love.

Inhale as the Beloved who draws unconditional and unlimited Love into herself, filling her being with Love as she holds the breath, and exhale as the Lover, whose being spreads itself throughout existence.

Lose all notion of Lover and Beloved as the inhaling and exhaling swirl in ecstatic union. "Lover" and "Beloved" make sense only to someone standing apart from both, whose point of view distinguishes between the indistinguishable. Those who are caught up in the embrace feel only Love. The unity of Love is perfectly clear, and all duality is only an appearance.

13. THE FIRE ELEMENT

When fire is produced, the heart naturally becomes warmer, and coldness, which is the common disease of every heart, begins to vanish. [Hazrat Inayat Khan][1]
The fire has its tendency to rise, therefore the flame goes up, even the smoke rises, and all objects in which fire predominates will show in them a rising tendency. [Hazrat Inayat Khan][2]

What Fire Is

Everything material is subject to gravity, but the natural inclination of some things is to rise against that force. For example, a seedling reaches upward, expending some of its precious energy in working against gravity. Smoke rises as the air above a fire is warmed. Mountains push up their jagged peaks, and volcanoes erupt to show that even the earth likes to rise. Lightning leaps up from the ground to neutralize the opposite charged particles rushing down.

In people, upward energy is all that is "uplifting," joyful, freeing, surprising, and exciting. Upward energy lifts the corners of the mouth, the eyebrows, and the forehead, makes the eyes sparkle, the arms rise, and the legs jump. It's an internal energy, yet it can be sparked externally. Fire energy can sweep through an audience, leaping from person to person as enthusiasm builds. We catch it from each other, then add it and circulate it again.

Within the body, Fire acts in the digestive system to convert food into warmth and energy. In the personality, Fire is seen in humor, in idealism, and in drive. The distortion of Fire is seen in

---

1 Khan, I. Githa 1, Esotericism, Zikr. *Esoteric Papers.*
2 *Ibid.,* Githa 1, Mysticism, The Form of the Elements.

destructive or aggressive behavior. The best of Fire is the power and freedom that ultimately come together in service to truth.

Fire as we think of it is only the beginning of what the Fire Element is. As the Fire Element evolves, it becomes light; as it evolves further, it becomes truth. The Fire Element of Heart Rhythm Meditation activates the Fire within by breath:

Breathe in and out from your stomach area, below your rib cage. As you breathe in, feel the expansion of your stomach area pushing against your belt. As you breathe out, the stomach area collapses, and your belt becomes several sizes too large. (Now loosen your belt.)

Draw every breath into your stomach, which produces a warm and comfortable feeling. Hold your inhalation in the stomach, then breathe out.

Your breath has two parts that are synchronized in the same rhythm: the air flow and the energy flow. The energy of the breath is being directed in and out of the stomach. The air flow can be directed separately. In this purification practice, you breathe in through your mouth and out through your nose. On every inhalation, part the lips slightly and sip the air, drawing it in so that it strikes the back of your throat. Then close your lips and hold your breath. Keep your mouth closed as you breathe out through your nose.

> Be aware of the fact that we are continually burning, continually in a state of combustion in our bodies and in our minds. [Vilayat Inayat Khan] [3]

After ten breaths like this, you will likely notice a definite warmth in your solar plexus. At this signal, shift your attention to your heart as you breathe out. This will allow the energy in your solar

---

3 Khan, V. (1980, 9)

plexus to rise into your chest as light, producing a softening or melting effect in your heart.

The solar plexus is the furnace in your body. Be directing your inhalation energy into it, you are blowing on the fire, making it rage. Your metabolism increases, enhancing your digestion, burn-

Figure 14: Using the Fire Breath to Generate Heat and Light

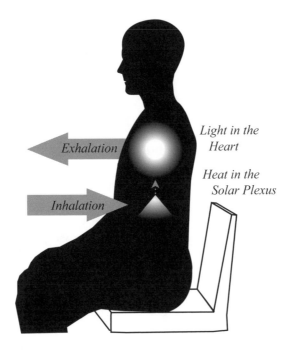

Exhalation

*Light in the
Heart*

*Heat in the
Solar Plexus*

Inhalation

ing up your body, and turning your substance into energy. The warmth stays in the solar plexus, but the energy given off by the "fire in the belly" spreads throughout the body, especially rising up your spine and filling your chest. The light of that fire, but not its heat, rises naturally up your spine to your heart. The heart is melted by light, not by heat.

MAKE YOUR STOMACH AREA SLIGHTLY WARM BY BREATHING OUT FULLY, USING THE FIRE ELE-MENT.

Increasing the Central Nervous System Activity

The gently-blowing wind kindles the fire of my heart. [Hazrat Inayat Khan][4]

The Fire Element of Heart Rhythm Meditation increases the metabolic rate and Central Nervous System Activity (CNA), resulting in enthusiasm, courage, and self-confidence.

> If your lips are as close as they can be while you are sucking in air, the current of air seems to hit the thyroid gland and the back of the throat. It vitalizes the whole combustion process in the body. [Vilayat Inayat Khan][5]

Breathing in through your mouth, which accentuates the inhalation, and thinking of your stomach/solar plexus as you do so, is a technique for increasing your metabolic rate. Just as blowing on a fire makes it burn faster and hotter, this practice consciously turns up the rate at which the substance of your body is converted into energy. Your CNA increases too, a further sign that meditation is affecting the basic functioning of your body and mind.

By this practice you can increase the number of calories you burn in a day, even at rest. You actually burn your flesh in the inner fire of metabolism. Clearly, some people burn up more calories in

---

4 www.hazrat-inayat-khan.org: Message: Sayings: Vadan: Alankaras
5 Khan, V. (1996, 31)

a day than others do. While there may be a genetic component of this difference, the greatest factor is the metabolic rate.

The body temperature is regulated by an unconscious mechanism, the autonomic nervous system. But laboratory experiments have shown that one can vary one's temperature, even the temperature in a finger or hand. Yogis, for example, are able to enhance the heat production of their bodies by controlling their metabolic rate. Immersing themselves in the cold water of the Ganges River 14,000 feet up in the Himalayas, then wrapping themselves in wet towels in this cold, they dry the towels by the heat of their bodies.[6]

> We have the ability to play some part in the outlay of energy in the form of heat. By stiffening our bodies and muscles, somehow we increase the temperature of our bodies. Even emotion can enhance the body temperature. For instance, when we get into a temper, we burn more intensely. The control over this is in the mind. Although it normally happens unconsciously, we can intensify it by thought. [Vilayat Inayat Khan][7]

People often find they gain weight as they age and become more sedentary. Some people prefer to carry some of this weight to buffer themselves against the disturbances of the world. But if you would like to reduce your weight, the Fire Element can help. In addition to eating healthy foods and getting regular exercise, the effect of changing your breath can be dramatic. In fact, the effect of a few minutes' exercise is small in comparison to the effect of breathing all day long. If you practice it every day, Fire Element breathing will linger longer and longer into your day, far beyond the conscious period of the practice itself.

The mental effect of the Fire Element is what you will probably notice first. The mind gets very bright and works very fast. When

---

6 Benson, et al. (1982); Ding-E Young, et al. (1998) provides an interesting theoretical framework and some scientific measurements taken from an advanced meditator; Cromie (2002) provides an accessible summary of some of this research.

7 Khan, V. (1996, 9)

the mind receives rising energy, it thinks completely differently, like the quick mind of a teenager or the mental power of a scientist. Your thinking will be much freer than usual, so your thoughts may surprise you with their freshness, creativity, insight, and clarity. You'll see why wit is associated with intelligence.

The emotional effect of the Fire Element is enthusiasm and joy. It lifts those burdens that have weighed you down. It reminds you of the inexhaustible source of energy that can never be taken from you. You'll smile as you feel energy snaking up your spine and turning on the light in your mind.

PAUL IS A *man in his seventies who studied Heart Rhythm Meditation with us. "I love the Fire Element," he told us, "but I can't do it very long." "Why not?" we asked. "Well, after five minutes, I've got so many great ideas, I can't sit still anymore. I've got to jump right up and get to them!" This is the* AHA! *experience of Heart Rhythm Meditation, and it's very compelling. But we recommend suppressing the impulse to jump up and act. If you suppress it, the impulse will disappear for a time, but it will rise again, changed. Then suppress it a second time. Each time you suppress the impulse, the idea will mature in your unconscious. When it becomes conscious again, it will be in an improved form. The third time it appears, hold on to it. Open your eyes, stop the practice, and keep that thought before you until you carry it out.*

If you should ever begin to feel afraid because the rising energy feels too strong, just change your breath back to the Water Element breath. That will immediately cause the energy flow to abate as the downward stream of water puts out the fire. Don't do the Fire Element practice at night until you have substantial experience with it, because it might make it difficult to sleep. Morning is a wonderful time for the Fire Element breath.

13. The Fire Element

Fire into Light

A candle is made to become entirely flame. In that annihilating moment it has no shadow. It is nothing but a tongue of flame describing a refuge. [Rumi] [8]

So far we have been working with heat and energy. But the Fire Element has even more value if the energy it stimulates is transformed into light.

Inhale with the mouth open and draw the breath into the solar plexus. As you hold the breath, let the light of the fire ascend from the solar plexus up the spine, to a point high in the back between the shoulder blades. Then exhale through the nose, and send the breath out in a forward direction from the heart.

Again breathe into the solar plexus, hold the breath while the energy rises as light to the middle of the chest, and radiate the light forward as you exhale.

Concentrate on the effect of each part of the breath on the energy flow. But the energy flows continuously: while you are concentrating on radiating from your heart, energy is still pouring into your solar plexus.

Now contemplate the energy flow and its synergy with your breath. The energy flow is boosted by your breath, and your breath is boosted by the energy flow. Energy rushing in fills your body with breath, and energy rushing out draws every bit of breath out of your body again.

Overall, this feels like a gentle current of electricity rising in your spine between the middle of your back and the top of your back.

---

8 Barks (1995, 43)

13. The Fire Element

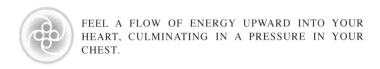

Purification by the Light Within

The Earth Element began the purification process by filtering; the Water Element continued it by washing. Now the Fire Element takes purification to a very intense level: a baptism by fire.

> I baptize you with water, but one comes after me who will baptize you with fire, and the Holy Spirit. [John the Baptist][9]

There is a progression of purifications here: the Earth Element strengthens your discrimination, the Water Element your mind and emotions. The Fire Element purifies your heart's intention. Each level of purification reveals more of your innate qualities and power, making them accessible and usable in your life. Every one of us longs to rectify our mistakes, to be released of our limitations, and to be forgiven for our shortcomings. We have all done things that we regret, and we all harbor thoughts and emotions that we aren't able to dispel. These are greatly alleviated by the self-discipline and mastery of earth and by the unconditional love of water that washes our hearts.

Yet something more lies beyond this alleviation. In the Catholic Church, it's called the sin of *o*mission, beyond the sin of *com*mission. It has to do with the most basic choice we make, behind our everyday choices, actions, and thoughts. "What is my life about?" That is the question we have avoided, even to the point where we deny that the purpose of our lives is something about which we have a choice. But the question concerns your very *intention,* the purpose to which you dedicate your life. You can discover it in the

---

9 *The Holy Bible.* Mark 1:8

thread that connects the events of your life, or in the theme of the drama you create by living the way you live. Everything else in your life flows from your intention, whether your intention is conscious or unconscious.

His bumper sticker *reads, "The guy with the most toys wins." Tom thought it humorous to express this most common intention shamelessly. It was a piece of satire; it didn't apply to himself. But when Tom looked at his life in the light of the Fire Element, he wasn't so sure. Maybe it was an expression of his unconscious, trying to get his conscious attention. He began to wonder what his intention in life was. Was there anything he actually did that demonstrated dissonance with the consumerist slogan? Did he ever give any toys away, or truly share them rather than show them off? Did he commit time to anything unrelated to the acquisition or use of toys? Wasn't even the time he spent with his kids a way of playing his own games, on his terms? What was Tom's real intention in his life?*

Some of the *people who know me are going to be surprised that I have written a book about meditation. My education and my professional work are in computer science. I spent years working for financial and mutual fund companies. I have five children and a wife to whom I am devoted. My co-workers, other parents at my children's schools, and my neighbors know me through the roles in which they see me. Through all these roles and activities, it is challenging for me to keep my intention clear, and sometimes I lose my direction. But over the course of decades, I can see that the choices I made were motivated by one intention: to make a contribution to the field of meditation. For that cause I have sacrificed relationships, jobs I loved, and substantial wealth. These sacrifices have tested my intention and strengthened my purpose.* Puran

13. The Fire Element

Consider what it is that you would give your life for. Because what you would die for is what makes your life worth living.
[Vilayat Inayat Khan]

There comes a time in our life when we must make our intention conscious, clarify it, test it, and strengthen it. Life itself compels us to do this, and the process will seem to be terribly inconvenient, annoying, perhaps even painful and traumatic, until we recognize it as the necessary purification of our intention. It is a trial by fire, in some terms. It looks different in every person's life, but it has a consistent theme.

If you consciously participate in the purification of intention, then your unconscious doesn't have to use extreme measures to get your attention. Conscious purification can be done with light, using the Fire Element Breath. Your intention needs inspiration. Your actions, even your moods and attitudes, are fairly evident to others. Your intention is less obvious. To see your intention, you have to "hold it up to the light"—that is, compare your life to your ideal.

First, you need a strong light. And you have to remember clearly what you have always thought was most important. Our ideals tend to fade in the grayness of practical life. They are replaced by what we like to call "realism" but is actually compromise. It takes a high-intensity state to remember, or perhaps discover for the first time, the mission or purpose that we would like our life to have. Without sufficient energy to pursue that purpose, we slip back into complacency, filling up the days of our lives with numbing busy-ness. But we will have to face our regrets eventually.

The two things people regret at the end of their lives are the things they haven't done and the person they haven't become.[10]

In a soft light, everything appears soft, without hard edges. In a strong light the edges are clear. A strong light creates strong dis-

---

10 Kübler-Ross (1969)

tinctions. Shadows are strong, distinct from areas of direct light. This is why the Fire Element, producing light, can cause a purification of your intention. The light shines through the murkiness of your life and exposes the truth. The energy of Fire lifts you and gives you the power to remember your original intention.

The fire in your solar plexus needs fuel to generate the inner light, and so you offer it the fuel of your own dark spots.

As you hold your breath, the fire in your solar plexus is raging and producing both heat and light within. This light gets concentrated in your heart. The light has the effect of lighting you up from the inside. This light is in every cell, in every part of your body. The intensity of this light in many places makes a sharp contrast to some dark areas within you where the light is less.

Visualize light within you, throughout your body, filling you with light internally and spilling out of you through your skin. (By visualizing what is actually happening, you enhance it.)

Light emerges inside you the way the sun peeks over a mountain at sunrise. First you can see a light area behind and around a very dark area. This is the period of discovery, and the visual image is a metaphor for what you might feel. When you start to think about light, you actually discover first what isn't light.

Then the sun rises a bit more, and the first rays of light spill over the edges of the dark area. The contrast between light and dark becomes extreme. For a while it can appear that the dark area will occlude the light area and the light won't be able to escape. This is a period of struggle and contrast. You feel now that there *is* some light within you, but you may feel unworthy of it, and you also feel an opaqueness within you that can never be light. Even worse, the dark part of you is now exposed by the brilliance of the contrasting light.

Anywhere you find an opaqueness, a part of yourself that is not light, gather it in and feed it to the fire in your solar plexus. The parts of yourself that you are not proud of, that do not contribute to illumination, that even attempt to hide the truth that you cannot deny, are very flammable; they make great fuel. Feed them to the fire.

That is to say, as you expose the ruse of the dark self-delusions, you receive a great inspiration. When a falsehood is exposed to the light of truth, it breaks up, producing even more light.

Whenever one of the human beings awakens from their ignorance and self-limitation, the ginns, angels and archangels break into a cosmic celebration. [Vilayat Inayat Khan][11]

Finally the sun peeks over the mountain, and the world is filled with its radiance. As you look at the sun, the dark area below can hardly be seen. It has no relevance; it cannot hold back the light. The sun is so bright, nothing else is comparable to it. Light is victorious; it has no equal. This is a period of breakthrough, accompanied by great joy.

At this point, the fire in your solar plexus is more than a furnace; it's a conflagration into which everything is drawn. A tremendous fire actually creates its own wind that feeds itself, drawing more fuel and oxygen into it. Let your whole self-concept, all that you thought was your person, be consumed in a purification. Everything about you that *can* burn, burns away.

Only then do you realize the extent to which you had been fooled. The truth about you cannot burn; it is released by burning. What you thought was important was only urgent. Much of what you thought was urgent was unnecessary. No blame. Throw everything into the fire, and then only that which doesn't burn will remain.

---

11 Khan, V. "The Cosmic Celebration", a pageant, drama and worship service involving all religions.

13. The Fire Element

THE ALCHEMIST RECEIVED *the apprentice, who offered for his training a large dirty chunk of metal ore. "Brush that off— let's see what we've got," she said. Much of it crumbled or broke off, and all the pieces were carefully caught and pulverized as much as possible, then separated by sifting into large pieces or powder. It was all moistened and examined over a moon's time. Some parts had smelled bad initially, but the odor subsided. Some had rusted, which was encouraged. "Bring me that lime, please," she asked, and she mixed the powder part into it. Adding a few drops of water, a reaction bubbled up. She added more lime until it was calm again.*

"Now wash it; let's see what dissolves." The apprentice spent a long time soaking and washing, and he succeeded in getting some of it into solution. "Store that," she said, "and let us try to melt the rest." A slow heat did indeed soften it, and some of it liquified and pooled at the bottom of the kettle. "I'll save that," she said, and poured the liquid off into a container.

"More fire is needed for the next step," she instructed, as she took the material to the forge. She heated it in a pan that was red hot, and the material began to vaporize. Above the pan, she caught the vapor in a hood that led to a tube that ran through an ice block and then down to a jar. Slowly, the distillate collected in that jar, until there was no further vaporization. Then, putting a new jar in place, she picked up the remaining chunk in long tongs. "Hold this in the fire," she instructed him, and he did, although the fire singed his hair and his hands burned. The metal sparked and spit, but still he held it tight. Eventually only a small, clear crystal was left. He was relieved to put down the hot tongs.

"We have found its essence, and now we can make what you came here to find," she told the apprentice. "But it's almost all gone," he said—"pulverized, rusted, dissolved, melted, or burned." "No," she said, "all the elements of it are still here, in more usable forms. But we will use of it only what we choose.

What is it you desire? Wealth, peace, power, admiration, knowledge?" The apprentice thought for a while and then said, "I want the power to right any wrong."

"Then I will make you a magic badge that makes you invulnerable; you will never be defeated by another," said the alchemist, and she cut the crystal and poured the distillate over it. The result was a very hard and very shiny disk that could be used to reflect the sun into the eyes of an enemy. All of this process was observed by a spy who took notes and tried to duplicate it for himself. But the disk he made from similar ore had no special powers and the first time he tried to use it, he was killed. What the spy hadn't seen was that the point of the whole Alchemical process was to describe a practice of the heart that the apprentice performed in his room each evening, after the alchemist's instructions that day in the coded language of chemistry.

What the apprentice brought was his own heart to be purified. The initial process was a surrender and a reprocessing, culminating in a purge of his acidic part with the patient tolerance of the alchemist until peace was restored. His tearful regret and sincere desire for forgiveness washed away some of his heart's trauma, and the rest of his heart's shell was dissolved by the unconditional love that the alchemist showed him. Then he was able to remember the burning desire of his life and that flame ignited his heart. The spirit of his being, that had been bound in captivity, was released and recognized in its essential purity. Finally, his intention had been tested in the fire of dedication that he endured through the pain of life. What was left of his heart was only his pure conviction: that which could never be taken from him. From this purification, his heart could be reformed according to what he most desired. The truth of his discovery of his soul became the light in his heart that made it so bright. The "magic" disk was just a badge he wore over the real power in his chest. The illuminated heart will never be defeated; it will always win in the end because it has vanquished the only enemy there is: one's own falsehood.

13. The Fire Element

At the psychological level, the Fire Element gives you zest. It gives you courage to stand by what you believe in and also courage to be absolutely up front and truthful. Consequently, truthfulness is often associated with a flame that burns intensely; it burns all impurities. Truthfulness purifies the psyche where there is deviousness and ambiguity. [Vilayat Inayat Khan] [12]

Be careful about "shoulds": you "should" do this, or you "should" not do that. The only standard to which you can dedicate your life is your own standard. Many things desperately need to be done in the world; you're looking for that which is *yours* to do. Be suspicious of the ideas the mind generates. No idea has enough power to sustain you. You need a conviction: an idea that cannot be countered or ignored. The Israelites had a pillar of fire to lead them through the darkness of the desert. When you allow your conviction to lead you, you too will have the power of Moses.

 DISCOVER THE INSPIRATION TO MAKE A SIGNIFICANT CHANGE IN YOUR SELF THAT ORIENTS YOUR LIFE TOWARD THE LIGHT OF TRUTH. (MAKE EXTERNAL CHANGES CAUTIOUSLY; THE MOST SIGNIFICANT CHANGES ARE IN YOUR ATTITUDE.)

Radiating Light

On earth, it is fire which is the substitute of the sun, for its flame gives light. Fire awakens the mind to the light within. [Hazrat Inayat Khan] [13]

---

12 Khan, V. (1996, 31)

13 www.hazrat-inayat-khan.org: Message: Vol 9, The Unity of Religious Ideals: Prophets and Religions: Zarathustra

13. The Fire Element

Now as you breathe out though your nose, imagine that you heart sends a powerful beam of light forward through your chest and out into the space in front of you. Breathe out all the way, to allow the maximum amount of light to emerge. Then open your lips, and draw the energy of breath into your solar plexus in the front. As you briefly hold the breath, the energy of the solar plexus rises as light, reaching your heart.

The circulation of breath operates like a pump of energy, building up heat below and light above. The more light the heart can send, the more the whole process builds.

The human body, like the bodies of most living things, does indeed emit light in the visible range. From direct measurements with a photon counter, we know that the emitted light is above the infrared range and that it occurs in a high-energy state. (With the supercooled photon counter, light from the body strikes a metal plate in a vacuum tube and causes an electrical current, a flow of electrons, in that tube.) That high-energy state also produces enthusiasm and ecstasy in the emotions, as well as brilliance and clarity in the mind.

To go further in the Fire Element of Heart Rhythm Meditation, you have to identify with *light,* the product of fire. Think of yourself as having a body of light. Your heart is the center of that body of light.

When you are excited, some of the electrons in your physical body make the leap to higher orbital levels and then fall back, emitting their extra energy as photons, or particles of light. The photons become part of a radiant aura of light that your body emits. When you reach that state of meditation in Heart Rhythm Meditation, your radiance is increased tremendously. When you are conscious of being light and sending that light to another person, the number of photons per second that your body emits increases ten thousand times, according to actual measurements in the visible range.

The light of your aura radiates into space in all directions. If the light escapes through a window, or if you're sitting outside, that light will travel across space and eventually reach the stars, whose light is simultaneously falling upon you. Multiple rays of light in the same space do not collide; they pass right through each other. Let yourself delight in this awareness of the intermingling light of beings and stars throughout the universe.

The human body is luminescent—that is, it gives off light, especially when inspired. The strongest source of this light is in the middle of the chest, apparently the heart. You can become aware of it by first imagining it, then discovering the reality, which is stronger than you probably ever imagined.

The increased metabolic rate and the experience of internal energy and power that you feel gives you an increased self-confidence and brings back to your mind all those ideals you've had but dismissed as unrealistic. Perhaps they *were* unrealistic in the usual state of consciousness and energy, but not in this state.

The cause-and-effect relationship between your energy and your ideals is the inverse of what you might expect. To be idealistic, you have to be in a high-energy state, but it's also true that idealism brings out the energy that serves your ideals. Notice how your internal sense of power in your chest increases as you dedicate yourself to that which is excellent, uplifting, inspiring, and good for the whole.

You can burn even brighter by dedicating yourself to "truth," however you understand it. Truth certainly incorporates honesty and personal integrity. It also includes your higher principles, those that you will not compromise. The clearer they are to you, the more they power your actions.

13. The Fire Element

You cannot just *think* about these things "in cold blood." You have to recapture the passion that allows you to remember that you have a purpose in life. You can recapture that passion using the Fire Element. Then your purpose will draw you to its fulfillment and help you to sustain the internal energy you need to accomplish it.

> Many in this world have undergone sacrifices; sufferings and pains have been inflicted on them, but it was only to put their virtue to the test, for every virtue has to prove itself by going through a testing fire. When it has proved itself in its trial it becomes a solid virtue. This can be practiced in every little thing one does in one's daily life. A person who says one moment one thing and another moment another thing, even his own heart begins to disbelieve him. [Hazrat Inayat Khan] [14]

Remember the ideal that was behind the various life-decisions you've made, like your choice to enter a career or to begin a relationship. That ideal will always be with you, and by recommitting to it, you can regain its strength.

The sense of the ideal that makes you burn brightly is very attractive to others. The higher principles to which you are dedicated are like a light in the darkness, and you become the radiant lantern. You can expect to gain business and attract associates according to the greatness of your ideal and your radiance of it.

Incorporating Light

A story of Moses relates that, while he was looking for a fire to bake bread, he happened to see a light on the top of a mountain. To get this fire, he climbed to the top of the mountain—but there the fire became lightning. Moses could not withstand that

---

[14] www.hazrat-inayat-khan.org: Message: Vol 3, Charater and Personality: 1. Character-Building

great flashing, and he fell to the ground. When he woke up, he began to communicate with God.

This story is allegorical. Moses was looking for light to make it his life's sustenance—but it was not possible to get it on earth where he stood. It was necessary that he climb to higher planes, to the top. There he found not only a light but lightning, a light that was beyond his power to withstand. He fell down. But what was this falling down? He became nothing, he became empty. When he reached that state of emptiness, his heart became sonorous, and he found communication with God through everything in the world. In the rock, tree, or plant, in the star, sun, or moon, in whatever he saw, he found communication with his soul. So everything revealed its nature and secret to Moses. [Hazrat Inayat Khan][15]

In this section, we will explore how to make light your life's sustenance—that is, how to recreate yourself from light continuously. Your heart is the key; it's the center of your body of light. As we've seen, the heart can radiate its light like a sun and create an aura around you.

There is another side to the experience of the aura. As we have so far experienced the aura, the physical body, especially around the heart, emits the body of light, the way some electrons emit energy as photons of light. The other side of this is that matter is somehow fabricated out of light. Light is the origin of matter. Not only does the body radiate an aura of light, but the body also absorbs the aura. The body is *refreshed* by light, continuously recreated by it. While the light emission of the human body has been measured, the opposite phenomenon, the absorption of light by the body and the transformation of that light into the substance of the body, has not been observed scientifically, to our knowledge. So we'll say that it's an inner experience that may or may not have a physical substantiation. But since light can cause an electric current to flow, the experience of being created out of light may have an undiscovered scientific basis.

---

15 www.hazrat-inayat-khan.org: Message: Vol 2, Cosmic Language: 13. Inspiration

13. The Fire Element

The light that is absorbed by the body has many sources. The light striking your body just now probably originated in the sun; light from electric lamps is probably also falling upon you. This light is also reflected off many surfaces, which affects its color and polarization. Still other light is emitted by all the people and things around you. There is also the light of the stars, not just at night but all the time. All this light is becoming part of your body. All the light that is absorbed into your body builds up that identity that you are. In meditation, it isn't that *you* are conscious of becoming a *star;* rather, you are conscious of the *star* becoming *you.* (The opposite action is occurring inside the star.)

Participate in your glorious continuous creation by experiencing how light focuses itself and how that focus of light develops a physical structure that becomes your body. Take the point of view of light. As you—light—breathe out, you send light into your body, which your body incorporates into its fabric. As you breathe in, you absorb the body into a field of light and wash it with light.

Contemplate how you, as light, create a physical body by an intense focus that condenses photons into matter. This physical creation is continuous; matter must be recreated every moment. As you breathe in, you are integrating every source of light in the universe, including the light of other people. As you breathe out, you are actually fabricating a body from light, a body that becomes your own physical structure.

Representing Fire and Light

When love's fire produces its flame, it illuminates like a torch the devotee's path in life, and all darkness vanishes. [Hazrat Inayat Khan] [16]

---

16 www.hazrat-inayat-khan.org: Message: Sayings: The Bowl of Saki: June 18

13. The Fire Element

In the state produced by the Fire Element, the way of fire will be natural to you. Fire has its own principles, very different from those of earth or water. At some time in every project, relationship, company, and path, the principles of fire are appropriate and necessary. Any attempt to apply the principles of water or earth at that time would fail. If fire is your nature, you will finally come into your element and achieve success. If fire is not easy for you, then you have the challenge of growth, and the asset of the Fire Element to meet that challenge. Some say that fire destroys, but actually it just radically changes the form of things, reducing them to their essence. Combustion breaks complex bonds in long molecular chains and releases the carbon in all carbon-based matter, in the form of carbon dioxide.

The following are some of the principles of fire:

- At some point things can no longer change incrementally; they have to change fundamentally. You run out of small steps, and you must take a big step. In order to change, you must feel disgust with the way things are. That emotion must be powerful if you are to make a true change. Otherwise, you will either take another small step, or else step back again after trying to make a larger change.

- What is truly yours cannot be taken from you. What you are truly connected to cannot be separated from you. But often the truth is hard to see. You can use the test of Fire to reveal the truth. Release the bounds that constrain freedom. What is yours will either remain or will come back to you. The rest will be lost or destroyed, but it was either superfluous or not yours to begin with. This is risk of the Fire Element. But the Fire Element doesn't see it as risk; it sees it as testing the truth of a situation.

- When the going is hard, you need more inspiration. More inspiration is the solution to all difficulties. Your inspiration, in turn, will leap to others as a spark leaps from one log to another. When people are energized and inspired, they act. Your ideal is your greatest inspiration. When your ideal is linked to the task at hand, there is no stopping you.

- The business principle of fire is to increase profitability by increasing the value and quality of the product or service, even beyond what is needed or expected. Do something that is desperately needed, especially if no one else is doing it. The Fire Element excels at competition, but it loves even more the situation where there is *no* competition.

- Be quick to smile, lifting your mouth; quick to encourage, lifting your forehead; quick to volunteer, lifting your hand; quick to sing praise, lifting your voice; quick to find humor, lifting your heart.

THE GERMANS HAVE *a saying, "Things are serious, but they're not bad."*

The Austrians have a saying, "Things are bad, but they're not serious."

The German saying expresses the Earth Element's perseverance and faith. The Austrian saying expresses the Fire Element's humor.

14. THE AIR ELEMENT

The greater evolution is to see from another man's point of view also. By seeing from his point of view you do not lose your own: your own point of view is still there; but the other point of view is added to yours, therefore, your knowledge becomes greater. It means a greater stretching of the heart and sometimes the heart feels pain when you stretch it. But by stretching the heart and by making it larger and larger, you turn your heart into the sacred Book. [Hazrat Inayat Khan] [1]

What Air Is

Energetically, the air element was the first, original element out of which the rest of the world was created. When a spark is added to air, fire results, which must be sustained by air. What is burned up in fire condenses again and falls as water. Water solidifies to ultimately form earth and is necessary for the earth to be fertile.

Thus activity of the air, clashing by the zigzag direction, produces electricity, the fire element of which may be seen in lightning, which is zigzag in form.

It is the activity of the Fire Element which rises above in clouds and turns into the water element and falls as rain, as the heat of the body is the cause of perspiration, and the heat of the mind accounts for tears.

It is the activity of the water element which solidifies and produces salt and minerals of different kinds, which develop into rocks and mountains, and then descend and make themselves a plain which is the part of the earth. This shows the origin of earth in the source of water. [Hazrat Inayat Khan] [2]

---

1 Khan, I. Githa 1, Mysticism 3, *Esoteric papers*.

2 *Ibid.* Githa 1, Asrar ul-Ansar 6.

Air is also the last element. Water dissolves the Earth Element, fire evaporates the Water Element, and air blows out the Fire Element. There is then a connection between earth, the ultimate element and goal of creation, and air, the original and final element.

This sequence is a metaphor for the process of creation. Air represents the original idea or concept. That concept must be carried into action (fire), and the activity must generate interest and desire in people (water). Ultimately this results in substance of some form (earth). The substance contains all of the thinking, effort, and creativity that culminated in its creation.

An idea must be crystallized if it is to be expressed, but even a concept that is given an embodiment continues to develop; it can never be fully captured. For example, a company is formed from an idea. But even as the company takes form, the idea behind it continues to evolve. As another example; infinite life is born in each infant, which then continues to evolve in abstract while also developing into a particular form in the growth of that child. Perhaps that child, when grown, will find a way to reconnect to its source element, the concept behind its form, and bring the updated version of its conception, which has continued to evolve, into its life. This is the idea behind the "second birth."

In your self, the Air Element produces intelligence. It is also seen in your freedom of thought, your wit, your insight, and your detachment. While everyone has this element to some degree, it can be developed further through the Air Element of Heart Rhythm Meditation.

A CERTAIN MAN CAUGHT *a bird in a trap. The bird said, "Sir, you have eaten many cows and sheep in your life, and you're still hungry. The little bit of meat on my bones won't satisfy you either. If you let me go, I'll give you three pieces of wisdom." The man was interested.*

He freed the bird and let it stand on his hand. "Number one: Do not believe an absurdity, no matter who says it." The bird flew and lit on the man's roof. "Number two:

Do not grieve over what is past. It's over. Never regret what has happened.

"By the way," the bird continued, "in my body there's a huge pearl weighing as much as ten copper coins. It was meant to be the inheritance of you and your children, but now you've lost it. You could have owned the largest pearl in existence!"

The man started wailing like a woman in childbirth. The bird said, "Didn't I just say, 'Do not grieve over what is past,' and also, 'Do not believe an absurdity?' My entire body doesn't weigh as much as ten copper coins. How could I have a pearl that heavy inside me?"

The man came to his senses. "All right, tell me number three." "Yes," the bird said, flying away. "You've made such good use of the first two." [Rumi][3]

In Rumi's story, the bird represents the Air Element, which is taunting and teaching the man's dense mind.

The Air Element and the Heart

In Heart Rhythm Meditation, the effect of the Air Element on the heart is three-fold.

First, the Air Element's gentle blowing on the heart makes the heart much more sensitive, especially to the vibrations of others, even at a distance, and to the atmosphere of a place.

The blowing rose brings to me Thy perfume, Beloved, which moves my heart to ecstasy. [Hazrat Inayat Khan][4]

Second, Air Element develops the heart's ability to express itself in words and to catch the feeling of others from their expression.

---

3 Rumi, in Barks (1995)

4 www.hazrat-inayat-khan.org: Message: Sayings: Vadan: Alankaras

14. The Air Element

Here is a story about the difficulty of expressing a deep feeling in words.

> There was a wall in a village that existed for ages, and many tried to climb it but few succeeded. Those who had climbed it saw something beyond, smiled, climbed over the wall and never returned. The people of the town began to wonder what magic could be there and what attraction, that whoever climbed over the wall never returned. So they said, "We must send someone who can reach the top, but we must tie him with a rope to hold him back." When the man they had thus sent reached the top of the wall, he smiled and tried to jump over it, but they pulled him back. When the people eagerly asked, "What did you see there?" he could not answer, he could only smile. [Hazrat Inayat Khan] [5]

It is not just pain and anguish that we have difficulty expressing; even visions of heaven are hard to express. But whether you can express it or not, you do have a feeling about an ideal of life beyond anything you've been able to find so far. This vision may remain submerged below your awareness for decades (on the other side of the wall) and then suddenly emerge when you finally have enough power in your heart to deal with it (to climb so high). The attractiveness of that place is so strong that once you see it, you will be willing to change yourself (by jumping over the wall). You must find a way to live in the state that you now know to be possible. At first, you cannot say much about it because it seems to be *another* place, distinct (on the other side) from the place where you live and where everyone you know lives. But if you cannot express *something* about why that ideal is so attractive, your friends and family will be left behind. That often happens, but it is not necessary. The way of the Air Element is to communicate to others, even though words are insufficient, your vision of the ideal, the way the world would be if people lived from the heart, as you

---

5 www.hazrat-inayat-khan.org: Message: Vol 8, Sufi Teachings

know it is possible to live because of your experience with your own heart.

The third effect of the Air Element on the heart is that it expands the heart the way warm air fills a hot-air balloon. A lifeless heap of fabric, as soon as air is warmed and blown into it, takes shape and rises into the sky. Your heart rises and finds its purpose in lifting your mental outlook out of pettiness into grandeur.

A great person will stretch your mind to the breadth of his own heart, and a small person will narrow it to the size of his own outlook. [Hazrat Inayat Khan][6]

The Air Element also increases the scope of the heart's influence and its inner capacity, its ability to grow in the future. Air creates space in your heart to give you more room before you bump into your limitations, the walls of your heart.

How did I rise above narrowness? My own walls began to hurt my elbows. [Hazrat Inayat Khan][7]

To obtain these three effects on the heart, you will first need to fully experience the Air Element and feel its effects, in the upward direction of Heart Rhythm Meditation. Then we will focus on the heart in the downward direction of the practice.

Purification by Expansion

The Air Element is expansive; it expands to fill any space it's given. We start the Air Breath with a purification by expansion. Each of the four elements performs its own kind of purification: earth performs filtration, water performs washing, fire performs melting. Now air performs the last purification: the air within all

---

6 www.hazrat-inayat-khan.org: Message: Sayings: Vadan: Tanas
7 www.hazrat-inayat-khan.org: Message: Sayings: Vadan: Gamakas

things expands when it is warmed, and that expansion allows for an inspection of the inner space within the substance.

In personal terms, air performs a microscopic analysis of the structure of your identity. It expands your psyche and spreads it across a vast space, allowing the light of intelligence to reach all its parts and examine the smallest features. The "black box" that is the psyche is now dismantled, and you may inspect it from within. Then you have no more mysteries about what it does, or how or why it does it. You can see every connection, trace the path of every impulse. The inner workings of the psyche are completely exposed to your understanding.

By going through this purification, you come to understand not only how *your* psyche works but how *the* psyche works. The more deeply your breath penetrates the intricacies of your own person, the more impersonal the knowledge becomes. Underneath the idiosyncrasies of each individual lies a vast common base of dynamic human experience.

This notion arises from the way of the heart. From the perspective of the mind, one stands back and categorizes human characteristics based on external observation; the heart feels the nature of the human condition by going within. Your own insight finds out *why* you feel the way you do, what stimuli within or without trigger that feeling, and how the feeling stimulates a chain of thoughts and behaviors. When you gain this knowledge about yourself, then you have gained knowledge of the human being in general. Your research laboratory is yourself. But for your discoveries to be relevant to others, you must find in yourself the essential basis that others share with you. The Air Element develops this insight by gently expanding the self to show you the beauty within the self that you're not aware of when you feel small, narrow, and limited.

Breathe in through your mouth, then out through your mouth, gently and silently. Make the rhythm of your breath very long, with no holding, so that the breath becomes imperceptibly fine. Be sure to

---

finish every breath by consciously extending your exhalation to reach the bottom of your breath.

Expand your heart with your breath; let your heart expand to fill your body on your exhalation, so that it feels like your whole body has become your heart; let your breath reach between the cells and even the molecules of your body, then blowing them outward in all directions like leaves upon the wind.

As you breathe out, you feel as if the cohesive force that holds your body together were loosened, allowing your body to expand and diffuse. As you breathe in, that force is restored causing your body to coalesce and concentrate itself once again around the center of your being: your heart.

This is a pleasant experience, removing the physical limitation that confines your body to a small space. Do not force any experience; just allow a gentle expansion of your heart in all directions.

The image of your body expanded to an enormous size, with great spaces within it, allows your heart to move freely within that space. Your consciousness is accustomed to being identified with your body. The expanded sense of body that you now have gives an equally broad scope to your consciousness. Your heart is as vast as your body is. It's important that you hold fast to the sensation of your heart beating; if you lose it, focus your attention on your heart. Placing a hand (or both hands) on your heart often helps.

This practice contrasts with the usual experience that "my consciousness is contained within a space defined by my skin that is small enough to locate my view at a single point, my own point of view." The expanded feeling of heart is the objective of this practice. The expanded sense of the body is a device to accomplish it.

14. The Air Element

In your vastly expanded state of heart, think of your body, your life, and your challenges. You have the experience of being the entire audience at a play, while your self has the appearance of being an actor on the stage. Look upon the actor with the understanding that comes from embracing all perspectives, your own, and those of all the others on the stage, as well as those of the audience. Your sense of understanding that arises from this state is very warm, as it comes from love. You feel and appreciate the forces that tug on the actors, causing the behavior you see so clearly.

The word *detachment* is often described as a goal of the spiritaul path, and this expanded state may seem like detachment. Yet detachment often feels very cool, while this state is suffused with the warmth of the heart. The heart loves to expand, loves to be great rather than small, and your heart comes awake when it rises and expands in all directions. In watching a play, though one is not personally acting, one puts oneself in the place of the actors, and yet one can see the actions of the other actors and gain an understanding of them as well. The way of the heart is the way of love, which is *attachment*, not detachment. Yet we want to make this experience of love truly expansive, beyond all sense of limitation.

The first sign of the expansion of your heart, so that it can become known to you, is the feeling that your life is being played out before you on a stage. You see your desires, impulses, emotions, actions, and so on, as common to all. You feel all the players on the stage, not just one of them, and you wish them the best, but your expanded heart allows you to see more deeply into their situation than even they can.

14. The Air Element

 ATTAIN THE EXPERIENCE OF AN EXPANSIVE HEART THAT ALLOWS YOU TO FEEL YOURSELF AS BOTH AN ACTOR ON A STAGE AND AS THE AUDIENCE.

Becoming Free

An extension of the experience of seeing your life on a stage is seeing all of life from the vantage point of a mountaintop or an airplane. Life looks much different from on high, but the Air Element gives you an experience that will surprise you: the effect of this mountaintop experience is a much greater sense of freedom in your heart.

Extend your expansive heart further still, to all of your life. Let your heart surround and pervade yourself, those you love, and all those with whom you come in contact. Let yourself observe and feel human life from this expanded place, with tremendous empathy but without narrow individual ownership. Appreciate all the struggles and challenges that you and all the others in your life go through. Feel how it changes you to see and feel things from this expanded state of heart.

This practice will invigorate and free your thinking, resulting in a newly intuited vision of how beautiful and fulfilled your life could be. At the end of the practice, focus this vision into practical reality.

Because of the Earth Element, you often feels responsible for the way things are in your life. You are responsible, of course, but your sense of ownership of these things creates a defensiveness that prevents you from seeing how they really are, or how they could be. In the Air Element you "own" nothing, so you're free both to criticize and to ignore criticism, and to observe constraints yet not be bound by them.

Some of the problems you have are characteristics of your ancestry and your culture. Both these sources are large systems that organize the elements within them through various forces that operate systemwide. For example, the genetic system creates models for men and women that ensure their mutual attraction and interdependence. These models are created not for the happiness or fulfillment of the individuals but for the growth and stability of the system as a whole. The cultural system does the same. America's cultural system is based on growth, which requires continual increases in consumption and expansion of influence. Consequently, stress is placed upon individuals in America, who must earn more money to be able to consume more; upon the resources of the world, which Americans consume disproportionately; and upon the individuals in other countries, who are overpowered. The cultural system must convince its members to espouse the values that it needs them to espouse. All systems must do this to survive.

You are a member of these two large systems, as well as the more specific subsystems of religion, ethnicity, region, occupation, social class, race, and gender. As such, you have accepted some or all of the models they promote. Some of these models may serve you as an individual by helping you to express and fulfill yourself. The genetic and cultural systems assign to men and women certain opportunities, through which they are challenged and receive great enjoyment. Being an American has many advantages. To the extent that you draw upon these various systems for help, security, or identity, you have a duty to perform some role in support of them. But these systems can also be quite oppressive in role definition.

Your objective here is to understand the complex web of influences upon you. This understanding will give you freedom: you can consciously choose your role. You may then have an effect upon the systems in which you are involved, to improve them.

LUKE HAD BEEN *very successful in his life. He started his own business and built it up to $100 million per year in revenue. He married a wonderful, intelligent woman and had several children. He became the president of his industry's trade association and the chairman of one of the country's best symphony orchestras. He was personally admired and respected, for he developed a good heart. All of the goals that he set for himself when he was in college were accomplished, and much more.*

Luke said to me, "I'm fifty-five. What do I do now? Should I just retire and sail my boat?" "No," I told him. "All that you've done so far has been practice, a preparation for your real mission, which is incomparably greater." "But how would I find out what that mission is?" he asked.

"Do you remember when you were in college and you developed the vision that you then spent thirty years achieving?" "I do remember it," Luke said. "It was a powerful inspiration." "The well from which that inspiration came is not dry," I told him. "You have to go back to the well." "You don't mean going back to college, do you," he stated. "No, the well is internal," I assured him.

"That kind of inspiration can be quite disruptive. It could change my life," he worried. "Yes," I agreed, "some change will be necessary to position you for the next phase of your life's contribution. But the next phase will likely use the resources and relationships you've established in this phase."

"I'm not free to go back to the well," Luke said. "I have too many responsibilities now." "That sounds like a man who's hiding from greatness among his habits and conventions," I said. "Surely you can continue the responsibilities that no one else can fulfill while shedding those that others would eagerly take up."

"No, I'm just not free to go into a process that would lead God knows where," Luke declared. "Well said," said I. "But you know as well as God does where you would be led. Don't you remember your longing, your dream?" "I'm not going to change

my life because of some dreams," said Luke. "Well then," I said, "imagine that you are about to die. Do you have any regrets?" "Yes," Luke said, "but I don't see what I can do about that."

"Okay, Luke," I said, "just put your life on autopilot, and enjoy drifting along. If you can stay awake under those conditions, you might notice that the current is carrying you toward your fulfillment, but it's unlikely that you'll reach it before you die unless you start rowing. You may be mentally limited by rules, roles, and obligations, but your unconscious is still free and still expanding. The desire to grow and evolve further cannot be ignored; it comes from your heart."

Change is hard. One often resists it for some time. Focusing on your heart helps you to embrace change, resulting in much greater harmony with life, whose purpose, after all, is growth and an ever-expanding quest to realize your infinite potential. After some years of resistance, Luke found his new purpose in building a new organization focused on microlending in developing countries. PURAN

In ordinary life, you only occasionally notice the existence of large-scale systems and their force upon you. But with the expansion of your heart, you see the people within these systems as, so to speak, corks floating on a river, moved by the currents. While the currents within the river are powerful, they have no effect upon the air, and this is the key to freedom: be air.

Your heart lifts you out of the swirling water by emphasizing becoming expansiveness, gaining a feeling of freedom and true independence through the recognition of interdependence, making you light and able to rise into the air.

In addition to the two large systems, genetics and culture, you are also molded by your own unique background. Your biography has been different from that of any of your siblings. Your place in the birth order makes a substantial difference. Your relationship with your parents and with other people to whom you've been close, the experiences you've had, and the choices you've made all contribute to your uniqueness.

As you continue the Air Element of Heart Rhythm Meditation, become aware that three overlapping influences have converged to form your psyche: your culture, your ancestry (genetics), and your life experience.

Look at an important moment in your life in the past or present, and see the simultaneous workings of these three influences. Perhaps you can see that at that moment you were acting or thinking as a typical woman (or man), a typical Smith (or your last name), a typical New Englander (or your region), a typical member of the technological elite (or your occupation), a typical middle-aged person (or your age group), a typical first-born (or your birth position), a typical Catholic (or your religion), and so on.

In order to free your heart, you must first become aware of how your heart is constrained.

BECOME AWARE OF WHAT IN YOUR BEING HAS COME FROM YOUR ANCESTRY, WHAT HAS COME FROM YOUR CULTURE, AND WHAT HAS COME FROM YOUR UNIQUE, PERSONAL LIFE EXPERIENCE.

Beyond these three influences, you still have some freedom to choose what you would like to be. You can certainly choose where to live and (within limits) where to work, what book to read, and whether to take an umbrella when you leave the house. But your choices of whom to marry, how much responsibility to take on at work, how much you weigh, and how to raise your children are almost entirely determined by these three influences. You *could* make free decisions if you could first see how your choices are predetermined.

Decide how you would like to respond to the situation you've recalled. In order to behave differently, you will have to see the situation differently. The Air Element can give you an experience of freedom that frees your thinking from the constraints of culture, genetics, and prior experience.

You'll know you are free when your thinking surprises you. Don't try to create a free thought; just let your thinking be inspired by the expansiveness of your heart as you do the Air Breath.

If you deliberately try to create a thought that is free, you'll find that you simply create a negative, or reverse, of the opinions around you. To have a free thought, you have to be free of your mental programming, especially your concept of yourself. All those systems to which you belong have sold you a self-concept in order to promote and sustain themselves. You bought that self-concept because it gave you a definition when you didn't have one, and it gave you a way to contribute to others. In meditation, you begin to discover your unique soul and your unique mission in life. This insight will give you independence from some of the models you've accepted from your culture, ancestry, and background.

14. The Air Element

When you have a really free thought, you'll be tremendously excited by it. It will be neither supported nor directly opposed by your culture, family, and friends. It's independent of those systems, like the third dimension in a two-dimensional space.

The consequence of the baptism of the Air is this tremendous freedom from the coercion of the body, the mind, the emotions, and the heredity. You experience freedom from the pressure of the ego, so it's freedom from what you do to yourself, not what the world does to you.

You are free from what in Buddhism is called "determination," from karma, because at this stage you overcome the law that binds.[8]

Switch from Particle to Wave

From the viewpoint of the Air Element, the whole world is vibration. Modern physics tells us that matter may appear to be either vibrations or particles, depending on what one looks for. If you look for evidence of particles, for example in a bubble chamber, matter will appear to be particles. If you look for evidence of matter as vibrations, for example in wave interference patterns, then matter will appear as vibrations. Matter never disappoints; it *is* the way you see it.

Thought, too, can be either particle-like or wave-like. Particle-like thoughts are discrete and specific; wave-like thoughts are general and global. Particle-like thoughts are identifiable by their specific subject matter: they are about a person, a place, or a point in time. (That covers almost all thoughts.) Wave-like thoughts are independent of person, place, and time. Nothing in them is individual; they have no personal context. The same wave-like thought

---

8 Khan, V. (1983, 15)

could occur to anyone, anywhere, in some other time, and probably has. (This paragraph expresses a wave-like thought.)

While particle-like thoughts are important for managing our lives, they are limited to their context, as a particle is limited to one point in space-time. Wave-like thoughts weave the facts of our lives together into an overall understanding. Without wave-like thoughts, the facts of life would be disconnected from each other, often colliding or scattering widely. As Plato said, you could see a thousand discrete tables without realizing the archetype, tableness, of which they are all examples. Many particle-like thoughts added together do not necessarily cause even one wave-like thought. But if we had only wave-like thoughts, we would not be existing as people with personal experiences in the passage of time.

A wave-like thought becomes particle-like when it is applied. A particle-like thought becomes wave-like when it is generalized.

Particle-like thought	*Wave-like thought*
Tim loves Camilla and wants to be with her.	Love draws people together.
Tim is afraid that Camilla will hurt him.	In the vulnerability of love, people can be easily hurt.
Tim is feeling criticized by Camilla.	People anticipate that which they fear.
Tim is trying to decide whether a relationship with Camilla will work for him at this point.	Any relationship will raise one's fears until those fears are understood independently of the relationship.

Our observations and experience deal almost entirely with particle-like thoughts. From them, we may create wave-like thoughts of understanding and insight. Most of our reasoning also deals with particle-like thoughts, even though they do not resolve into conclusions without a wave-like thought. It is futile to try to make a decision with particle-like thinking. Tim is not going to be able to decide about Camilla based on particle-like reasoning. He will probably allow her to decide, or some circumstance to force a decision.

The Air Element fosters wave-like thinking, resulting in greater understanding and insight.

As you exhale through the mouth, you no longer have to use your breath to disperse the particles of your body, since your body is already dispersed throughout the universe in its wave aspect, along with every object around you, every person and object you've ever seen, and every person and object you've ever heard of. They are all coexistent in space, just as separate radio broadcasts share the same space yet remain distinct.

Be aware of the wave aspect of matter as you breathe out. As you breathe in through the mouth, shift back to the particle aspect. The particles of matter are localized in space, but the waves of matter are boundary-less and coexist with all other waves. Therefore, the space occupied by the particles of your body is also filled with part of the wave aspect of every object in the universe. In your wave aspect, you are coexistent with the sun, the moon, and all the stars, as well as with every person alive anywhere.

Remember your heartbeat. The beating of your heart is both particle and wave, both individual and yet big enough to contain all thought, all emotion, all being.

The reality of the coexistence of matter has an effect on your thinking. As you continue the Air Element of Heart Rhythm Meditation, you notice that "your" thoughts and feelings are wave-like, not particle-like.

14. The Air Element

Earlier, we used the concept of an expanded physical body to create an expanded consciousness. Just so, we are now using the concept of the wave aspect of matter to create wave-like thinking. The way we think about matter affects the way we think generally.

A milestone in this practice is the experience of limitlessness. As the wave aspect of your body spreads throughout the universe, infinity becomes an actual experience.

Using Intuition

Now apply your wave-like state to the practical problems facing you. As you remember what those problems are, your interest in them will collect the thought waves into thought particles. This is the process of intuition, not reasoning. Reasoning comes from processing particle-like thoughts, weighting specific facts, like inputs into a computer. Intuition comes from nonspecific, global waves of feeling that are suddenly focused into the moment.

Rather than trying to make a decision or form a conclusion, let your wave-like feelings settle down into particle-like thoughts. Don't direct them. Your vastly expanded heart will do the work, taking into account all the knowledge there is, not just what you consciously know. You just have to watch the thinking process with detachment.

When you want to use intuition, you have to suspend your judgment faculty because judgment uses particle-like thoughts. That means that if you have a preferred decision, outcome, or conclusion in mind, you can't use intuition because your judgment faculty would steer the intuitive process toward your desired result. Your intuition would be distorted to suit your judgement.

14. The Air Element

Intuition is a powerful and accurate faculty that is innate and natural in everyone. It never fails you, but you have to know how to discriminate between intuition and reasoning. The two processes are as different as any two processes could be. You will feel the difference more and more as you gain experience with the process of intuition.

Thoughts Without a Thinker

So far you have been using the Air Element to scatter your physical body. Now repeat this diffusion with your mind. Even wave-like thoughts require a thinker.

A further step in the experience of the Air Element is: a moment of non-thought. You approach it by further expanding your heart to achieve a compassionate concern in the present that has no prejudice about the outcome in the future.

- First your heart's expansion made your notion of your own self much larger.
- Then you expanded your thought and feeling of everyone and everything that you know.
- Now you expand your sense of thinking and feeling as processes.

Your sense of identity is a cohesive force that draws your thoughts into a recognizable and characteristic set of patterns with which you identify. That is, you say, "These are *my* thoughts," identifying with the thinker. Actually, they are simply thoughts, generated by a computer-like, high-speed neural circuit from sensations and associative memory. The cohesive force for your thoughts is your interest in them. The thoughts that do not attract your interest dissipate naturally, while the thoughts that interest you are retained.

As you exhale through your mouth using the Air Breath, look upon your thinking with the expansion that comes from your vast heart: from the input of your memory and sensations, the computer-brain can create nothing more than thoughts, like endless ripples on the surface of water.

Focus your attention on the process itself; unify with the ocean of feeling beneath your thinking. All thoughts come from your interests, which come from your heart. This view allows *the* thoughts (not *your* thoughts anymore) to dissipate, and you begin to sense some space between the thoughts in your mind.

For a moment, at the end of your exhalation, you may sense that you are free of thoughts. You can't think that you are, or imagine it; you can only "sense" it. At this point, use the inhalation through the mouth simply as a place-holder between exhalations. The next exhalation scatters the thoughts even further and produces more space of nonthought.

After a few minutes of using the exhalation this way, you may sense that the space of nonthought is no longer increasing. At this point, turn attention to the inhalation. As you breathe in, look for your thoughts with new interest: "What am I thinking now?" It's a real discovery to notice yourself thinking about something.

Still on the inhalation, try to trace where your thought came from. Is it a continuation of a previous train of thought, or was it triggered by a sensation? If not, if it seems to have risen spontaneously, then it is a "message" from your heart. This kind of thought could be very valuable, as it represents "new," unconditioned thinking instead of recirculation of your "old" thinking. Each message from your heart is important, and taking note of these messages will bring you a much closer connection with your heart.

The combination of scattering your thoughts with on your exhalation and attracting new thinking on your inhalation refreshes your mind and produces surprising, innovative ideas. When one of these ideas comes, watch it long enough to be able to recall it later, then discard it, as one throws a little fish back in order to get a bigger one. With practice, the AHA! experience will come more and more often.

Existence Without a Center

So far, this practice has been person-centered. While you were expanding and contracting, your center was unchanged.

Now we are going to expand and contract without a center. Instead of thinking that you are breathing, take a passive perspective and allow yourself to be breathed.

Identify with the breath that flows into and out of your body. When the breath flows into the body, like an incoming wave on the beach, the lungs expand to accept it. When the breath flows out again, the lungs collapse as they are emptied. The same breath flows into and out of all other breathable organisms. If you can make this leap in identity, you gain a kind of thinking/experiencing that is impersonal and therefore not limited by your personal perspective.

As you breathe in, you realize that you are picking up the software of the universe in your thinking. As you breathe out, you realize that your thinking is the thinking of the universe, and your feeling is the feeling of the universe.

14. The Air Element

> "Now you discover that your mind *is* the mind of the universe. It is not a fraction of it."[9] This is the experience of unity.
>
> Finally, consider your current puzzle/dilemma at work. With the wisdom of all experience to draw upon, but without the limitation of your interpretation of that experience, let your mind receive your heart's wisdom through the discovery of a solution that surprises you.

Expanding Your Heart

Now we turn to directly applying the Air Element to the development of your heart. Heart Rhythm Meditation proceeds into the downward-directed phase. The experience of unity is followed directly by recreating an individual center. The center you want to create is your heart. Your heart then becomes the focus of all that you know yourself to be in this expanded and unified consciousness.

> As you exhale through the mouth, imagine that you are blowing the Air Element gently into your heart, to create a focus of all that you are. Your heart can't be limited to the shape and characteristics of your physical body. This heart that your exhalation is forming is enormous.
>
> Now switch your identity from the infinite source of the breath to your heart, the receptacle of the breath. You can do this on the inhalation, which is also through the mouth. This heart is not within you; you are within it. The heart in this condition occupies a vast space, like the body that was dispersed earlier in the Air Element.

---

9 Khan, V. (1988, 82)

This gives you an unusual and very wonderful experience of literally being inside your heart. Your "heart" is so large that you can walk around within it. Try that: while blowing into your heart on your exhalation and drawing the breath into your heart on your inhalation, get up, walk around the room, then out of the room but inside the building, and notice that everywhere you go, you are within the space of your heart. Everything and everyone you see is also within your heart. When someone comes toward you, they come into your heart. When they walk away from you, they carry the blessing of your heart with them. All of what the heart contains is connected so that it is integral within, united in feeling, experience, understanding and purpose.

This is what it means to be "*in* love." Everywhere you go, this vast heart remains around you, and you, and everyone near you, live within its love.

This is a crucial experience in living from the heart, for it experientially demonstrates that the heart is a "capacity," a capacity for love. Here is a wonderful description of the experience of the Air Element of the heart:

Every form I see is Thine own form, my Lord,
And every sound I hear is Thine own voice;
In the perfume of flowers I perceive the fragrance of Thy spirit;
In every word spoken to me I hear Thy voice, my Lord.
All that touches me is Thine own touch;
In everything I taste I enjoy the savor of Thy delicious spirit;
In every place I feel Thy presence, Beloved;
In every word that falls on my ears I hear Thy message.
Everything that touches me, thrills me with the joy of Thy kiss;
Wherever I roam, I meet Thee; wherever I reach, I find Thee,
my Lord;

14. The Air Element

Wherever I look, I see Thy glorious vision;
Whatever I touch, I touch Thy beloved hand.
Whomsoever I see, I see Thee in his soul;
Whoever aught gives to me, I take it from Thee.
To whomsoever I give, I humbly offer it to Thee, Lord;
Whoever comes to me, it is Thou who comest;
On whomsoever I call, I call on thee. [Hazrat Inayat Khan] [10]

Representing the Air Element

The Air Element is represented in life by the vastness of your heart and is focused through your glance. When you are able to focus the vastness of your heart into your eyes, you develop a powerful glance.

Coming out of the Air practice—with the feeling of your mind merged with the universe's software and your heart expanded to include all that you care about in the world—your open eyes become windows between the finite and the infinite. Instead of receiving the image of the world *into* your eyes, the luminous light of your heart streams *out of* your eyes. It's as if your eyes are lamps, lit by the light of consciousness. You have the feeling of being behind your eyes, looking through the windows at a transfigured world that opens up as your heart pours into it.

Your eyes have the ability to illuminate things in such a way that you can see into their nature. This glance doesn't just pick up the light that is reflected off of an object's surface, as in normal sight. It illuminates things with a kind of X-ray light. This is only a metaphor because what you want to see is not the inside of an object but the *nature* of the object.

---

10 www.hazrat-inayat-khan.org: Message: Sayings: Vadan: Ragas

For example,

- When looking at a flower, you see the beauty, life, grace, and so on that the flower represents.
- When looking at a person, your glance reveals not just their appearance and their current condition but their qualities and their potentials.
- When looking at a situation, your glance reveals the cause behind the apparent cause, and the purpose the situation serves.
- In every issue, you see its context. The issue appears as the focus of a larger issue. Addressing the larger issue in the particular case allows you to make wise decisions.

The most amazing thing about this glance, its greatest power, is that the glance is *creative:* it creates what it sees. People actually become more like the way you see them. Situations unfold according to your understanding of them. You yourself become what you know yourself to be.

The challenge is to keep your eyes charged with light and to avoid self-deception. You can recharge your eyes with creative vision by using the Air Element. You avoid self-deception by not assuming that you create your thoughts. Thinking of your thoughts as your own is a self-deception because the ego generally distorts the one, single reality by its concept of individuality.

The thinking you can trust is based on harmony:

By a study of life the Sufi learns and practices the nature of its harmony. He establishes harmony with the self, with others, with the universe and with the infinite. He identifies himself with another, he sees himself, so to speak, in every other being. He cares for neither blame nor praise, considering both as coming from himself. [Hazrat Inayat Khan][11]

How can you develop this attitude? Not by your will, but rather this attitude of harmony with others comes only from the experience of unity. It is tested by life's difficulties, but the one who has seen the truth of unity cannot think any other way.

If a person were to drop a heavy weight, and in so doing hurt his own foot, he would not blame his hand for having dropped it, realizing himself in both the hand and the foot. In like manner the Sufi is tolerant when harmed by another, thinking that the harm has come from himself alone. [Hazrat Inayat Khan][12]

If others are not harmonious with you, you can still harmonize yourself with them. What difference does it make whether you change or the other changes? For the Air Element, change is natural. As you see wider and deeper, you understand more about how to work with people of all kinds, making music that includes their note, not excluding or overpowering it.

[The Sufi] uses counterpoint by blending the undesirable talk of the friend and making it into a fugue. [Hazrat Inayat Khan][13]

You naturally feel that the care of your expanded heart is your responsibility and your desire, since whatever happens in your heart happens to you. Your feelings fill the space of your heart and then continue to vibrate and ring within your heart for a long, long

---

11 www.hazrat-inayat-khan.org: Message: Vol 2, The Mysticism of Sound: Harmony

12 *Ibid.*

13 *Ibid.*

time. You live in the atmosphere of your heart, whatever the atmosphere is like, so you have an interest in making it loving.

The more you understand, the more interesting life becomes. What you see is the vision your heart creates, and what your heart creates is the life you live.

Part 4

CONTINUING
YOUR
PRACTICE FOR
A LIFETIME

15. COMMON PROBLEMS WITH MEDITATION

When people are learning Heart Rhythm Meditation, they encounter certain typical problems. Many have gone down this path before you, so practically all of the problems you have or will have are known to experienced teachers. Since this book is serving as an imperfect teacher, unable to respond to a query, at least some of the problems that you are likely to ask about must be listed here. If you don't have any problems with the practice now, you will later, so you can save this chapter for then.

Getting to It

> "My problem is that I just can't find time for this. It seems like such a big commitment, and I'm not sure I'm going to like it. I enjoy reading about it, but I don't think I'm ready to actually do it."

First of all, if you're thinking about meditating, that counts for something. Without feeling guilty for what you're *not* doing, appreciate that you *are* thinking about doing it. Try to think about it more. Remember the stories and concepts you've heard. Consider what makes you uncomfortable about meditating, and what attracts you.

You could slip into it gradually. Some of the instructions can be done informally, anywhere: while driving a car, watching television, putting the kids to bed, sitting in a meeting, standing in line. You can be aware of your breath at any time. You can try making your breath rhythmic or extending your exhalation whenever you think about it. If you become comfortable doing it in an informal setting, then you'll be encouraged to try it in a formal posture.

You always have all you need to do these practices: your breath and your heartbeat. No special equipment is required. Whenever you think of your breath, you benefit. If you can catch your heartbeat, you're blessed.

If you wake up at night and can't sleep, sit up on your pillow and do the rhythmic breath until you get sleepy again. If your unconscious is regularly waking you up at night to meditate, perhaps you'd better pay attention to this message and start practicing deliberately.

If you want some help in getting to it, make a schedule. Creating a routine will strengthen your ability to "sit," overcoming the first and worst hurdle in Heart Rhythm Meditation. You establish the routine in a mood of determination and wise dedication. Then when you're in a different mood—in the morning, when you have to get up and resist the call of the morning paper—your resolve will come back to help you.

My MIND IS *bright and busy in the morning. As I shower, my mind is preparing plans for the day and solutions to problems left over from yesterday. As I get dressed, my mind is already at work. Then my stomach chimes in and demands food. I promise to deliver but ask for its patience. I'm interested in what my wife is saying: insights from her dreams, continuations of last night's discussions, coordinations about the day to come. I wake up my 12-year-old son and hug him despite his protests. The dog needs to be walked. To act on the ideas I had in the shower, I'll have to find a few papers to take with me on the train.*

My meditation stool calls to me, and I hear it. I walk into the Meditation Room (how fortunate we are to have one) and take off my shoes. I'm operating on faith here because if I had to think about whether I should take this time or not, I might not do it. My mind is supporting the interests I have, as always, and I'm interested in all the things around me. But as soon as I sit down, my mind begins to change. Now I remember how I built up the faith that meditation is something I need to do despite my mind's arguments. Waves of energy wash over me, and gratitude rises from my heart. I almost missed this—how thankful I am that I didn't!

What a pleasure it is to meditate in the morning when I'm alert and not sleepy. My mind enjoys it too, always following my interest. It delights in going through the steps of the practice, finding my heart's beat and then rediscovering the elements as if for the first time. PURAN

Finding even one other person to practice with will change your experience substantially. A small group that meets regularly is best. In the safety of numbers the "terrors" of having a conscious heart will subside. Eventually, the practice will call you, and you'll be drawn to it without resistance.

Can't Sit Still

"I can't sit still long enough to get any benefit from this."

The body is made for motion, and holding it still can seem like torture. If sitting still seems like torture to you, then you can combine breath practice with movement. The simplest form of this is the most effective: the Walking Breath Practice (Chapter 6).

When you sit down, your nervous system undergoes a change that is conducive to meditation. Also, it is very difficult to feel the heart beat while you are moving, unless you are considerably exerting yourself. Of course, the pressure sensors remain fully on, so you never have relief from sensory overload. The fine breath does not occur with motion; the finer emotions are overwhelmed. For all these reasons, it is preferable to sit down and make the body still. You can do this with a body-friendly attitude if you watch your breath and look for your heartbeat.

Once you have discovered the heartbeat, it is much less difficult to sit still. The heartbeat is your entrance to the world within.

You can build up your sitting time gradually. Start with five minutes. You might like to set an alarm to announce the end of the period. Then you can move up to ten minutes.

It is only the entranceway to the world within that looks foreboding. Inside it's a palace, although from the outside it appears to be in ruins. It is a palace that you have visited before only while asleep. In the dark it can look frightening, but a light inside reveals the beauty of the place. Actually, it is your real home, and it holds for you all that "home" is. It is safe inside; the palace has never been breached; the wars outside have not corrupted it inside.

Thoughts in the Way

"Whenever I try to do the Heart Rhythm Meditation, my thoughts and the noises around me distract me and get in the way of my meditation."

First of all, accept that your mind will continually produce thoughts. That's its job. Your mind is like a computer that is constantly displaying images for your delight. You cannot turn it off. What you can do is focus it on your practice.

I would never want to insult your mind. It is a faculty at the seat of identity; we identify with our minds. It's our unique memory of life that gives us our individuality. But there are levels of mind—there is logic, intuition, and the subtle sense of mind. Mind can be focused on an example of a table; on the use of a table; on memories associated with a table; on the construction of tables; on the archetype of the table, tableness; on the archetype of tableness, objectness; and so on.

How do you tune your mind to a "higher" level that allows you to discover the essence of your own nature? It takes training, and that training has steps. Your thoughts sometimes come from the depth of your heart, reflected in your mind; this is wonderful, like listening to a Bach mass on the radio. Other times the mind produces the equivalent of a radio advertisement, or even the noise of a bad reception.

First of all, consider the ordinary level of your thinking as comparable to the noisy conversation of children. We are not generally disturbed by children. They enjoy their play, and they like to use their voices. Their minds are like new toys, and they love to see what they can do. You can sit among the voices of the children in your mind and not be disturbed by them because you know they're children.

Another image that I like to use is that the output of my mind is like the display of a computer. Isn't is marvelous what can be done with computers? I make my living by my mind, but I'm aware of its great limitations. If it is not fed from a deep well of emotion, it becomes quite mechanical. All the images that the mind draws on its screen have a similarity. They are all screen images, and one gets tired of screen images. Even though the computer cannot be turned off, you can move the screen so it displays to the wall.

When you devalue your thoughts, they lose their appeal and their compellingness. To "change the channel," you must be able to deselect the current show. This is a key step in tuning your mind.

Say you're sitting in meditation, and a fire truck goes by outside. Part of your mind rushes to the window, like a child, and generates many thoughts about the fire truck, about fires, about houses, about your house, and so on. The more mature part of your mind is uninterested in the sound of the siren. That disinterest is freeing. This is one half of the training of the mind: the mind produces only thoughts, and no thought can be very interesting.

The second half of the training directs the mind to support the practice. Then your thoughts are the focalization of your consciousness. They accompany you on the journey within, almost the whole way. (At a very high level of meditation, consciousness becomes completely unfocused, and so the thoughts, which are the focalization of consciousness, disperse. Until you reach that level, however, and afterward, your thoughts are always with you.) When you are interested in what you are experiencing through your senses, your thoughts are there. When your interest turns to what you are experiencing within, your thoughts are there. When the Heart Rhythm Meditation is interesting to you, your thoughts are on it.

Your interest directs your mind. So to keep your mind on the practice, you have to make the practice interesting. You can do that by remembering why you wanted to learn to meditate. The more specific your goal, the stronger motivation it creates.

Another part of the training is to build up your ability to control your mind at all. The first step in that training is to sit still.

A person who lacks control over his nervous and his muscular systems has no control over his mind; he eventually loses it. But by having control over one's muscular and nervous systems one gets control over the mind also. [Hazrat Inayat Khan] [1]

Once you have developed disinterest and interest and have built up your mental control, then the thoughts that come to you during Heart Rhythm Meditation will be important; consider them with respect. This is the time when the unconscious speaks to the conscious, so be aware of the meaning of your thoughts.

You may get a thought that comes like a directive: "Do this!" Such thoughts typically carry one away because they seem to be so inspired. How can you tell whether a thought is an unusually clever display of the computer or a genuinely valuable piece of inner guidance? Put it to the test.

---

1 www.hazrat-inayat-khan.org: Message: Vol 8, Health and Order of Body and Mind: Physical Control

1. Whenever a thought occurs that has great specificity, creativity, and an apparent solution to your problems, note it and then suppress it—force it back into the unconscious, under the surface of the conscious mind.
2. After a while, it will come again. It will be different this time, but still recognizable as the evolution of the first thought. It has benefited both from being noticed consciously and from being forced back into the source, where it has matured and drawn upon a wider scope. Now, having evolved, it is a wiser thought. Now suppress this thought a second time.
3. When it reemerges again, take it. The third version is the right one.

This process may occur over a single meditation or over many meditations. The thoughts that remain after this process are rare and special thoughts; take note of them.

Can't Get Enough Breath

"While doing the Square Breath or any long breath, I find that I run out of air, so I have to take a few ordinary breaths before the next breath of the practice."

This problem has two general causes: incomplete exhalation and strong emotion. First, check your breathing technique. If you want to get more breath, you need to exhale more fully. Even a small extension of your exhalation will make a big difference in the next inhalation. Second, check your posture. If you are slumped forward even slightly, your lungs will be constricted and won't be able to fill completely.

But if you're having an attack of anxiety during meditation, you need to follow the opposite advice. Anxiety is aggravated by full exhalation and by holding the inhalation. If anxiety comes up, it is important to know how to reduce it. By learning how to increase and decrease your anxiety, you gain control over this emotion—control you can exercise whenever anxiety occurs in your life.

Decrease anxiety by keeping your breath rhythmic, in and out without stopping. Do not hold your breath at all, and do not extend your exhalation. Use the normal range of breathing, but make it very rhythmic, like a pendulum swinging in and out. You will usually find that when anxiety starts, your breath stops moving.

There are many other emotions you could also experience during meditation. All emotions except peace require extra breath. When you feel anxious, joyful, or sad, you will need more air. If you become worried about doing the breathing practice correctly, it can become a worsening spiral: the worry requires more breath, which interrupts the gentle, rhythmic flow and makes you gasp, which makes you worry more about your performance. When this happens, just take a big sigh and blow away the judgment.

Emotions can be experienced as gross or fine by the relative amount of breath they require. Gross emotions require big breaths, and fine emotions require only a little air. Every emotion has a gross and a fine version, for example:

Emotion	Gross Form	Fine Form
Love	Passion	Admiration and respect
Anger	Rage	Determination
Fear	Panic	Alert caution
Joy	Hilarity	Bliss

As it is often difficult to be aware of our feelings at all, we are generally aware of only our gross emotions. With the Heart Rhythm Meditation you become more aware of your fine feelings, and those feelings expand to become vast and deep. One of the characteristics of living from the heart is living in these fine emotions.

To live in the gross emotions is like living on the earth; to live in the fine emotions is like living in heaven.

Breathing consciously and rhythmically and making your breath fine will make your emotions fine as well. When this happens, your breath will become even finer.

The Latin word for "spirit" is the same as the Latin word for "breath." The Sermon on the Mount thus speaks of the blessing of living in the fine emotions:

Blessed are the poor [fine] in spirit [breath].[2]

Getting Sleepy During Meditation

"I find myself nodding out while sitting. I don't notice it coming, but I suddenly realize I've been asleep."

It is very common to get sleepy during meditation. Concentration is strenuous. Once sleepiness is present, it serves as a ceiling for your consciousness. You can't get "up" through it, you just black out again. You can come "down," in the sense that you become more aware of your body and mind, more awake. But actual spiritual awakening is far away.

The first approach to this problem is to take a break. If you can take a nap, then do: you'll get a wonderful rest. Slipping into sleep from a meditation state is blissful.

It is not necessary that they should do their meditation trying to avoid sleep; if by doing meditation they can sleep so much the better, for the meditation continues through sleep in the subconsciousness. [Hazrat Inayat Khan][3]

Even if you prescribe to a student to do a certain meditation at night before going to sleep and through that meditation to sleep, it would make a hundred times greater effect than if the

---

2 *The Holy Bible.* Matthew 5:3

3 Khan, I. Sangitha. *Esoteric Papers.*

student engaged himself in doing different things between his meditation and sleep. [Hazrat Inayat Khan]⁴

The second approach is to take the Fire Breath. Sleepiness is an impenetrable barrier to higher consciousness, but you can jump over the barrier if you have enough energy.

Sleepiness may be happening because you have "blown your fuses," as Pir Vilayat Inayat Khan puts it. Reality won't fit into any of the compartments in which we store our ideas; it cannot be encapsulated by our concepts. It is overwhelming; it blows our concepts away. When you have a particularly close brush with reality—a large dose of the truth—it cannot be readily incorporated or integrated. The mind shuts down, in a harmless way, for a short time.

Losing Track of Time

"When I did the practice, I was surprised at how much time had gone by. I thought it was only a few minutes, but it was half an hour."

Unconsciously, we measure time by counting our heartbeats and breaths. When you meditate, your breaths will be longer than normal, so you will take fewer breaths per minute. Normally, you may take 12 to 15 shallow breaths a minute, but when you're meditating, a single breath may take up to 25 seconds or even longer, which is 2.4 breaths per minute; a more typical meditative rhythm would be 4 to 6 breaths per minute. At 12 breaths per minute, you're expecting a half hour to take 360 breaths, but when you're breathing 4 breaths a minute, a half hour takes only 120 breaths. Normally, 120 breaths would take 10 minutes. Your unconscious breath counter has calculated only a third of the actual time of 30 minutes.

An additional problem with time determination is that when your breath and heartbeats become conscious, your unconscious

---

4 *Ibid.*

counter of breath and heartbeats is disabled. The breath and heart are either conscious or unconscious. When you do Heart Rhythm Meditation, your conscious mind takes control of your breathing and to some extent your heart rhythm also, so your unconscious, which is usually your timekeeper, doesn't have access to its clocks. Your usual method of gauging time becomes inoperative. Consequently, even less than forty percent of the actual time may seem to elapse. As discussed in Chapter 7, it can seem that time stops completely.

If you have to stop your practice at a certain time—to catch a train to go to work, for example—then you should set an alarm. This has the added benefit of removing a potential source of anxiety. Knowing that the alarm will end the meditation will free you up internally. An alarm also serves a valuable function of making you commit to a certain length of time that you'll meditate. If you're meditating without a place to be afterward, try setting the timer to a bit longer than what you're accustomed to, and don't stop until the timer goes off. This will give your practice session a sense of intentionality and help you build mastery.

Headaches

"When I meditate, I get a headache in my forehead."

A forehead ache is not uncommon for beginning meditators. After more experience, it becomes a feeling of pressure, without pain. Finally it ceases altogether. It comes from being unable to handle the rising energy that reaches the head, especially in the Fire Breath. There are three solutions we can recommend:

1. Kneel and place your forehead on the floor. When the highest point in the body, the head, is placed on the same level as the lowest point in the body, the feet, the energy "shorts out." Imagine that the energy inside the head spills out through your forehead. This will give quick relief, although it wastes the energy.

2. Incline your head down slightly, and place both hands on the heart. Make a conscious effort to move the breath through the heart, rather than allowing it to rise to the head. Allow the sense of your heart to expand so that it includes your entire body.

3. Do the Water Breath, the antidote to strange energy experiences. It is especially good as a preventative measure. If you are prone to headaches, emphasize the Water Breath and discontinue the Fire Breath.

Heart Aches

"Since I've been meditating, I occasionally get an intense pain in my chest."

This is a problem we've had and have seen in others many times. It can occur at an advanced stage of practice. It can happen while you're walking, driving, or doing anything at any time. The pain is sharp and very localized, either in the physical heart on the left side of the chest, or in the center of the chest at the level of the heart. It is so painful, it's hard to breathe. After two or three minutes, certainly less than ten, it disappears completely.

This pain feels like a heart attack. Of course, you should immediately have your heart checked because it could *be* a heart attack. But in my experience, it is not physical, and the medical doctors are never able to find anything. It is caused by an opening in the poetic *heart*.

At the concentration level of the Heart Rhythm Meditation, you are conscious of the heart inside your body. At the contemplation level, you are conscious of being inside the heart. At the meditation level, the heart that you are inside is the heart of humanity, and you begin to feel all that is in that heart. You feel these vast and intense feelings in and through your own physical heart, which is like trying to pour the ocean through a funnel into a cup. The individual heart cannot contain all the emotion, from love to pain, so it cramps.

If you can recall what you were thinking about just before the pain occurred, you will probably find that it was a thought of compassion and concern for others. It was not the feeling of worry, of loss of control, or performance anxiety. Those give one a pain in the stomach. Heart pain occurs at a moment when the heart of the world touches your own heart.

This is a sign of a living heart.

That person is living whose heart is living, and that heart is living which has wakened to sympathy. The heart void of sympathy is worse than rock, for the rock is useful, but the heart void of sympathy produces antipathy. [Hazrat Inayat Khan] [5]

A heart that has become open and sensitive is a heart that can feel genuine sympathy for others. Where do you feel the heart ache of others? In your own heart, as a physical pain, as a heart ache of your own. As you develop, your heart becomes bigger—that is, it develops a larger capacity for emotion—and then the pain subsides.

Think of this pain as a growing pain of the heart.

Crying

"Whenever I meditate, tears fill my eyes, and I can't stop them."

This is the problem of too much of the downward stream of love (see Water Breath in Chapter 12). It can occur in very creative people and in people with a sensitive heart. The rest of us would welcome such a flood of emotional experience and much prefer it to the desert of non-emotion, but to those who can't stop crying, that is no solace. As desirable as it is to be able to touch the heart, we want to maintain some control over our state of being.

---

5 www.hazrat-inayat-khan.org: Message: Vol 13, Gathas: Metaphysics: 3.2 Sympathy

The tears may come early in your meditation experience or later. They may express your heart's intense longing to return "home." They may come to wash your heart after a heart wound is uncovered. They may signal the opening of your heart—one of the breakthrough experiences of inner development.

We don't recommend trying to harden your heart so that you are less sensitive to emotion. That is probably what you do all day long. Your meditation time is when you can enjoy the natural quality of your heart. All you need is a way to tune your heart to a higher pitch so that you can stay in the heart without being swamped. The way to do that is to meditate more.

The Air Breath is the key to developing a finer emotion. By refining your breath, you become more vast, and your experience becomes more diffuse. Your emotion doesn't go away; it becomes more impersonal. The tears will stop, but your heart will remain open. (See also the problem above, "Can't Get Enough Breath.")

Inability to Sleep

"If I meditate at night, I'm not able to sleep afterward."

Early in the morning and late at night are two of the best times to meditate. However, you must choose the practice appropriate to the time. In the morning you want those practices that produce awakening, inspiration, and power. In the evening you want expansion, receptivity, and light. Practices that produce peace or love can be done anytime. If you don't have time to meditate at night, then you can do any practice in the morning.

In the evening just before you go to bed, do the Air Breath. Then lie down while you still feel the experience of it, and slip into sleep. Avoid the Fire Breath late at night.

15. Common Problems With Meditation

Distaste for the Philosophy

"I do the practices you describe, but I don't care for your philosophical commentary."

It is unnecessary for you to accept any philosophy that you find in this book. The philosophy supports and arises from the methodology, but is not required. If there's something in this book you don't like, disregard it. Perhaps a different part of the book will be useful to you. It's not a package; you can take what you like and leave the rest.

16. INDIVIDUAL AND
GROUP PRACTICE

Unless you are already connected to a group of Heart Rhythm Meditators, it's likely that you'll try Heart Rhythm Meditation on your own first. Once you learn the Heart Rhythm Meditation, you can certainly maintain it alone. Some people are able to learn and sustain it on their own. Most people, however, need help in mastering the practice.

There are many advantages to sharing the Heart Rhythm Meditation with a group, either with or without a teacher. If someone recommended this book to you, you've been given a great advantage. You have someone to discuss it with, to share your experiences and questions. I hope you make opportunities to do the practice together with your friend. Then you'll find what every meditator finds—that the experience is very much stronger in a group than it is alone.

Perhaps you'll even feel that you can pass this advantage along to others by offering to host or support a Heart Rhythm Meditation group. If you would like to find or offer a group, please visit the website of the Institute for Applied Meditation: IAMheart.org. We will be glad to help you find others in your area who are interested in Heart Rhythm Meditation.

The experiences of doing Heart Rhythm Meditation alone, with a teacherless group, and with a teacher are quite different, and each represents its own challenges and opportunities.

Meditating Alone

It is difficult to master Heart Rhythm Meditation on your own, but you can gain a great deal by trying. The only obstacles you'll have are the ones you yourself create, so you'll receive the benefit of overcoming inner obstacles as well as the benefit of the practice. Your mind is very clever, and it may feel threatened by the experience of meditation, which is not logical and not strictly personal. So it will create all kinds of excuses and diversions. It may tell you, for example:

- "Meditating is so selfish. Why spend so much time on yourself?"
- "Meditation is for the wealthy who have leisure time."
- "Meditation doesn't sound like much fun."
- "It's not for you. You've done things like this before, and they don't work for you."
- "How could such simple practices produce any valuable experience?"
- "You're just going to end up frustrated, so why start?"
- "You're not good enough to do something so advanced."
- "You're much too important to spend your precious time this way."
- "You know everything in this book, so you must be beyond these practices."
- "No one else knows what you should be doing."

And innumerable versions and combinations of the above.

These excuses will test your intention. If you're able to overcome them, you'll show your commitment to living from your heart.

Make an Objective

The way to succeed when you're practicing alone is to formulate a clear objective. This objective might be one that Heart

16. Individual and Group Practice

Rhythm Meditation can help you accomplish: "to make a change in your life," or "to gain a certain capability or quality" like those described in Chapter 2. Alternatively, your objective might be to learn Heart Rhythm Meditation itself. The goals offered throughout the book are intended to serve as these objectives.

Here are some further examples of objectives related to learning the practice:

- To be able to do Heart Rhythm Meditation for 20 minutes on your own
- To be able to do one of the four Element Breaths alone
- To be able to attain the stage of contemplation with Heart Rhythm Meditation
- To be able to attain the stage of meditation with Heart Rhythm Meditation
- To be able to do Heart Rhythm Meditation with your eyes open, while working.

To accomplish such objectives, you'll need to know how to solve the frequently encountered problems described in Chapter 15.

Make a Schedule

[A person] has to learn how to recharge. Instead, he usually argues that he "has not the time" for meditation. Yet meditation is the very thing that will give him the time, and most of all for his own self, for his own welfare. [Hazrat Inayat Khan][1]

If there is constant activity and if there is all attention to the world outside, how can man ever come face to face with himself? Instead he grows older with the years and displays loss of vitality so very often. For not only when body is fatigued or

---

1 Khan, I. (1989, 239)

mind tired does this loss manifest, but in every display of emotion also. [Hazrat Inayat Khan][2]

When working alone, it is essential that you make a schedule for yourself. A schedule is helpful if you're working with a group as well, but if you're doing it alone, it's necessary. You have to make time to do the practice, every day, by not doing something else that you're used to doing now. You'll need the help that a schedule will give you.

If you follow these simple directions, you will enjoy the results. For once you actually sit down on your bench or pillow, you'll sigh, as I do, in thankfulness that you didn't miss this moment, this feeling, and this opportunity.

> There is some benefit when meditation is performed constantly in one place. . . . Such a place offers the right accommodations for the highest and finest vibrations and establishes an atmosphere of stillness. This makes it easier for others who come to such a place. [Hazrat Inayat Khan][3]

Step one. Select a place in your home to be your meditation spot. Always sit in the same spot. Keep there whatever you sit on: a pillow, a bench, or a chair.

You could say that the meditation period takes on a life of its own. Your intention conceived it; your repetition feeds it; your own breakthroughs make it grow.

> The meditation attracts wonderful, unseen beings who gather at the appointed time to enjoy the atmosphere of sacredness. If you change the time and place, or don't hold a meeting, these beings leave disappointed and it will be some time before they return again. [Vilayat Inayat Khan][4]

---

2 Khan, I. Sangitha. *Esoteric Papers.*

3 *Ibid.*

4 Khan, V. (1983)

Step two. Determine the time of day you're going to meditate. Make it specific—for example, "6:15 A.M." or "9:30 P.M.," not "after my shower" or "before breakfast."

> It is best to meditate regularly at a certain hour, every day if possible. This adds to the music of life also. [Hazrat Inayat Khan][5]

Perhaps your life doesn't have so much rhythm that you can be specific. In that case, a good place to start is to set a definite time for meditation. Then the rest of your day can revolve around that. Your meditation time becomes the stake in the sands of life.

Consider times for your practice both in the morning and in the evening.

> It must be prescribed to the student to do his exercises as he wakes in the morning, and just before he goes to bed. The importance of the process is in engraving all he practices in his subconscious mind, for that is where the phenomenon is hidden. [Hazrat Inayat Khan][6]

Step three. Set a timer for 15 to 20 minutes. This will allow you to put aside the concern that you will lose track of time. You *will* lose track of time, but the timer won't. You don't have to stop when the timer goes off, but you can.

> Fifteen minutes a day regularly will help one much more than two hours a day at one's convenience. [Hazrat Inayat Khan][7]

The question of whether to practice for 15, 20, or 30 minutes can be resolved experientially. It is important to get to the "monolithic sensation" described in Chapter 3. That physiological condition may occur as early as 10 minutes or as late as 30 minutes. If you

---

5 Khan, I. Sangitha. *Esoteric Papers.*

6 *Ibid.*

7 *Ibid.*

sit very still and are experienced with it, the sensation will occur earlier. Movement and inexperience delay it.

If you can't practice for 15 minutes, then do 5 minutes. If you can't even do 5 minutes, do at least 3 breaths. Three breaths will maintain the practice—barely. Repetition is important. The effects of meditation are cumulative: they build up.

> The effect of spiritual practices is gained like interest on capital. The practices do not always produce an effect when a person is doing them, but practices once done are never lost. They are seeds sown on the soil of one's subconscious mind and must bear fruit in due course of time. No doubt, conditions may be against, which may delay the result of practices, but it does not often happen. [Hazrat Inayat Khan][8]

Step four. Keep the daily schedule for six days a week. Meditate at the same time, in the same place. If you're traveling, keep the schedule, adjusted for the time zone. On the seventh day, meditate whenever you want to. Perhaps you'll want to meditate longer that day.

> As the whole body, mind and soul unite in meditation, it is important to have a fixed hour or fixed periods for meditation, to arrange one's time so there are hours for work, play and eating, studying and meditation, and to keep these hours as much as possible. [Hazrat Inayat Khan][9]

Step five. Progress through the chapters of this book in order, going only up to the first goal in each chapter. Leave the rest for the next step. Write out a schedule for yourself like the following, but with specific dates:

---

8 *Ibid.*
9 *Ibid.*

16. Individual and Group Practice

Step six. After doing Heart Rhythm Meditation for half a year on your own, it is strongly recommended that you find a teacher and get feedback and advice. You can do this by attending a course or seminar in your area. If that is not possible, we also have online courses where you get individualized feedback and instruction from one of our certified instructors in an intimate setting; most classes are limited to 25 students. We also offer individual instruction in our mentoring program; more information at IAMheart.org.

Step seven. For the second half of the first year, your schedule would depend on the advice of your teacher. One possibility would be to revisit each section, this time going all the way through it.

Week	Chapter
27	All of Chapter 3
28	All of Chapter 4
29-37	All of Chapters 5 through 14, going deeply into each section
38	Earth, Water, Fire, Air Breaths
39-52	Earth, Water, Fire, Air Breaths, followed by an unstructured meditation that takes off from there

Step eight. Pause at each goal in the book, and verify for yourself that you can do what the goal describes, before going on to the next goal.

Step nine. When you finish the last goal in the Air Breath, you're ready for the next course in Heart Rhythm Meditation. To receive credit for your accomplishment, you would need to take a Heart Rhythm Meditation course or demonstrate your proficiency to one of our certified teachers in an individual session. (See "Benefits of Having a Teacher" in this chapter for a description of the verification process.)

A Teacherless Group

Benefits of Practicing Together

Here are some general benefits of being in a Heart Rhythm Meditation group.

First, another person in your group can verify your experience with Heart Rhythm Meditation. A simple electronic instrument is commonly available that indicates when your heart beats. It allows you to demonstrate that you can feel your heart beat and receive verification. With the instrument attached to your finger but its flashing light out of your sight, the other person asks you to make a tone whenever you feel your heart beat. The other person can then verify that your tones correspond to the instrument's flashing light, both while you hold your breath and while your breath moves.

Another way to verify your heartbeat is to observe your Square Breath while watching the heartbeat instrument. If you've been doing this practice, you know that success with it requires more than simply knowing the technique. The ability to maintain the Square Breath, in which the heartbeat and the breath rate are in harmony, requires harmony and stability in your emotions, and peace in place of fear. Achieving it is a great accomplishment of personal and spiritual integration.

The second reason to do Heart Rhythm Meditation in a group is that meditation is much easier in a group than alone, especially when you're first learning it. Learning doesn't require a teacher as much as a group of other people who are committed to it.

> Spiritual students, by combining their efforts, collectively build an atmosphere, an area of calm and quiet, the center of fine vibrations, which becomes a healing center. People often imagine about healing pilgrimages and some do not believe in the miraculous cures, but this is a mistake. The faith of the people, their prayers, build up this atmosphere, and the healthy ones who go there actually heal the sick, and the sick, in the area of those purified atoms, become well. [Hazrat Inayat Khan][10]

> There is a reason why people meditate in a group, with or without a teacher or leader. The teacher or leader serves to draw them closer together, to harmonize them, like the conductor of the orchestra harmonizes the musicians and their instruments. In the orchestra it is not only the instruments which are brought into attunement to each other but the players themselves. In the meditation hall the atmosphere serves to tune the hearts of the devotees, to bring them, so to speak, into consonant pitch. [Hazrat Inayat Khan][11]

---

10 *Ibid.*

11 *Ibid.*

Problems will arise with your meditations; others may be able to remember the solutions from their own experience or from a different understanding of the instructions in this book. Problems will arise in life too, and others may be able to help you apply Heart Rhythm Meditation to the challenges you face.

Third, you'll get to know some wonderful people. You'll feel disarmed, at ease, vulnerable, and understood by a group of people with whom you share a profound and deeply moving experience. It is a vital experience for living from the heart.

Forming a Group

One way to find a Heart Rhythm group is to put up a note in a bookstore that carries this book. Another way is to post a note on the Institute for Applied Meditation Website.

If possible, your group should set aside a room exclusively for Heart Rhythm Meditation, or use a room that is dedicated solely to meditation. This room will develop a wonderful feeling. A second choice would be to use a room that is used for quiet and contemplative purposes, like a room at a church, temple, or library. A third choice would be to use a room that is used for other purposes but is consistently available to the group, like a room in the home of one member. A fourth choice would be a general-purpose room in a public facility like a school or community center.

Every aspect of forming a group is itself practice in living from the heart. You'll need to involve all the elements of the heart in your group, developing, for example:

Qualities of the Group	Elements
Desire to understand yourself and this practice deeply	Air
Enthusiasm for the practice	Fire
Friendliness and acceptance	Water
Security and commitment	Earth

Security means both confidentiality and privacy as well as the group's reliability and steadiness. Meet at the same time and place every week. (See "Make a Schedule" in this chapter.) *Friendliness* among the members and toward newcomers is a natural characteristic of the heart. *Enthusiasm* comes from knowing how important the practice is to both your practical and your spiritual life. Your happiness is to share this practice with others: to help them and to be challenged and helped by them. All of this supports the objective of *understanding*—how do breath and heart rhythms affect yourself and others? With this understanding you can have better health, deeper relationships, be more genuine and more fulfilled, and more useful to others.

The material you have to work with is the experience of the group with the practice, both in the room and outside the room in life. After a practice, share your experience with the group. It is helpful and supportive for the others to hear of both your difficulties and your successes with it. Share also how the practice works in your life, as specifically as you can. Stay with your experience; that's what is real, and more helpful than any commentary.

We suggest you rotate the leadership of the group. When it's your turn to lead, your thoughts should be of how to serve. First decide what preparation is necessary beforehand. It's a good idea to do some physical movement before you get started. An ideal way to do this is to follow along with the Heart Rhythm Movement DVD led by Susanna Bair, which includes exercises which lengthen and tone the body gently, while energizing the heart. Atmosphere may be established using music, or incense, or silence, or friendly hugs, according to your feeling. You may review instructions from earlier chapters of the book, leading up to the current chapter.

Then select what part of the current chapter to read and what to say in your own words. Establish the pace of the practice so that the group is able to follow it and yet doesn't become impatient. You may have to accommodate members of the group who have started earlier or later than the others and therefore have different capabilities. After the practice is over, you can draw out those who want to share their experience.

When you are leading, the most important thing you do is to communicate the feeling of your own heart through your voice. Your voice will help the others find their hearts, go into the feelings there, honor what they find there, and feel safe in the Heart Rhythm Meditation.

The benefit to you as the group leader is that you will learn the most. Even if you knew the practice before, you will learn what you have learned. We don't know how much we know until we have to teach it.

The group can discuss whether to repeat the same chapter next week or advance to another one. This discussion, too, is a way of practicing living from the heart. There is no need to rush through; it is better to bring everyone in the group along. Everyone will progress at a different speed, depending on their experience and their nature. Sometimes, if the experience of one chapter is eluding you, the best way to "get it" is to go on to the next one.

In determining the pace of the group, you also need to balance learning the practice with applying it. Some people will want to stay with a chapter, like the one on full exhalation, until they see proof of its effect in their lives. Others will be content just to learn how to do full exhalation, trusting that the results will come. These are different modes of learning, and both must be accommodated.

An Example

Anyville. A teacherless Heart Rhythm group is assembling. Some of the people have been friends for years and discovered a joint interest in meditation. Some of them met by taking courses or seminars with the Institute for Applied Meditation. The mother of one member initially came at her daughter's urging, then found she loved it. A notice that one of them posted on their church's bulletin board brought another person. It was no problem to assemble a group of ten, some seven of whom come in any one week. The stability of the group is helped by keeping constant the place it meets.

The leadership rotates, for several reasons. First, no one feels knowledgeable enough to take on the responsibility of being a "teacher." Second, the group is generally wary of "groups," and no one is seeking to "join" anything. Third, an opportunity to share the leadership is part of the attraction.

The group begins with an invocation, or statement of belief and shared goal:

> Toward the One, the perfection of love, harmony and beauty, the Only Being, united with all the illuminated souls who form the embodiment of the Master, the spirit of guidance. [Hazrat Inayat Khan] [12]

After the invocation, the group members check in. "Does anyone have anything they would like to share before the practice begins?" today's leader asks. "Numerous issues can get in the way of listening to the heart's beat." One person speaks about his struggles with his schedule; another speaks of difficulties in her marriage. Never is there blame for another. The challenges of life are all seen as internal dilemmas. There is no discussion of people's reports except maybe a question of clarification. But everyone is moved by the sharing of the others, and by expressing their feelings, they offer their support and compassion for each other.

Tonight it's David's turn to lead. He's thought about it all week since the last meeting, but he hasn't "prepared" anything. He trusts his heart, especially as it has been directed by a week's focus and inspired by daily meditations on his own. The group has been meeting for a year, so they've gone through all the chapters of this book, having spent from one to three weeks on each one. Now they're on Part 3 on their second pass. They support each other in attempting to achieve the goals of each chapter, but they don't al-

---

12 www.hazrat-inayat-khan.org: Message: Sayings: Invocation

ways achieve them. The group goes on anyway, and often a person gets it later. If not, there's always the next pass through. They'll keep doing this until they all get it, or they decide to go on to the next course.

David is reading a section that stimulates discussion. When the group started out, the members used to try to outdo each other with their zeal, or the intensity of the phenomena they experienced, or their clearness, or their level of understanding. Some of that competitiveness remains, but they've all learned how a voice that speaks from real experience sounds, so that real voice has become the standard. The voices of opinion and guessing have become obvious by contrast. The members keep their comments real by talking about their own experiences in meditation and in applying them to life. The common objective is to be able to work with and relate to others using Heart Rhythm Meditation. They've found that, to various degrees, they can recall this state in the midst of life, when they need it. It has given everyone hope that they can change the things they want to change and accomplish the things they desire to accomplish.

David reads the instructions for the practice, starting at the beginning and skipping through the early stages as he feels necessary, then concentrating on the new instructions. It's a help to have them read aloud so everyone else can keep their eyes closed. David's own meditative state, transmitted behind his words, inspires everyone further. They all say the same thing—that meditating in a group is consistently much easier and better than meditating alone. Something happens there that everyone shares in creating and receiving. But they also practice alone to build up their experience and ability.

Through the process, they've built up a set of common, shared experiences that rarely develops in groups, and this process has drawn them closely together. Having shared the beats of their hearts, they find it easy to express their hearts with each other. They are not guarded, but are open and vulnerable. They have become expert at the most vulnerable sharing, silence, and the most intimate exchange, breath and heartbeat. They've looked at each other through eyes that are opened by their inner awareness and seen the face behind the face—the beautiful countenance of one another's soul. Having glimpsed what one has always been, it is easier to see what one will be. This is the sacred trust they uphold with each other—to remember who they are when they forget. "I remember who you are when you forget, and you remember who I am when I forget." They can do this because of their Heart Rhythm Meditation.

A Group with a Teacher

If you think of your teacher as your brother or sister, it is true; if you think of your teacher as your friend, it is true also; and if you think of your spiritual teacher as your servant, it is also true. Besides this, there is no place for any other discussion. [Hazrat Inayat Khan] [13]

The teacher's work is to help another person to find out for himself or herself; to develop, and to discover what is true and what is not. There are no doctrines to impart. There are no principles to lay down. There are no tenets to which the lives of pupils must be restricted. The teacher is just a guide along the path. The teacher is the one who kindles the light that is already in the pupil. [Hazrat Inayat Khan] [14]

Benefits of Having a Teacher

Meditating in a group is easier than meditating alone, and meditating with a teacher is easier still. A teacher is someone who is thoroughly experienced with a practice and how to teach the practice. A teacher was first a student. He or she is appointed as a teacher when they have demonstrated their mastery of the practice, both in

---

13 www.hazrat-inayat-khan.org: Message: The Supplementary Papers: Class for Mureeds 1

14 www.hazrat-inayat-khan.org: Message: The Supplementary Papers: Mysticism VII

technique and in application. The Institute for Applied Meditation offers several levels of certification for teachers.

> It is easy to become a teacher, but difficult to become a pupil. [Hazrat Inayat Khan] [15]

There are primarily four benefits from working with a teacher.

First, a teacher "opens the window," affecting the entire group's experience of higher consciousness. The "window" is a limit that normally exists in people's ability to attain a meditative state. The teacher has learned not only how to meditate but how to hold open the window for a whole group of people. A specific technique that teachers learn allows the group to easily go beyond their normal limits.

> The teacher can, by his/her presence, make the accommodation for still finer vibrations. So there is at least one advantage to having a teacher who is more than a leader, who can elevate the feeling of a room. Yet the faith of people, their prayers and their attitudes also help to strengthen the atmosphere of a chapel, a hall or a temple. [Hazrat Inayat Khan] [16]

> The breath of the teacher is, so to speak, the ladder by means of which the student climbs on his way to God. The breath of the teacher helps to establish rhythm in meditation and also to refine the atmosphere. The finer the vibrations that are received into the atmosphere, the more beneficial is it to those who participate in the silence. If the pupil is able to adjust his breath to that of the teacher it is most helpful. At the same time the teacher does what he can to reach the heart of every pupil in his presence. [Hazrat Inayat Khan] [17]

Before you have learned how to attain the meditative state, it is very difficult to imagine what it's like.

---

15 www.hazrat-inayat-khan.org: Message: Sayings: Gayan: Boulas
16 Khan, I. Sangitha. *Esoteric Papers.*
17 *Ibid.*

I REMEMBER WHEN *my eldest son was a toddler, encountering a pool of water for the first time; he was afraid of it, confused by it, and had no idea what to do with it. With one hand under his belly, I held him up while he paddled around. He was ecstatic! It obviously felt good, and he had a feeling that he could actually swim! Meditating with a teacher is like that. It requires very little effort, it's completely safe, and it feels wonderful.* PURAN

After one or many such experiences, the new student will desire to learn how to do it alone. Then the contribution of the teacher shifts from the direct intervention, "opening the window," to teaching the techniques and attitudes needed to open one's own window.

The second advantage of having a teacher is that the teacher can verify the group members' experience with the Element Breaths. This verification is done when the teacher sits directly opposite a member and meditates with the member. The teacher experiences sensations inside himself or herself that resonate to the energy the member experiences within. Consequently, the teacher can feel the spreading, steady magnetic field of another's heart in their Earth Breath, the descending stream of energy in them during their Water Breath, the light of their heart in their Fire Breath, and the atmosphere of sacredness in their Air Breath. No instruments to measure these phenomena currently exist, but one can learn to sense them, and that is what teachers of Heart Rhythm Meditation are trained to do.

Third, the teacher models how to relate to the Heart Rhythm Meditation. He or she is an example of someone who is trying to live from the heart.

To even state this as an objective is remarkable and opens the teacher to criticism. Having a high ideal is a (fire) element of the heart, and as we learn to live from the heart, we want to have our ideals inspired and confirmed by a living example. However, the teacher may have a different ideal, may be working on different aspects of living from the heart, or may simply fall short, as everyone does at times. When they consider the teacher's example, the group can show that compassion and acceptance are also (water) elements of living from the heart. You should keep your ideals, but apply them to yourself, apply compassion and acceptance to others, even to your teachers.

Finally, the thought of your teacher will make your own meditation easier when you're alone. Something about meditation can't be taught, but it can be caught. When you sit down to practice, think that you are linking up with your teacher and that you are meditating as he or she is. You'll find that your usual obstacles are removed.

> The more the student sits in silence before the teacher, the easier it is to adjust the breath of teacher and pupil. It is by this means that the pupil receives the blessing from the teacher. This may be no special knowledge. However it does mean that the heart becomes more sensitive and through its sensitivity it can grow in wisdom, insight, compassion and love. [Hazrat Inayat Khan] [18]

Finding a Teacher

Throughout the United States and Europe are capable teachers who share the methodology of Heart Rhythm Meditation as it is described in this book. Some of these teachers are certified by the Institute for Applied Meditation and follow this method carefully. Their insights are fed back through the Institute and will enrich and extend the practice. Teachers in other schools use the material here to augment the method they have learned.

Anyone who has been certified as a Heart Rhythm Meditation teacher is part of the Institute's faculty. The faculty all use the same materials, including this book, for Heart Rhythm Meditation; its teacher manual; and drafts of future books for the later courses in Heart Rhythm Meditation. The fees for the courses and for indi-

---

18 *Ibid.*

vidual feedback and advice are standardized throughout the faculty. The Institute for Applied Meditation will help you locate a teacher near you through our website, IAMheart.org.

An Example

We're leading a small group of meditators for a course in Heart Rhythm Meditation. As the hour approaches, the group starts to assemble. Bill and Ken drive in together from a distance. Alima picks up Duncan on her way. Liz walks over. Terry is taking the course as a follow-up to a Heart Rhythm Meditation training course he took at work. Teresa was referred by her neurologist. Lynn and Dave like to come together, but sometimes they take turns. Lisa has phoned her regrets. Charlie comes right from work. Gail and Steve found out about us online and started a week late.

People settle into their meditative posture, spines straight, hands relaxed on the thighs. Some do a few neck and shoulder rolls to relax any tension. We sit in a rough circle so all can be seen. Everyone has their eyes closed. We quickly settle into our inner quietness. One or the other of us leads the meditation, speaking softly to the group about the stages we need to go through.

PURAN: When I'm leading, I like to remember being on retreat, facing the sun and filling it with light from my heart so it can shine. Each person in the group becomes a sun for me, and we interact in silence through the breath and the heartbeat.

The focus of each person is on what is happening inside themselves. Whatever this energy is that we are sharing, it seems to be emerging from within each of us, not coming from outside. The energy gives a very definite physical sensation, but the more glorious experience is happening in our minds and in our emotions. The meditation is changing the way we think about ourselves; as it does so it's solving problems, answering questions, clearing away obstacles, and building up a powerful engine of the heart.

16. Individual and Group Practice.

We do this together, and we can tell what is happening in the group because it is happening in each one of us in the same way. Sometimes Susanna is inspired to speak when I am silent, and she raises the pitch, so to speak. Sometimes I speak again, describing the experience I'm having or giving an instruction that will cause a further change.

An hour goes by without anyone noticing. An hour and a half may pass if the group is experienced, with no one suffering from the absolute stillness or getting lost in the ethers of the mind. An occasional word, reminding us all of the technique or the application of this state, keeps us in rhythm with our hearts.

Then we move a little more, and the eyes see the outside of that world that we have been feeling from the inside. The most beautiful sight is the eyes of each other.

APPENDIX 1: THE SOURCE OF HEART RHYTHM MEDITATION

BASIC RHYTHMS

Our mother's heartbeat is our earliest experience in the womb. Our first breath is experienced as we exit her womb, and our last breath defines the end of our life.

It must have been one of the earliest observances of ancient contemplatives that the body has two rhythms: the breath rate and the heart rate, the coordination of which produces an experience of integration that is essentially spiritual.

The method of Heart Rhythm Meditation consists of a conscious, deep, full breath that is in rhythm with the breath, with a concentration on the energetic heart as the center of existence. Parts of this method emerge from many contemplative traditions. Two that we know of are the Christian and Sufi traditions.

THE CHRISTIAN TRADITION

In the time of the Apostles of Christ, there was a practice called the *prayer of the heart*. By the seventh century, this practice became known as the *Jesus Prayer*, and some variation of this practice has been used in monasteries ever since. In the Jesus Prayer, the words *Kyrie Eleison, Christe Eleison*, (Lord have mercy on me, Christ have mercy on me) are said with an awareness of the heart, while breathing consciously. This practice is the topic of the book, *The Way of a Pilgrim*, written by an anonymous Russian mystic.

Appendix 1: The Source of Heart Rhythm Meditation

The oldest description we have of the Jesus Prayer is by Abba Philemon, a student and companion of the holy Apostle Paul, who died in 54 AD. A sixth century book called *The Life of Abba Philemon* gives the following instructions:

> With the help of your imagination find the place of the heart and stay there with attention. Lead the mind from the head into the heart and say, "Lord Jesus Christ, have mercy on me," quietly with the lips or mentally, whichever is more convenient; say the prayer slowly and reverently. As much as possible guard the attention of your mind and do not allow any thoughts to enter in.

Here we see the use of the homonym "heart" to mean both the physical and emotional heart, a key aspect of Heart Rhythm Meditation. The Christian practice developed further over the centuries as the saints stressed four fundamentals in their descriptions of how to practice the Jesus Prayer:

1. Concentration on the heart

2. Concentration on the breath

3. Sincere, devotional, emotion

4. Invocation of Jesus Christ

The first three of these are fundamental to Heart Rhythm Meditation. Especially important is the emphasis on emotion. In Heart Rhythm Meditation, we are working with more than consciousness; we are working with energy, which is experienced as strong emotion.

In the quotation above, Abba Philemon did not mention breath, but it was an early part of the practice, as Houlden writes:

At some point these desert contemplatives began to use the name of Jesus as their invocation. In the fourth century text, *The Life of Anthony*, by Athanasius of Alexandria (c. 293-373), there was already a practice of invoking Christ in a repetitive prayer, even linking the breath to its repetition, as if the one who prayed was actually breathing Jesus: 'Anthony called his two companions... and said to them, "Always breathe Christ."[1]

Athanasius, relating the death of Anthony, gives Anthony's final words: (Schaff 519)

For ye know the treachery of the demons, how fierce they are, but how little power they have. Wherefore fear them not, but rather *ever breathe Christ*, and trust Him. Live as though dying daily.

The emphasis is on being in the heart rather than the head, through concentration on Jesus Christ. St. John Climacus (525-606 AD), author of *The Ladder of Divine Ascent*, affirms the importances of the breath, writing simply "May the memory of Jesus be united with your breathing; then you will understand the use of silence."[2]

Not every writer in the Christian tradition mentions all the fundamentals listed above, nor do they place equal emphasis on them. For example, Philotheus of Sinai stresses concentration and emotion when he writes:

Let us go forward with the heart completely attentive and the soul fully conscious. For if attentiveness and prayer are daily joined together, they become like Elias' fire-bearing chariot, raising us to heaven. What do I mean? A spiritual heaven, with sun, moon and stars, is formed in the blessed heart of one who has reach a state of awareness, or who strives to attain it.

The goal of the one who strives after righteousness, on which his mind should be firmly set, is to treasure the presence of God in his heart as a priceless pearl or some other precious jewel. He should disregard everything, even his present life, for the sake of having God in his heart.

And so every hour and every moment let us zealously guard our heart from thoughts that obscure the mirror of our soul, which

1 Houlden (2003, 815)

2 Kaldoubovsky (1992, 193)

should only reflect the radiant image of Jesus Christ, who is the wisdom and the power of God the Father. Let us continuously seek the kingdom within our heart and we will certainly find the seed, the pearl, and the yeast and everything else if we purify the eye of our mind; for Christ said, "The kingdom of God is within you" (Luke 17:20).

The 19th century Saint John of Kronstadt lays great emphasis on the emotion:

When you pray, keep to the rule that it is better to say five words from the depth of your heart than ten thousand words with your tongue only.[3]

Saint Hesychius of Jerusalem draws attention to the link between emotion and concentration:

To call on Jesus perpetually with warm desire, full of sweetness and joy, fills the air of the heart with joyous stillness; and this comes from extreme attention.[4]

It becomes clear what is meant by the heart in the Christian tradition in the writing of a modern scholar: "The heart is man's feelings (affect). The heart is man's volition (will). The heart is man's mind (cognition). These three elements are together in one unbreakable unity."[5]

In the words of Saint Callistus we see that the concentration on the heart is incredibly profound, for the heart is capable of union with God:

---

3 *ibid.* 52

4 Kaldoubovsky (1992, 297)

5 Logothetis (1982, 17)

> A monk should always live with the name of Lord Jesus, so that the heart absorbs the Lord and the Lord the heart, and the two become one.[6]

St Ignatius reveals that the way to find this state of union within the heart is through repeated invocation:

> Do not estrange your heart from God, but abide in Him and always guard your heart by remembering our lord Jesus Christ, until the name of the Lord becomes rooted in the heart and you cease to think of anything else. May Christ be glorified in you.[7]

St Dorotheus provides another perspective on how the repetition of sincere prayer from the heart unfolds:

> Do you wish to learn to pray with the mind and heart? I will teach you. At first you should make the prayer of Jesus with your voice, that is, with your lips, tongue and speech, aloud by yourself. When the lips, tongue and senses are satisfied with prayer pronounced vocally, then vocal prayer stops and it begins to be said in a whisper. After this, one should contemplate with the mind, and always regard and attend diligently to the feeling in the throat. The mental Prayer of the Heart constantly begins to rise automatically by the nod (of God – i.e., by the action of divine grace) – begins to be carried about and act at all times, during every kind of work, in every place.'[8]

The prayer of the heart that all these saints describe is designed to create the perfection of love in your heart, as described in Corinthians 1:13:

Love suffers long and is kind; love does not envy; love does not parade itself, is not puffed up; does not behave rudely,

---

6 Kaldoubovsky (1992, 193)

7 *ibid.*

8 Brianchaninov (1995, 51)

does not seek its own, is not provoked, thinks no evil; does not rejoice in iniquity, but rejoices in the truth; bears all things, believes all things, hopes all things, endures all things. Love never fails... And now abide faith, hope, love, these three; but the greatest of these is love.

Only in a heart that is overflowing with love can it have meaning to "rejoice always, pray without ceasing, [and] in everything give thanks", as it says in Thessalonians 5:16-23.

It is the love of the Divine Being that leads to the perfection of love in a human being. In the words of St Isaac the Syrian: "Love incited by something external is like a small lamp whose flame is fed with oil, or like a stream fed by rains where flow stops when the rains cease. But love whose object is God, is like a fountain gushing forth from the earth. Its flow never ceases, for He Himself is the source of this love and also its food which never grows scarce."[9]

Later, in the 13th century, St Gregory of Sinai affirms the importance of the breath, specifically a rhythmic breath, writing:

Regulate your breathing also, because rhythmic breathing can disperse distracting thoughts.[10]

One of St Gregory's fellow monks on Mount Athos was Nicephorus the Solitary, who offered even clearer instruction, writing:

You know that we only exhale our breath, the air that we inhale, because of our heart. Sit down, recollect your spirit, introduce it—I mean your spirit—into your nostrils; that is the route your breath takes to reach the heart. Pull it in, forcing it to descend to your heart at the same time as the air is breathed in... do not

---

9 Kaldoubovsky (1992, 257)
10 *ibid.* 275-6

> have any occupation or meditation other than the cry, *Lord Jesus Christ, Son of God, have mercy on me!* No truce, not at any price.

From what was written and preserved of the methods of prayer in the mystical Christian tradition, we can see that all the fundamentals of Heart Rhythm Meditation were developed. Yet it would be a mistake to think that this method is somehow doctrinal or sectarian. On the contrary, since everyone has a heart, it is for everyone, and it will work for anyone, religion or no religion. The Christian mystics used the name of Christ because his name was sacred to them. If you don't feel the same way about Jesus Christ, then choose a name that is sacred to you; perhaps that word is a name from another religious tradition, like "Buddha" or "Moses", or perhaps it's a name that has no connection to an established religion, but connects you to a divine quality, like "Peace" or "Love".

Though the method of Heart Rhythm Meditation has roots in the Christian tradition, no doubt its roots are far older, as it seems clear that the methods used by Jesus Christ, John the Baptist, and others at that time go back to the older Egyptian schools.[11] Perhaps it's the way of the modern world to rediscover the knowledge that was held by the wise long ago. Certainly new features have been added to the practice in the intervening centuries.

SUFISM

We learned the method of Heart Rhythm Meditation from our meditation teacher, Pir Vilayat Inayat Khan (1917-2004). He learned the method from his father, Hazrat Inayat Khan, the first Sufi to teach in the US and Europe, starting in 1910. The Sufis are mystics who have gone through a training to attain to an extraordinarily beautiful state of character development. They are not con-

---

11 Baigent (2006, 133-179)

fined to any religion, although they are comfortable in any religion or any non-religious group of people who look deeply into life.

For thousands of years, researchers have been exploring the nature and limits of the human being through direct experimentation. Some of this exploration we call scientific, some of it we call spiritual, some of it we call psychological. All of this research contributes to our ability to fulfill the grand human goal of the development of the heart, and ultimately to the experience of unity.

One special group of researchers are the mystics, those who have a direct, personal experience of the oneness of reality and who can recapture that experience at will. The experience of mystics is the basis for all religion and philosophy. In stark contrast to the popular conception of mystics as otherworldly, a mystic is ultimately concerned about how to live a better life here in this reality on this planet at this time, and how to help those who seek help.

An example of an American mystic is Walt Whitman, who wrote:

In all people I see myself—none more, and not one a barleycorn less; And the good or bad I say of myself, I say of them.[12]

Whitman expresses the mystic's view of unity: the unified experience of life in which every person affects every other person, every action rebounds in every other action, every thought echos in every person's thinking, and every heart feels all that every heart feels. In this view, the flowers floating on top of a pond, that seem to be separate and distinct plants, are actually one water lily connected by the common network of stems and roots beneath the surface.

The mystical experience may occur spontaneously to anyone, or it may develop slowly over a lifetime of study and reflection upon life. It is the goal of every life to know by personal experience that this life is one. Everyone comes to this realization sooner or later. When it comes before death, it is a great benefit, for it makes sense of life.

---

12 Whitman (1900), Song of Myself, Verse 395

Appendix 1: The Source of Heart Rhythm Meditation

The development of the heart is a crucial landmark in the progression of a mystic. The demonstration of the forms of love through one's personality is the mark of a mystic. A special group of mystics are called "Sufis." Technically, Sufis are mystics who formally learn mysticism as students of a teacher. Through their own discipleship, each Sufi has learned at least one way to develop the mystical state and thereby to progress on the spiritual path toward the Truth that underlies appearances. Through their experience, students may eventually become teachers themselves. Since the Sufis had to learn mysticism through a conscious process, they value the stages of the process and can recognize the mark of authentic spiritual experience in another. The companionship of a teacher makes the lifelong journey toward mysticism into a caravan of deep friendship among kindred souls who aspire to the same destination.

Hazrat Inayat Khan writes, "a Sufi is one who seeks Truth, in any tradition or outside of any tradition. Everyone wants to claim Truth for their own group, but it cannot be narrowed or contained for it is the essence of wisdom; it comes from pure experience and it abides by no dogma or rules."

Hazrat Inayat Khan stressed that his approach was free from any ties to any established doctrine:

The lineage we follow originated from the ancient school of Egyptian mysteries, a school which existed even before Abraham, the father of three great religions: Christianity, Judaism, and Islam. Sufism is neither a religion nor a philosophy, neither deism nor atheism, nor is it a moral, nor a special kind of mysticism, being free from the usual religious sectarianism. If ever it could be called a religion, it would only be as a religion of love, harmony, and beauty.

The highest heaven is our own heart, and that which man generally knows as love, to us is God. Different people have thought of the Deity as the Creator, as the Judge, as the King, as the Supreme Being; but we call him the Beloved. Are there any dogmas, are there any rituals or ceremonies which we adhere to? There is nothing which restricts us. At the same time we are free to make use of any ritual, any ceremony that we thinks suited to our purpose.[13]

Sufism is thought of by Muslims as the mystical side of Islam, and indeed many Sufis have been Muslims, but Sufis can be found in every tradition. One of the greatest Sufis recognized by Islam was Jelal-ud-Din Rumi, of Konya, Turkey, founder of the Mevlana Order of "Whirling Dervishes." He said,

I am neither Christian, nor Jew, nor Hindu, nor Moslem.
I am not of the East, nor of the West, nor of the Land, nor of the Sea... I have put duality away; I have seen that the two worlds are one.[14]

Another Sufi revered by Islam was Moinuddin Chisti, who emigrated from Iran to India and taught Sufism to Hindus. Muslims say he brought Islam to India, but Hindus say he just taught Hinduism. His tomb is one of the rare spots in all of India that is a pilgrimage point for both religions.

The Sufis have often been punished and even killed by religious authorities for their unorthodox views. One of the greatest Sufi teachers, Ibn Mansur Al Hallaj, was tortured and then crucified by Muslim clerics. Sometimes Christians applied the label "Muslim" to those, like the early Transcendentalists and Unitarians, whom they wanted to defame. Modern Sufis are respectful of the label "Islamic" and are just as respectful of "Christian," "Neoplatonist," "New Age," and any of the many other labels they've been given. But the truth is that Sufis eschew all labels and titles, even the title "Sufi," as they eschew all dogma. They worship love, harmony, and beauty; their scripture is the book of nature, and their altar is the heart.

One Westerner whom we honor as a Sufi is Saint Francis, who encountered eastern Sufis in the crusades and who brought Sufism

---

13 www.hazrat-inayat-khan.org: Message: Vol 9, The Unity of Religious Ideals: The Ideal of the Sufi

14 Jelal-ud-din Rumi, in Nicholson (1898, II)

to many others, including Saint Claire.[15] The back-to-the-essence form of Christianity that he taught is a characteristically Sufi approach. But identifying Sufis is difficult because they themselves don't always use the name "Sufi."

Walt Whitman didn't have a living teacher and didn't have students who became mystics as he was. He never identified his inspirational source as Sufi, even though the three books that he read over and over again throughout his life, The *Rubiyat* of Omar Khayyám, *One Thousand and One Tales of Arabian Nights*, and the works of Shakespeare[16], are all Sufi teaching materials. The same truth can be expressed in any religion, or in the language of science, poetry, or music.

Because all mystical traditions recognize unity as the truth, there are "Sufis" in all religions and traditions, and in no tradition. There are Muslims who are Sufis, and there are Buddhists and Christians and Jews and Native Americans who are Sufis. Not every practitioner of a religion becomes a Sufi—only those who recognize, as Thomas Merton did, the kinship among all who seek the heart. Father Merton left his Trappist monastery and found a deep brotherhood with the Tibetan Buddhists, among whom he died. While some come to Sufism through religion, philosophy, or science, others call themselves Sufis because they have recognized all paths as one path and have linked themselves to a Sufi teacher.

I ONCE INTRODUCED *Heart Rhythm Meditation to a rabbi. He told me, "You have become Elijah for me. You bring me this method of the heart like the wine in Elijah's cup." At another time, I taught a Jesuit priest who exclaimed, "After twenty years of searching, I have found Jesus by the help of a Sufi." These statements are themselves typical of the sentiments of Sufis, which the rabbi and the priest had become. A Sufi is always a*

---

15 Shah (1977, 257)

16 It is an interesting coincidence that Muslim Sufis are sometimes organized into schools headed by a *Pir*, or elder, who may have one or more senior students called a *Sheik*. The head of the school may then be referred to as the *Sheiks' Pir*, a homonym for the poet's name.

student and recognizes the One Teacher everywhere. Regardless of what is actually taught, the real student is inspired to find that for which he is currently searching. I was only talking about the heart, but the rabbi found the wine of Elijah, and the priest found the presence of Christ. PURAN

Our discovery of Heart Rhythm Meditation came out of decades of practice with a Sufi school. What does a Sufi school teach? A method by which one may experience much more than one normally experiences and, from the integration of that experience, form a more holistic understanding of himself or herself. A Sufi doesn't study a religion or even all religions; a Sufi studies religion, for there is only one. This religion is the softening of the heart, making it easily moved by beauty and able to convey love. It is what causes the ego to bow and the ideal to soar. It is what causes one to remember the awe and wonder of the universe. It is the religion of the heart. Who are the prophets of this religion? Whoever has attained the realization of unity, for no matter what culture or race or gender a mystic belongs to, the experience of unity is one and the same. A Sufi finds it unnecessary to debate the various approaches of different traditions. People have different understandings according to their various experiences and their interpretations of those experiences. Rather than debate, the Sufi loves to dialogue about what each one has truly discovered about reality, beyond opinions, and to share together their methods of discovery.

Beyond that, Sufis find the very presence of each other incredibly uplifting. They may play music, or sing, or sit in silence, or try to say what they are just barely capable of expressing in words, or none of the above, for all they really need to do is remind each other of the heart.

As unbroken lines of teacher-to-student-become-teacher through thousands of years and many cultures, Sufis are a living treasure chest of humanity's spiritual discoveries and practices. A Sufi school will teach the methods used for personal and spiritual exploration by the hierophants of ancient Egypt, the Zoroastrian magi who initiated Christ, the hermit Hesychasts of the fourth century A.D. who formulated the "Kyrie Eleison" chant, the Jewish

Kabbalists who developed the "Tree of Life," and the alchemists who linked ancient Egyptian mysteries with Christian mysticism. The spiritual treasures of the great prophets, masters, and saints are not kept by the Sufis as historians catalog artifacts. The treasures of their methods of self-discovery are kept alive by those who hold them in their hearts and continue the practices of their spiritual ancestors while pushing ahead into new realms of spirituality in their own time.

In 1910 a renowned musician and Sufi teacher in India was asked by his teacher to go to the West. As a result, Hazrat Inayat Khan became the first Sufi to teach in America. His son, Vilayat, took up his father's mission of teaching meditation and the philosophy of the Sufis and has become internationally known for his integration of mysticism, science, and psychology. Their caravan is the one to which we belong.

With the maturity of his soul, a man desires to probe the depths of life, he desires to discover the power latent within him, he longs to know the sources and goal of his life, he yearns to understand the aim and meaning of his life, he wishes to understand the inner significance of things, and he wants to uncover all that is covered by name and form.

He seeks insight into cause and effect, he wants to touch the mystery of time and space, and he wishes to find the missing link between God and man—where man ends, where God begins. [17]

---

17 www.hazrat-inayat-khan.org: Message: Vol 9, The Unity of Religious Ideals: 5 Desires of Man: 4. Desire to Probe the Depths of Life

APPENDIX 2: GOALS AND LANDMARKS OF HEART RHYTHM MEDITATION

The following list gives the goals and landmarks of Heart Rhythm Meditation in the order presented in the text, for easy reference.

Appendix 2: Goals and Landmarks of Heart Rhythm Meditation

BECOME AWARE OF WHAT IN YOUR BEING HAS   292
COME FROM YOUR ANCESTRY, WHAT HAS COME
FROM YOUR CULTURE, AND WHAT HAS COME FROM
YOUR UNIQUE, PERSONAL LIFE EXPERIENCE.

APPENDIX 3: THE WORKS OF HAZRAT INAYAT KHAN

Hazrat Inayat Khan (1883-1927) was an Indian musician and sage who lectured in the United States and Europe on the unity of all religions, presenting a comprehensive method of developing the heart. His teachings form the single most important influence to our work at the Institute for Applied Meditation and the material in this book.

IAM has created an online database of Hazrat Inayat Khan's teaching so that it can be easily accessed and studied. All the references in this book to his teachings can be found on this database, at www.hazrat-inayat-khan.org.

The system of referencing used in this book for Hazrat Inayat Khan's lectures and poetry is designed to make it easy to find on the website. For example, the quote:

Rocks will open and make way for the lover.

This quote is referenced as:

www.hazrat-inayat-khan.org: Message: Complete Works: Sayings: Gayan: Boulas.

The passage can also be found using the search function.

REFERENCES

Baigent, Michael. (2006) *The Jesus Papers: Exposing the Greatest Cover-Up in History*. New York: HarperCollins.

Bair, Puran and Susanna. (2007) *Energize Your Heart in Four Dimensions*. Tucson, AZ: Living Heart Media.

Barks, Coleman, trans. (1995) *The Essential Rumi*. San Francisco: Harper.

Basu, Shrabani. (2007) *Spy Princess: The Life of Noor Inayat Khan*. New Lebanon, NY: Omega Publications.

Benson, Herbert. (1976) *The Relaxation Response*. New York: William Morris.

Benson, Herbert; Lehmann, John W.; Malhotra, M. S., Goldman, Ralph F.; Hopkins, Jeffrey; Epstein, Mark D. (1982) "Body temperature changes during the practice of g Tum-mo yoga". *Nature*. 295: 234 - 236

Benson, Herbert, and Mary Stark. (1996) *Timeless Healing: The Power and Biology of Belief*. New York: Scribner.

Bentov, Itzhak. (1977) *Stalking the Wild Pendulum: On the Mechanics of Consciousness*. Rochester, Vt.: Destiny Books.

Brianchaninov, Ignatius. (1995) *On the Prayer of Jesus*. St John of Kronstadt Press.

Cromie, William J. (2002) "Research: Meditation changes temperatures: Mind controls body in extreme experiments". Cambridge, MA: *Harvard University Gazette*, 18 April 2002 http://www.hno.harvard.edu/gazette/2002/04.18/09-tummo.html

Dieker, Bernadette and Jonathan Montaldo, eds. (2003) *Merton on Hesychasm - The Prayer of the Heart*. Fons Vitae.

Ding-E Young, John and Taylor, Eugene (1998) "Meditation as a Voluntary Hypometabolic State of Biological Estivation". *News in Physiological Sciences*, Vol. 13, No. 3, 149-153, June 1998

Epstein, Mark. (1995) *Thoughts Without a Thinker: Psychotherapy from a Buddhist Perspective*. New York: Harper Collins.

Fuller, Jean Overton. (1971) *Noor-un-nisa Inayat Khan (Madeleine)*. Rotterdam: East-West Publications.

Guillaume-Schamhart, Elise and Munira van Voorst van Beest, eds. (1979) *Biography of Pir-o-Murshid Hazrat Inayat Khan*. London: East-West Publications.

Hester, David. (2001) *The Jesus Prayer*. Conciliar Press.

Houlden, James L. (2003) *Jesus in History, Thought, and Culture*. Vol 2, p 815

Kaldoubovsky, E. and G.E.H. Palmer, trans. (1992) *Writings from the Philokalia on Prayer of the Heart*. Faber & Faber.

Khan, Inayat. *Complete Works*. www.hazrat-inayat-khan.org

—. (1960-64) *The Sufi Message of Hazrat Inayat Khan, Volumes 1-13*. London: Barrie and Rockcliff.

—. (1978) *The Complete Sayings of Hazrat Inayat Khan*. New Lebanon, NY: Omega Publications.

—. (1980) Tales Told by Hazrat Inayat Khan. New Lebanon, New York: Sufi Order Publications.

—. (1989) *Complete Works of Pir-o-Murshid Hazrat Inayat Khan, Original Texts: Lectures on Sufism, 1923 I: January-June*. London/The Hague: East-West Publications.

—. (1990) *Complete Works of Pir-o-Murshid Hazrat Inayat Khan, Original Texts: Lectures on Sufism, 1922 I: January-August*. London/The Hague: East-West Publications.

—. *Esoteric Papers* (unpublished).

Khan, Vilayat Inayat. (1974) *Toward the One*. New York: Harper and Row.

—. (1978) *The Message of Our Time: The Life and Teachings of the Sufi Master Pir-o-Murshid Hazrat Inayat Khan*. San Francisco: Harper and Row.

—. (1983) *Retreat Manual*. Unpublished manuscript.

—. (1988) *Rehearsal for Life*. Unpublished manuscript.

—. (1996) *Tools of Meditation*. Seattle: Sufi Order International.

Kotsonis, John K. (2007) *An Orthodox Christian Study on Unceasing Prayer*. Theandros. 4: 3. www.theandros.com

Kronstadt, St John. (1994) *On Prayer*. Holy Trinity Monastery.

Kübler-Ross, Elizabeth. (1969) *On Death and Dying*. New York: Macmillan.

LeShan, Lawrence. (1974) *How to Meditate: A Guide to Self-Discovery*. Boston: Little, Brown & Co.

Levinson, Daniel. (1986) *Seasons of a Man's Life*. Ballantine.

Logothetis, Spyridon. (1982) *The Heart: An Orthodox Christian Spiritual Guide*. Holy Transfiguration Monastery, 1982

Nicholson, Reynold A., ed. (1898) *Selected Poems from the Divani Shamsi Tabriz*. London: Cambridge University Press.

Ryan, William. *Breathing Yeshua: Christian Meditation in the Way of the Heart*.
http://www.avalon-counseling.com/breathing_yeshua1.pdf

Schaff, Phillip, ed. (1892) *Athanasius: Select Works and Letters*. Grand Rapids, MI: Christian Classicas Ethereal Library.
http://www.ccel.org/ccel/schaff/npnf204.pdf

Shah, Indries. (1971) *The Sufis*. New York: Anchor & Doubleday.

Tompkins, Peter. (1973) *The Secret Life of Plants*. New York: Harper and Row.

Whitman, Walt. (1900) *Leaves of Grass*. Philadelphia, PA: David McKay. Bartleby.com, 1999. www.bartleby.com/142

INDEX

Hazrat Inayat Khan (see *Khan, Inayat*)
Head cold, 8
Health,
    Attitude and, 218
    Elements and, 218-220
    Rhythm and, 148
Heart,
    Cardiac plexus, 33
    Chakra, 33
    Dimensions of the, 211-213
    Directing the energy of the, 194, 254
    Energetic field of the, 6
    Guidance of the, 25, 41, 44
    Height of the, 180-182
    Living from the, 14, 17, 184
    Message of the, 44, 153
    Monitor, electronic, 9
    Pain of the feeling, 32-34, 219, 320-321
    Poetic, 6
    Power of the, 26, 61, 67, 70, 219
    Recharging another person's, 255-256
    Speaking from the, 5
    Strength of the, 223
    Sun-like nature of the, 15, 72
    Universal, 49
    Wounds of the, 133, 140
Heart Rate Variability, 30
Heart Rhythm Meditation,
    Atmosphere created by, 2, 28, 29, 112, 246
    Difficulties, 13, 26, 99
    Discovery of, 15-16
    Effects of
        Cardiovascular health, 2, 6
        Creativity, 23
        Enhancing self-confidence, 2
        State of stillness, 2
        Mental, 2
    Goals of, 15, 33, 94-96
    Learning,

Individually, 325-331
    With a group, 331-338
    With a teacher, 338-343
Noisy environments and, 146
Practice, 14
States of, 34-59
    Channel of the Heart (Contemplation), 48-49, 51
    Heart Focused (Concentration), 37-42, 51, 162
    Heart Centered (Contemplation), 42-44, 51, 163
    Representative of the Heart (Concentration), 49-52
    Universal Heart (Meditation), 44-47, 51, 139, 157, 163
Uses of
    To achieve success, 1
    To express harmony, 1
    To get in touch with your feelings, 1, 9, 74-76, 243
    To handle stress, 16
    To heal oneself, 7, 8, 199-208
    To know yourself, 91-92
    To move through emotion, 9, 16, 74-75
    To reduce sleep, 69-70
    To read the emotions of others, 76-77
Heartbeat,
    As a self-diagnostic health signal, 7, 9, 186
    As a signal about your emotions, 8, 9
    Convergence of in group of people meditating, 10
    Earth's, 10, 15
    Feeling your, 11, 12, 183-187
    Infinite, 52, 58
    Sending waves of peace on your, 50
    Strength of your, 10, 186
    Variations in your, 7

Hedonism, (see *Happiness, Relation to hedonism*)
Hell, 133
Hercules, 154
Hesychius of Jerusalem (saint), 348
Himalayan Institute, 54
Hospital, 76
Howard, 168-169
Humor, 279
Hyperventilation, preventing, 174
Idealism, 84, 91, 115, 171, 212, 213, 218, 251, 256, 258, 267, 274-275, 278-279, 283, 340-341, 356
Identity, sense of, 36, 58
Ignatius, (saint), 349
Impermanence,
    Critique of the Buddhist notion of, 32
Individuality,
    Consciousness and, 31
    Nature of, 31
    Particle-like vs wave-like understanding of, 53
Infinity (see *Meditation, Key concepts that initiate*)
Insight, development of, 85, 180
Inspiration (see *Breath, Inhalation*), 158
Institute for Applied Meditation, *xiii*, 17, 18, 324, 333, 335, 339, 341, 342, 362
Integrity, 62, 87, 91-92, 96, 223, 274
Intention, 4, 25, 27, 31, 45, 54-56, 87, 265-268, 271, 319, 325, 327
Intuition, development and use of, 85-87, 95, 297-298
Irritation, rising above, 179-180
Isaac the Syrian, (saint) 350
Isaiah, 49
Islam, 31
Israelites, 272
Jack, 87-88

Jesus (see *Christ*)
Jesus Prayer (aka *The Prayer of the Heart*), 15, 345-346, 349
Jim, 84-85
Joan, 4-5
John, 86
John of Kronstadt, (saint), 348
John the Baptist, 265, 351
Journal writing, 131
Judaism, 31
Julius Caesar, 86
King, 24, 49-50, 147
Kingdom, heavenly, 24
Kabbalah, 357
Kathy, 89-90
Ken, 11, 342
Khan, Inayat, *ix, x, xiv*, 6, 21, 29, 33, 37, 46, 47, 51, 60, 79, 80, 81, 109, 115, 116, 119, 120, 126, 127, 135, 138, 141, 142, 143, 144, 145, 148, 150, 155, 156, 163, 166, 167, 175, 176, 180, 183, 184, 185, 186, 187, 188, 189, 192, 193, 203, 214, 216, 217, 218, 219, 221, 236, 239, 242, 243, 247, 249, 256, 258, 259, 261, 262, 263, 267, 269, 272, 275, 276, 277, 280, 282, 283, 284, 303, 306, 314, 317, 318, 321, 326, 327, 328, 329, 332, 336, 338, 339, 341, 351, 353, 354, 357, 362, 363
Khan, Vilayat Inayat, *ix*, 25-26, 33, 42, 47 note 14, 54, 77 note 3, 80 note 6, 112, 239, 243, 249, 259, 261, 262, 267, 269, 272, 318, 327, 351, 357
Khayyám, Omar, 355
Kyrie Eleison, Christe Eleison, 345, 356
Laura, 77
Lawyer, 4-5
Levinson, Daniel, 150
Light, 51-52, 170-171, 182, 259-260, 264-267, 272-278
Lisa, 342